LIVING IN ROMANTIC BAGHDAD

Contemporary Issues in the Middle East

LIVING IN ROMANTIC BAGHDAD

An American Memoir of Teaching
and Travel in Iraq, 1924–1947

Foreword by John Joseph

IDA DONGES STAUDT

Edited by
John Joseph

Syracuse University Press

"Living in Romantic Baghdad" by Ida Donges Staudt is published with permission
from the Evangelical and Reformed Historical Society, Lancaster, PA.

∞ The paper used in this publication meets the minimum requirements
of the American National Standard for Information Sciences—Permanence
of Paper for Printed Library Materials, ANSI Z39.48-1992.

For a listing of books published and distributed by Syracuse University Press,
visit our Web site at SyracuseUniversityPress.syr.edu.

ISBN: 978-0-8156-0994-0

Library of Congress Cataloging-in-Publication Data

Staudt, Ida Donges, 1875–1952.
Living in romantic Baghdad : an American memoir of teaching and travel in Iraq,
1924–1947 / Ida Donges Staudt ; foreword by John Joseph ;
edited by John Joseph. — 1st ed.
p. cm. — (Contemporary issues in the Middle East)
Includes bibliographical references and index.
ISBN 978-0-8156-0994-0 (cloth : alk. paper) 1. Staudt, Ida Donges, 1875–1952—
Travel—Iraq.   2. Iraq—Description and travel.   3. Iraq—History—Hashemite
Kingdom, 1921–1958.   4. Americans—Iraq—Biography.   5. Teachers—Iraq—Biography.
6. American School for Boys (Baghdad, Iraq)—History.   I. Joseph, John. II. Title.
DS70.65.S73 2012
956.7′47042092—dc23
[B]   2012018984

Manufactured in the United States of America

[King Faisal I] shook hands with us, and asked us to sit down with him. He said he was delighted to know that we had come all the way from America to open a school and assist in the educational work in his realm.

—IDA DONGES STAUDT

IDA DONGES STAUDT was born and raised in Myerstown, Pennsylvania. Her father, a prominent businessman, owned the town's hardware store and served as a member of the Board of Trustees of its Palatinate College, from which young Ida graduated. Interested in elegant expression, she took courses in elocution at Philadelphia's Neff College of Oratory. After marrying Calvin K. Staudt, whom she had first met at Palatinate, she received her Bachelor's degree from the University of Chicago while her husband worked on his PhD dissertation.

In 1919 the Staudts launched their Middle Eastern educational adventure in Beirut, Lebanon. In 1924 they founded the American School for Boys in Baghdad, a unique educational institution that flourished in the newly created Iraq. The eminent American broadcaster Lowell Thomas, a member of the school's Board of Trustees, referred to the author as the "dynamo" that runs the school.

Mrs. Staudt died in 1952, a year after the death of her husband.

JOHN JOSEPH graduated from the American School for Boys in Baghdad in 1941 and taught there for the next four years. He graduated from Franklin and Marshall College in Lancaster, Pennsylvania, in 1950 and taught there for twenty-seven years (1961–88). Princeton University, where he received his PhD in 1957, published his dissertation in 1961 *(The Nestorians and Their Muslim Neighbors)*. His *Muslim-Christian Relations and Inter-Christian Rivalries* (1983) was among the American Library Association's *Choice* magazine's Outstanding Academic Books for 1983–84. In 2000 a revised and expanded version of his *Nestorians* was published under the title *The Modern Assyrians* as volume 26 of the series *Studies in Christian Mission*.

Joseph retired in 1988 and lives in Lancaster with his wife of fifty-five years. They have three children and four grandchildren. After his retirement one of his former students, a retired CEO of Reynolds American, financed the building of an international center in Lancaster and wanted it named after him; it is now the Joseph International Center.

CONTENTS

ILLUSTRATIONS

EDITOR'S FOREWORD

Why is this memoir published posthumously, almost sixty years after it was written? The author, Ida Donges Staudt (1875–1952), and her husband, Calvin K. Staudt (1876–1951), who cofounded the American School for Boys in Baghdad in 1924, retired in 1947. They accepted the invitation of their lifelong friend Harvey C. Bickel, a prominent retired lawyer and judge of the city of Baltimore, to share his home with him. In Judge Bickel's hospitable home, Ida Staudt found the time to rest, reminisce, and review her diaries of twenty-five years. She finished recording this engrossing chronicle in 1951; we do not know what happened to her diaries.

I graduated from the American School for Boys in 1941 and taught in its intermediate division for the next four years. With the Staudts' help I received a full scholarship at Franklin and Marshall College. Eventually I joined the faculty there and taught Middle Eastern history for twenty-seven years.

In a letter to me dated December 31, 1950, responding to a message that I had enclosed with a Christmas card, Ida Staudt described her American home as "very cheerful in its Christmas decorations, the fire on the hearth will soon be burning brightly . . . It's all lovely." But she had "attacks" of nostalgia for Baghdad. "Christmas time," she wrote, "we are in Baghdad"—thinking of Christmases past.[1]

Sadly, all was not well in Baghdad. The American School, mismanaged by their successor, was closed in June 1950. In a letter sent that summer to a friend and benefactor of the school, a distressed Dr. Staudt pointed out

---

1. For Staudt's comments on Christmases spent in Iraq, see chapter 6.

that the Board of Trustees of the school had sent out to Baghdad "a man who in one year ruined what it took [us] to build up in twenty-three years."

A still-hopeful Mrs. Staudt wrote me on that last day of 1950, "We have only one wish: the opening of that School . . . We'll believe this to be true. In this faith we'll greet 1951." In a kindly overpraise she added, "I wish that the mantle of my husband would fall on your shoulders, John; you would wear it worthily."

Judging from letters that I have recently read, it was evident by early 1951 that Dr. Staudt's desperate efforts to reopen the school had hopelessly failed. Dispirited, he passed away in April of that year at the age of seventy-five. Eight months later his wife and co-laborer suffered a stroke that robbed her of her gifted speech. She was cared for briefly at the home of a nephew and his wife, Elwood and Irene Staudt, and died early in 1952 at the age of seventy-seven.

Among the few mementos from Iraq that the young Staudts had in their possession was a copy of their aunt's typescript. Busy raising a family in the early 1950s, they kept their inheritance from Baghdad in a carton in their attic, set aside there and forgotten until they moved to a retirement community in 2006. At that time they donated their gifts from Iraq to their church's historical society, The Evangelical and Reformed Historical Society, at the Lancaster Theological Seminary.

The archives of the society already had a few files of correspondence and documents on the Baghdad school, material with which I was familiar since I used the library often. The archivist kindly notified me of the Staudt memoir soon after it was acquired. I was encouraged to feel free to edit it in any way I saw fit to assure accuracy. What a great opportunity this was for me to pay at least a part of my debt to the Staudts. And what a pleasant surprise to find that the title of the chapter devoted to the American School for Boys was a phrase from my Christmas card message of 1950.

The Staudts were of Pennsylvania German stock, born and raised in that state's beautiful countryside between Reading and Lebanon—he from Wernersville, she from Myerstown. Ida Staudt was a graduate of Palatinate College, located in her own hometown. In her opening chapter she describes Palatinate as a small college, "only a little more than a preparatory school." Dr. Staudt, who met his future wife at Palatinate, graduated from Franklin and Marshall College in 1900 and then attended Lancaster Theological Seminary, finishing in 1903, the year when the couple was also married. Four years later, he received his PhD from the University of Chicago, where his wife took enough courses to earn her PhB (Bachelor of Philosophy).

Prior to the First World War the couple moved to Tacoma, Washington, where Dr. Staudt taught at Whitworth College and served as a pastor of a congregation there. During the war he served with the YMCA and for a time was educational and religious director at Camp Dix, New Jersey.

I have not been able to find information on what Mrs. Staudt did prior to teaching in Beirut and Baghdad. She probably was a public school teacher at Tacoma. We know that both she and her husband were teaching in Beirut, Lebanon, where we find them soon after the First World War ended. For three years (1919–22), Dr. Staudt taught at both the American University of Beirut and the American Community College, then known as Preparatory School. Mrs. Staudt taught at the American Girls School, an experience that she cherished and remembers here at the end of her days.

The memoir that Ida Staudt wrote is an impressive firsthand record of their life and times in Iraq. Their daily contacts for twenty-three years were not only with their students but frequently also with many of the students' parents and with the varied communities from which they came. The school's boarding department made it possible for a number of students from all over Iraq to attend the renowned American School for Boys in the capital. We often read in these pages about the Staudts being hosted and entertained by parents of their students in the remote regions of the land, be it among the Kurds, Shiahs, Sunnis, or Bedouin tribesmen. In the author's own words, "I had an unusual opportunity to gather my material. In our work and in our travels and through the open door of our house, we had the rare privilege of coming in touch with the heterogeneous groups that make up the population of the country . . . Besides, all kinds of homes, ranging from the royal palace to the refugee huts and the Bedouin tents, were open to us. We were fortunate, too, in personally knowing many of the tribal leaders and practically all the men who guided the new nation state."

Impressed by the free flow of this memoir, written by a well-informed and perceptive observer with years of local experience in Iraq, I have limited my comments to a few citations and annotations that I thought would be helpful. Bearing in mind that the author did not intend to write a history but to record an account of her and her husband's work and travels in Iraq, I have deleted or edited what was redundant or judged to be superfluous. In two cases the historical accounts were misleading, largely because academic research done since Staudt wrote has corrected or expanded our knowledge of the subject under discussion. I have identified these passages with an explanatory note.

The title of the book is of Ida Staudt's choosing; the subtitle is mine, as are all of its notes. It should be pointed out that the author used "Romantic Baghdad" with due consideration. "These beginning days," she wrote, "were great days for us when we lived, not, of course, in the city depicted in storybooks and in Arab history, but in the present Baghdad—a Baghdad, nevertheless, which to us at the time appeared equally great, since we saw it with our inner eye and could, through rose-colored glasses as it were, behold the splendor that once was here."[2]

Present at the creation of modern Iraq, Ida Staudt has also depicted here a sociopolitical profile of the country that she saw come of age, struggling with the establishment of a modern nation-state. The most serious problem facing Iraq and the rest of the newly created Arab states of the region was their relationship with Britain and France. Soon after the First World War ended, these two superpowers began to extend their declining colonial rule into these heartlands of the Arab world. It soon became known that during the war, the Allies had reached secret agreements that would divide the Arab provinces of the Ottoman Empire between them (Sykes-Picot Agreement, 1915). Disclosed also were negotiations between representatives of Zionist organizations and the British Foreign Office, declaring the British government's "sympathy with Jewish Zionist aspirations" in Palestine (Balfour Declaration, 1917).

Palestine became a subject of controversy soon after it was "freed" from the Turks. As the British General Edmund H. H. Allenby walked triumphantly into liberated Jerusalem, these boasting words were attributed

---

2. See chapter 1.

to him: "Today ended the Crusades." Even the staid *London Times* seems to have lost restraint: "Saladin entered Jerusalem in triumph," it wrote, "as Allenby enters it today."[3] By 1920 Arab nationalist agitation had spread throughout the newborn states. In Iraq anti-British sentiment was strongest among the Shiahs, erupting that year in an uprising led by Muhammad al-Sadr, a son of the Grand Ayatollah Hasan al-Sadr of Kadhimain, working together with the conglomerate of religious leaders of Najaf and Karbala.[4]

As the Iraq war of 2003 comes to an end, Americans wonder how they can avoid involvement in future Middle East conflicts. Meanwhile, let us briefly look to the past to understand why the British occupation of Iraq in the 1920s and its recent American occupation have been violently opposed. The past often informs the present and the future—especially if we take into consideration how it is remembered and viewed by the people concerned. The conquerors and the vanquished always have different versions of the same event depending on how its history is told by the storytellers of each passing generation.

During the few decades prior to the First World War, we find the historic Tigris and Euphrates Valley, modern Iraq, attracting the special attention of the West. The country's fertile soil, abundant water, rich natural resources, and strategic location are often commented upon by scholars, diplomats, and military strategists as well as by the financiers and speculators of the day. This is also the period of Ottoman history when the central government in Istanbul tried to assert itself, starting with the reforms of Sultan Mahmud II early in the nineteenth century (1808–39); these were followed by the Tanzimat movement and the efforts of the state to introduce secular reforms on a number of fronts: educational, legal, political, military, and industrial. By 1860 Baghdad was linked with Istanbul by telegraph lines; postal service reached the country in the 1880s. Railroads came a little later, pioneered by Germany. The Ottoman

3. For details, see footnote 2 in chapter 18.

4. The young cleric Muqtada al-Sadr, who has headed an anti-American insurgency in the Iraq war, is a scion of the al-Sadr clan. His father, Ayatollah Muhammad Sadeq al-Sadr, and two of his brothers were executed in 1999 by agents of Saddam Hussein.

state, which had been ruling Iraq since the early sixteenth century, tried also to bring under its control the remote provinces of the empire, including the three provinces of Mosul, Baghdad, and Basra, referred to in the West as Mesopotamia until the early 1920s, when the name Iraq was formally used.[5]

By the mid-1800s Mesopotamia was also the focus of worldwide attention. By then archaeological excavations had unearthed the remains of the ancient Babylonian and Assyrian civilization to the wondering eyes of the world. Starting in 1843, the French consular agent at Mosul, Paul Emile Botta, uncovered the ruins of the magnificent palace of Sargon II, king of Assyria (722–705 BC). That same year the British excavations, under Austin Henry Layard, discovered the majestic palace of Shalmaneser I (ca. 884–860 BC) with its winged bulls, followed by the palace of Ashurbanipal (668–626 BC) with his library's vast collection of cuneiform tablets. These and other splendid collections soon became major attractions in the museums of London, Paris, and Berlin. Before long the mysterious cuneiform writing was deciphered; Assyrian texts, in the Akkadian language, were soon read by scholars with the same certainty as Hebrew and Aramaic (O'Leary 1923, 1; Wright 1966, 14).[6]

In 1860 the great corpus *The Cuneiform Inscriptions of Western Asia* was published and a lost chapter in the history of civilization was retrieved. Until the second half of the nineteenth century, the only detailed account of these ancients, written by contemporaries, came from the Hebrew Bible,

---

5. The Greek term "Mesopotamia" means "[Land] between two rivers"; it is used as a geographical nomenclature in the Septuagint, the Greek translation of the Hebrew Bible, done in the third century BC for the Hellenized Jews of Alexandria, Egypt. The Authorized Version of the Bible continued to use the term "Mesopotamia." In 1970 translators of the New English Bible preferred the original Hebrew name—Aram Naharaim—"Aram of the two rivers." The New Testament, originally written in Greek, continued the Greek terminology of the Septuagint: Mesopotamia. (See Acts 2:9; Genesis 24:10.) "Iraq" was the name long used by Arab geographers for this region.

6. Akkadian is closer to Hebrew and Arabic than to Aramaic, which comes a close third. According to De Lacy O'Leary, "A much closer relationship exists between Hebrew, Arabic and Aramaic, than between Hebrew and Akkadian."

the history of whose people was fatally entangled with that of Assyria and Babylon: northern and southern Iraq of today. Perhaps the major reason why the Christian West was so fascinated by these Mesopotamian discoveries was that, in some cases, the cuneiform inscriptions confirmed the authenticity of the Bible, at a time when "biblical criticism" in the West was flourishing. Mesopotamia came to be called The Cradle of Civilization.[7] In her opening chapter, Ida Staudt relates how fascinated she was in college in the late 1890s by the newly found history of ancient Iraq. She daydreamed of going there one day.

The 1800s also had their dark side; that is the century when Western imperialism began anew "scrambling" for new territories, annexing and dominating new lands—other people's lands. The whole of the African continent was parceled out among a few European countries. Toward the end of the century, the northern rim of Africa bordering on the Mediterranean, Arab and Muslim, was ruled by France and Britain, the former declaring Algeria an integral part of France as early as 1848. After suppressing a mutiny in India in 1857, involving both Muslims and Hindus, the British government took over the English East India Company, and Queen Victoria formally became the empress of India.

How did Iran and "Ottoman Iraq" fare in this scrambling? Austin Henry Layard was among those who drew attention to this corner of the globe. Years after his excavations in Mesopotamia, Layard was appointed British ambassador to the Ottoman Empire (1877–80). During his first year in Istanbul, he warned his government of Russian expansion through Transcaucasia, which was mainly at the expense of Iran and the Ottoman Empire. He was concerned that Russia's advances toward Iran and beyond would mean that even "the great valley of the Euphrates and Tigris" would "inevitably fall into her hands in the course of time." Uppermost on Layard's mind was the effect that Russia's creeping encroachment would have upon Great Britain's possessions in India.

Unlike other European countries, Russia built its empire in its own backyard, eventually pushing its boundaries all the way to the Pacific

---

7. For details summarized here, see Joseph 2000, 15–16.

Ocean, unilaterally declaring the countries involved as part of its empire. Along their way Russians acquired the Muslim heartlands of Central Asia and Caucasus, embroiling them in a bloody and ruthless civil war. For years these lands were in a state of perpetual rebellion, suppressed by the Tsarist armies with a brutality that saw the extermination of entire tribes, burning their villages and confiscating their cattle.

Muslim leaders, using the only means they had, tried to rekindle the religious feelings of their flocks and to incite their followers to fight a holy war against the occupiers. Shiah pilgrims from Iran, who visited the holy cities of Ottoman Iraq, carried with them accounts of persecution and dangers to which Muslims were exposed under Russian yoke. Ayatollahs of Karbala and Najaf, we read, were implored to urge the shah to take up arms in defense of his insulted religion. He was threatened with curses and everlasting perdition if he failed to take up arms in the holy cause (Allen and Muratoff 1953; Kazemzadeh 1951; Joseph 2000).

Defeated by Japan in the war of 1905, Tsarist Russia was no longer a threat to British India or to Mesopotamia. It was now Britain that sought to secure her position in both the Persian Gulf and "the great valley of the Euphrates and Tigris rivers." A new rival, Germany, was now threatening the growing British interests there. In her enticing and informative chapter "The Story of Oil," Staudt writes that "[f]rom the Paris Peace Conference that followed World War I, to the later treaties pertaining to Iraq, we detect the smell of oil." That whiff was first detected in the Persian Gulf in 1908, and Britain lost no time "to dig herself in."

Britain was certainly no stranger to the region; as early as the late eighteenth century, the English East India Company had established a trading post at the Iranian seaport of Bushehr,[8] not far from Iraq's port of Basra. By the early 1900s the Persian Gulf, already a sphere of influence of British India, gained greater importance. In 1909 the Anglo-Persian Oil Company was established, and a pipeline was built from the oil fields to a

---

8. A century later, present-day Bushehr is reportedly the site where Iran has a plant, built with Russian help, to enrich uranium. See the *Guardian,* Feb. 26, 2009.

refinery located in nearby Abadan. By 1912 the Royal Navy had switched from coal to oil.[9]

These "foreign aggrandizements" did not go unnoticed by the politically conscious. In 1905, prior to the discovery of oil, the Basra newspaper *al-'Alam al-Islami* (The Islamic World) published an article in which Germany was accused of following in the footsteps of Great Britain, trying to create a German Iraq, just as Britain had created a British Egypt in 1882 (Great Britain 1905). The British consul in Basra warned his government in India in 1910 of anti-British sentiment; citing from the translation of an Arabic newspaper of the city, he wrote, "At whatever part of Basra you look, a thousand different things connected with England will immediately strike your attention and you will feel how deep the claws of English influence have sunk into our country's flesh." The article warned that the British intended to do in Iraq what they had done in India (Great Britain 1912; Cohen 1976).

We even hear from America's own vice-consul, A. E. C. Bird, stationed in "Baghdad, Turkey." He commented on conditions in the southern part of the country about one hundred years ago, calling the region "a stronghold of Islamism," mentioning the Shiah holy cities of Karbala, Najaf, Samarra, and Kadhimain, names that the current Iraq war has made familiar.[10]

During the turbulent 1920s, whether in Iraq or the rest of the Arab states, the development of stable societies was inhibited by tensions and treacheries. The only expressions of helpfulness and trust that these heartlands of the Muslim world heard from the West came from America. Even

9. In Iraq, oil in large quantities was discovered near Kirkuk in 1927. Prior to the First World War, there was a Turkish petroleum company made up of a consortium of oil companies; it became Iraq Petroleum Company in the late 1920s. For more on the production of oil in Iraq, see chapter 19.

10. Vice-consul Bird wrote to caution against the intent of some Jewish organizations to settle Jewish victims of persecution in Romania on land in southern Iraq. Such a project, Bird wrote, could not be carried out "without arousing Mohammedan fanaticism to an extent that would plunge the country into bloodshed and anarchy" (Bird 1987).

XX   EDITOR'S FOREWORD

when the United States entered the First World War, it did not declare war on the Ottoman Empire, an ally of Germany, because of the large number of Americans who lived and served there as teachers in American schools for both boys and girls, as professors in American colleges and universities, or as scores of missionaries, physicians, nurses, and others (Joseph 2000, 65 seq.).[11] The wartime American president, Woodrow Wilson, was especially admired because of his Fourteen Points, whose principle of self-determination proclaimed the right of peoples to determine freely their own political status.

Ida Donges Staudt, Calvin K. Staudt, and the many other American men and women in Beirut, Istanbul, Cairo, Baghdad, and smaller cities and towns of the region helped create "a gigantic reservoir of good will" for America and its people (Willkie 1943, 158–59).[12] Ida Staudt's memoir on their life and work in Iraq provides "an educational adventure" and is an uplifting historical backdrop to the present predicament facing the United States there.

11. For the Staudts' early association with Christian missions, see chapter 2.

12. I well remember reading Wendell Willkie's words cited above at the age of twenty, when they appeared in the English-language newspaper *Baghdad Times*. Willkie was interviewed by that newspaper when he passed through Baghdad on his world tour in 1943. He was the Republican Party's candidate for president of the United States in the 1940 elections, running against Franklin Delano Roosevelt.

EDITOR'S ACKNOWLEDGMENTS

First I would like to express my debt and gratitude to those who helped restore to life Ida Donges Staudt's fifty-five-year-old typescript: Elwood and Irene Staudt. They safeguarded their aunt-in-law's memoir and, years later, preserved it at the archives of The Evangelical and Reformed Historical Society, located at Lancaster Theological Seminary in Lancaster, Pennsylvania. I thank them also for providing me with the pictures of the Staudts that appear in this memoir.

I am grateful to the director of The Evangelical and Reformed Historical Society, Dr. Richard R. Berg, for bringing the Staudt transcript to my attention soon after it was acquired; it gave me the opportunity to pay back to the author and her husband—well known in Baghdad as "Dr. and Mrs. Staudt"—some of the debt that I owe them.

At the Lancaster Theological Seminary, its associate librarian, Mr. Chris Belden, has kindly scanned the original typescript onto the computer, greatly facilitating my work. Dr. Christina Ravert, school psychologist for Manheim Township School District, has efficiently and patiently attended to the numerous details involved in the preparation of this chronicle, especially its electronic version.

Dr. Louis L. Athey, Charles A. Dana Emeritus Professor of History, has read the foreword and offered me detailed comments on it, akin to the judicious advice that I have received from him throughout our years together as colleagues and friends at Franklin and Marshall College.

I am grateful to Mr. Paul Rascoe, Government Documents, Maps, and Electronic Information Services librarian of University of Texas Libraries, who cordially and promptly provided me with the digital map of Iraq that I have used here.

Closer to home, my special thanks to my wife, Betty, for her patience and support, now and through the years. More than once she has read this text as it passed through its various stages, sharing her generally sound observations with me. My daughter Deena I thank for her forthright comments on my introductory piece. My son Larry has clarified for me a number of legal intricacies issued by Syracuse University Press.

For whatever flaws that the reader may yet detect in this book, I am, unquestionably, the responsible one.

PREFACE

This book chronicles interesting and colorful incidents of my life in Baghdad and Iraq. It gives my observations and experiences and reactions in a reborn land as it was trying to adjust itself to a new world with its surging influences and problems. My life in Iraq, as it was framed between two memorable garden parties, had all the color and fascination of the romantic Baghdad of long ago.

But the real value and interest of the book lies in the social, political, and historic background, and the never-changing and ever-changeless Baghdad. What I have written should therefore be informing and enlightening as well as make absorbing reading.

I lived in Baghdad during an interesting and significant period. My husband and I began our life there when Iraq was newly born; actually, we landed and set foot on its soil the very day and the same hour that the Constituent Assembly had convened in Baghdad to frame a constitution for the new nation. And we were an intimate part of this growing life for twenty-three years, sharing with the people the joys and pains incident to growth.

Upon my arrival, I was at once fascinated with Baghdad. Those early days made an indelible impression upon me. Baghdad was then still purely an Oriental city, and for me it had all the charms of the *Arabian Nights Entertainment.* Somehow, I always felt I was living, not in the present Baghdad but in the Baghdad of the golden age of the caliphs. That is why these lovely customs and the inherited traditions are so fully described.

I had an unusual opportunity to gather my material. In our work and in our travels and through the open door of our house, we had the rare privilege of coming in touch with the heterogeneous groups that make up the population of the country. In our school alone, we scarcely ever had less than twenty ethnicities and nationalities, and an equal number of religious communities. Besides, all kinds of homes, ranging from the royal palace to the refugee huts and the Bedouin tents, were open to us. Our contacts were not only with the Arabs of the land, who are in the majority, but also with all the minority groups, who form a quarter of the population.

We were fortunate, too, in personally knowing many of the tribal leaders and practically all the men who guided the new nation-state. Those who lived and ruled in the earlier years of Iraq's history were outstanding men, men with statesmanlike qualities, many of whom also were picturesque characters. Foremost among them, of course, was King Faisal I.

We followed the oil industry, which was an economic asset to the country; saw how Iraq again became a crossroads of the world; traced the tremendous changes that took place, which, however, did not increase the sum total of human happiness; traced the impact of the West upon the East, which, unfortunately, was not always an unalloyed blessing; sensed the social and intellectual ferment; suffered with the people because of the Nazi infiltration; and passed with them through the various stages in Iraq's struggle for independence.

Most of the material for this book was gathered and assembled while I was still living in Baghdad. I am naturally indebted, to a certain extent, to friends and books. But first and foremost, I gratefully acknowledge my husband's help, who collaborated with me in every way. Without his generous aid and contribution of time and labor, and his steadfast faith in the value and importance of the material and its colorful incidents, the book would never have been written. The quotation from Reginald L. Hine appearing in chapter 19 is from his *Confessions of an Un-Common Attorney* (1947, 167), and is used by permission of Macmillan Company, New York.

LIVING IN ROMANTIC BAGHDAD

1

ARRIVING IN BAGHDAD, 1924

When I was graduated from a small college, which was only a little more than a preparatory school, I was not yet sixteen. The town was small and its two major influences were the college and the church. I grew up rather unsophisticated and knew much less of the general ways of the world than the fifteen-year-old today. I was inordinately proud of the degree of M.A. which was conferred upon the lady graduates as Mistress of Arts. My husband teasingly would say that this had given me an advanced academic degree before I had earned and received my bachelor's degree. When I became aware of this inverted order, my self-complacency was jolted; no longer was I the prodigy who at the age of fifteen had acquired an M.A.

A recent reading of my commencement essay eliminated entirely the word "prodigy" from any connection with myself; the essay was astonishingly puerile. Yet I recall that my mother heard a clergyman sitting beside her say when I had concluded the reading of it, "*Wunderschön.*"[1] My bent at the time was "elocution," and I likely had weighted the insaneness of the material with an elocutionary fervor which moved the hearers and hypnotized their thinking.[2] Others have been guilty of doing the same. I carried away from that college, however, a love of history, especially the history of the ancient world. In the margin of the textbook of my Ancient History I found I had written one day while studying about Babylon, "I

1. German words are still occasionally used in everyday speech by Pennsylvanians of German ancestry, not to be confused with the sectarian Amish. I have met relatives of the Staudts who have a distinct "Pennsylvania Dutch" accent.

2. After graduating from Palatinate College, Staudt attended Neff College of Oratory in Philadelphia, which offered courses in elocution and dramatic arts.

1

1. Ida Donges Staudt in her younger years.

wonder where I will be ten years from now?" I wonder what induced me to write these words.

As I became more mature, I acquired an extensive knowledge of the region now known as the Middle East, and in particular Mesopotamia, which is today called Iraq. I began to understand the place and importance of Mesopotamia in the history of the world. I got a clear perception of Iraq's incredibly rich past and learned that of the six thousand years of written history, one-half was chartered here. I became aware that here was the cradle of civilization, and that here Arab culture had reached its highest level. Besides, I was impressed by Iraq's geographical position: the country's strategic location and her future possibilities in oil and soil.

These two things, then, had influenced me as I grew into woman-hood: the survival of a far distant past in my psychic life and a clear perception of the place and importance of Mesopotamia and her future possibilities. Consequently, the most natural course for me to take then was to live and labor where my youthful longings and my later reflections had directed me.

It was wonderful that in the spring of 1924, my husband and I should arrive in Mesopotamia, with unforeseen suddenness and storylike pre-cipitancy, having been commissioned to open educational work there.[3] Wonderful that for nearly a quarter of a century we lived and labored in the old, fabled city of Baghdad.

Babylon had always been more familiar to me than Baghdad; never-theless, the city of the *Arabian Nights* tales began to take on flesh in the three years we had lived in Beirut, Lebanon, before going to the storied city. My husband taught at the American University of Beirut, and while there, a party from the university drove by automobile to Palmyra in the desert. It was said that our automobiles were the first passenger cars to enter the once great caravan city of Zenobia. Standing in the colonnaded street of these remarkable ruins, I turned eastward and said, "Baghdad lies in this direction; we have come almost half-way; why not drive on?" Hap-pily and providentially, our wish was fulfilled.

Two years after our adventurous trip to Palmyra we found ourselves, to our amazement, in Baghdad. It was the latter part of March 1924, about six o'clock in the evening, when we alighted from the train that had brought us from Basrah to Baghdad. We looked about to see what kind of conveyances would take us into the city after our arrival. Many carriages (*'arabanas*) drawn by two horses were awaiting the passengers, and in one of these we seated ourselves rather excitedly. Our long voyage by way of the Pacific had come to an end. Our destination having been reached, we drove with eager expectancy toward our new home.

3. For details on the Staudts' "commission," see chapter 2.

2. Dr. Calvin K. Staudt in their favorite *serdab,* ca. 1940.

The railway station was then located on the outer edge of the city, and between the station and the main part of Baghdad was a broad street, which is now a fine boulevard. This street led to a pontoon bridge, called Maude Bridge in honor of the British general who had freed the land from the Turks. The road was bordered with gardens in which, at that time of the year, roses, cannas, hollyhocks, and other garden flowers displayed their blooms; the ever-present palm trees lifted their fronds high in the air.

Near the bridge overlooking the Tigris River were the open-air coffeehouses crowded with men, and men only. In these open spaces they sat, pensively drinking coffee out of tiny cups, or drawing smoke from slender, bubbling *nargilas,* or playing backgammon. While the women were not seen in the coffeehouses, they certainly were noticed on the bridge, a scene which from a distance looked like a flower garden. The bridge was a mass of bright, variegated colors that moved, and in the colors was the glittering of gold! Jewish and Christian women had come out of the stuffy courts of their houses to *shamm al-hawa* (smell the air). The Muslim women of the city, always swathed in black when they were on the street, did not have this freedom. These women on the bridge were covered from head to foot with heavy silk 'izars or 'abayas, woven on the Baghdad looms in various shades.

The 'izars, which were worn only by married Christian or Jewish women, were of solid colors with marvelous borders of deep and contrasting colors interwoven with threads of gold. The colors were largely pastel shades: cream, lavender, rose, blue, and pink. The garment was made by sewing together two lengths of silk, the solid colors meeting, leaving the borders to cover the head and decorate the lower edge. The unmarried girls wore sleeveless 'abas which hung from their heads.[4] These, too, were of various colors, but the designs were woven into the entire piece. These lovely garments are now a thing of memory only. In their day they were beautiful and colorful, and brightened the monotonous drab of a city built of clay bricks, the color of the desert earth.

We crossed the bridge of boats in an 'arabana (a two-horse carriage). How wide the Tigris was! It was a great river in a thirsty land, greater by far than I had anticipated.[5] Neither did the shoreline disappoint me. The

---

4. 'Aba is short for 'abaya.

5. During the summer season the Tigris that so impressed Ida Staudt in 1923 can be crossed in 2009 from one bank to the other by walking and island-hopping on its drying bed. Its water flow has been choked by the dams, hydroelectric plants, and tunnels that the Turkish government has been building in southeastern Anatolia. In that region of Turkey the headwaters of the Tigris and the Euphrates have for centuries gushed and cascaded southward to carve "the land between two rivers" and to help create "the Cradle of Civilization" there. On its way to Iraq, the Euphrates winds its course into eastern Syria first, tempting its government to build, in recent decades, its own lesser dams. An

houses with overhanging balconies were built as close to the water's edge as the time of flood would permit. Blue-faienced minarets lifted themselves into the blue of the sky. On the river itself were seen the various river crafts: round, old-as-time *guffa*s, like the ark of Moses, made of wicker and daubed on the outside with bitumen; *mahaila*s with graceful sails; rowboats aplenty, and a few launches the worse for wear.

Had our entrance into Baghdad been carefully planned—the time of the year, the time of the day, even the day itself in the hope that first impressions would not mar the picture the imagination had conjured up of this once famed city—it could not have been more perfect. Palm groves, gardens, crowds of men in the coffeehouses, a riot of colors on the bridge, blue-tiled minarets, overhanging balconies, river crafts, the noble Tigris: all had a genuine "Oriental" flavor. Whatever I surveyed from the 'arabana that evening was wondrously different from what I had been accustomed to. It was a world not yet influenced, or just slightly touched, by the West. That something that was within me which seemed akin to this old world responded to it. At once, I knew I would like it and that I would happily adjust myself to it.

When we reached the little hotel that was only a stone's throw from the bridge, and a few steps from the main thoroughfare, a strangeness suddenly engulfed me. Was it really I who had come to Baghdad? Or had I temporarily exchanged myself with someone else for the Mesopotamian experience and adventure? Or had my youthful concepts of the land been magically transformed into merely an illusory reality? Could it be possible that it was I who was in the land that had so long held my unflagging interest and in whose bygone greatness I had reveled?

I had traced the course of the two mighty rivers, the Tigris and the Euphrates, that have redeemed the land, long before this day that my eyes lighted upon them. I had hung over the pictures of the palaces of Babylon

---

extensive bibliography can be found online on the Tigris-Euphrates dispute, a controversy between Iraq, Turkey, and Syria, whose tensions exacerbate the conflicts that are already plaguing the whole region.

and Nineveh and marveled at the minds that could conceive so greatly. With difficulty did I bring myself down to earth and believe that I was now, in the body, in Iraq; and in the verily existing city of Baghdad, which had hitherto been to me only a city reared by magic and dissolved by magic. The very idea that I was now here partook of magic itself.

There was, however, not the slightest suggestion of magic in the little hotel that harbored us for a time. It had obviously not been reared by the jinn for a prince's palace, though its name was Palace. It was indeed most commonplace; and when I climbed its high, irregular steps, up which I wished I could be hoisted, I was brought down to solid earth and no longer had any doubt as to my identity.

Remarks concerning the weather of Mesopotamia were beginning to perturb me. We had come to Iraq via the Pacific, and landing in Calcutta, we had crossed India to Bombay by rail. It was March, and India was humidly hot. Its discomforts being on my mind, I made it the subject of conversation. Talking about it to a British officer who had come into our compartment on the train, I became curious when he remarked that he knew of only one place hotter. Wondering where that might be, I received the staggering reply "Iraq." That certainly was a blow! We recovered by hopefully believing he was mistaken, and in a certain way he was. It is true that the heat of Mesopotamia registers higher, but because it is a dry heat, it is far more endurable. Happily, my faith in the decency of the climate of Iraq steadily mounted on our voyage from Bombay. It was early spring, the Indian Ocean was at its best, the Persian Gulf belied its reputation of being an inferno, and the Shatt-al-Arab, the river formed by the combined waters of the Tigris and the Euphrates, behaved perfectly. Palm groves stretched along both sides of the river, and those on the Iraqi shore were separated by little irrigation ditches that opened glimpses of the desert behind the groves. This dark green border that ornamented the river was very attractive.

At Basrah, we left the ship to set foot on the ancient and historic soil of Mesopotamia. "Sinbad's Bossorah" had been important as a shipping port for centuries, and became more so during World War II when much of the lend-lease aid to Russia and the Middle East was discharged here. It is now an important airport as well.

Our landing was auspicious not only as to weather; it took place on the very day we set foot in Mesopotamia, and at the same time when the Constituent Assembly of a hundred delegated members were meeting in Baghdad, organizing themselves for the purpose of framing a constitution for Iraq. This coincidence was made possible because of an earlier sailing from Bombay than we had expected. The cabin we occupied had been assigned to the Agha Khan, the head of the Ismaeli Muslims. His mother being indisposed, he cancelled his passage shortly before the boat sailed, and the cabin was offered to us.

The train from Basrah to Baghdad passed through the land where civilization began. This region, though now largely a desert, insisted that we recognize its mighty past and demanded that we acknowledge the debt which the world for all time owes it. A few miles from Ur Junction dwelt Abraham in the city of Ur of the Chaldees, where the moon god was worshipped; there the priests ascended the great ziggurat by a triple stairway to sing the hymns of praise to the god who lifted himself in overawing splendor from the horizon, flooding the alluvial plain with his glory. The mound on which Nebuchadnezzar had reared his palaces fairly shouted at us, proclaiming its days of greatness as the train passed by. And when we crossed the Euphrates, one of the rivers that had watered the Garden of Eden, the river boldly glared at us as if we dared question the garden that flourished along its banks.

Nothing can "down" the history of Mesopotamia. The ruins are forever a testimony to the glories that once were the colossal achievements of bygone days. The desert wastes and the undeveloped resources seemed to scoff and snarl at those who tread the land today, as if to say, "Will you ever be able to build another Babylon, another Kish, another Erech, or another Ur?" And while the list of names of famous cities and civilizations trailed on, the train pulled into the station of the capital of Iraq, not the Baghdad of the caliphs, but the Baghdad that is today.

For two weeks we busied ourselves exploring the city. As we were thus occupying our time while staying at the misnamed Palace Hotel, we had warnings from the people that this paradise-like weather would not last much longer. We therefore stopped nosing about. Taking time by the forelock, we attended to the business of settling. We first sought advice concerning the kind of house we wanted, inasmuch as we were quite ignorant of the requirements for, at least, a minimum of comfort. And what a house we eventually moved into!

This dwelling was in the heart of the densely crowded Christian quarter. It was built, as were all the houses at that time, around an open court but it lacked the very essentials for the endurance of the heat which was coming on apace. Nearly all Baghdad houses then had a *serdab*, a room below the level of the court, where the temperature was lower. Before there were electric fans, a serdab was a saving refuge in the summer. This house, unfortunately, had no serdab and no real room downstairs except the kitchen, which, being windowless, had nothing in it but a crude charcoal stove and a small hole in the middle of the floor for drainage. I did my best to make the house livable as the thermometer soared; but I failed, and it nearly broke me.

The house had been my first problem; my second was needed help. The solicitous person who had recommended his relative to assist in the general work and do the marketing soon discovered that I knew the difference between honest work and shirking, and between what I should have had for my money and what was actually brought me. On that shamming and profiteering I slammed down with spirit. Then, just as I was about to succumb to the unyielding torments—the heat, the rodents that bored holes beside the closed ones, the roaches that were on nightly parade, the mosquitoes that made directly for me—there was brought to the house to help me one of the sweetest women that ever graced a home of ours. She belonged to a refugee people, called Assyrians, who had fled from their native land in the First World War. Her name was Sonia.

Sonia had lost all of her family in a terrorizing flight except one son who had gone to America. I wrote to him for her, and not only did she later join him, but she was also provided with a comfortable home by a fellow countryman who had recognized her worth. Sonia could not control heat and vermin and general discomfort any more than I, but her faithfulness and kindness and willingness to work revived my spirits and my courage. Her short stay with us had taught us where to turn for help when needed, so that throughout the years that followed, the Assyrian helpers were, because of their reliability, their versatility, and their efficiency, pillars in our home and in the school which we opened.[6]

In June 1924 a large house that stood by the river was temporarily offered to us. It had been built for comfort, and we thoroughly enjoyed it. Here we started really to live. In the middle of the day we retreated into the cool serdab. In the evening we found it restful and enchanting just to sit on the balcony facing the river and watch the lights sparkling on the pontoon bridge and "along the shadowy shore." In the night we slept on the roof under the star-studded heavens, and the morning's first gift was the sight of the river with the sun striking the buildings on the opposite shore; Omar Khayyam's lines came to mind:

> Wake! For the Sun who scatter'd into flight
> The Stars before him from the Field of Night,
> Drives Night along with them from Heav'n, and strikes
> The Sultan's Turret with a Shaft of Light.

Two servants belonged to this house whom we had to adopt: a Goa cook and a general servant of Arab extraction.[7] The latter was so thin and wore such a huge headgear that I always feared for his balance. A Baghdad house of ample size was built on the presumption of having servants. The city, which had no paved streets when we arrived and was innocent of sprinkling, made constant cleaning a necessity. The kitchen in this house was downstairs, while the dining room was upstairs, and the ceilings were

---

6. Because of this genuine gratitude and high regard with which the author held their Assyrian helpers, she devoted a whole chapter to them, examining in some detail their complicated history, something avoided in this memoir when covering other communities of the land. Because we know the complex history of this ancient Christian, Syriac-speaking minority more than we did over fifty-five years ago, I have either taken the liberty of trimming Ida Staudt's account wherever I judged it unsubstantiated or have qualified her information with a brief footnote (Joseph 2000, 9–15).

7. Goa was a tiny Portuguese colony on the west coast of India; it was peacefully taken back by India in 1947.

high. In a land where you must bargain or haggle over the purchase of even an onion, a foreigner cannot do the family buying unless she is well versed in Arabic and has lots of leisure and patience.

My schooling during these few months in someone else's house was an excellent preparation for the setting up of our own establishment and enabled me to arrive at some definite decisions. I would not keep groceries under lock and key and dole them out every morning. When Anthony the cook asked for a certain number of eggs and a certain amount of sugar for the day, how could I know how much went into the food, and how much went away with them in the evening? Neither would I notify the cook when I intended to come to the kitchen: I would enter when I chose. That summer we had three American young men visiting us. Not knowing the rule, one of them who was domestically inclined one morning stepped into the kitchen where he surprised Anthony at his bath standing over the drainage hole pouring water over himself. Then, too, I decided to be boss. Complete "bossdom" I never fully attained. Spasmodically, when I stormed, every one walked softly and humbly and obediently for a few days, but it never lasted.

While living in this improved state we were frequently called upon by Ibrahim the carpenter. He told us of a big house near his home, which he called a *qasr*, which literally means a castle but is also commonly applied to a large and commodious house. The house had just been vacated by the British high mess. It was in a newer part of the city surrounded by palm groves. Ibrahim wanted us to come and look at it, which we did. It certainly took my eye, and we rented it at once, and with our moving into it in fall our active life in Baghdad began. The house was exactly suited for our purpose, though not a few had thought it was too far out. Today it is in the center of the city. So has Baghdad grown and expanded.

It was indeed a big house with twenty large rooms built around an open court around which ran wide balconies. On one of these balconies three hundred boys could easily be seated. Here we conducted our morning assemblies and many of the school functions were held here. The house also had domed serdabs that had a cloistered air and spacious rooms upstairs with high ceilings. The house was large enough for both a residence and a school: an inspiring house. I felt like a titled lady as I walked about this spacious qasr, and I truly believe that it, to a certain extent, remade me and obliged me to become what the house demanded of me. One felt lordly in it and acted accordingly. This gave me, who am small of stature, an authoritative air greatly needed in the school. One day a friend said to me, "You won't change the East, but the East will change you." That was not altogether true; it worked both ways.

In the center of the open court of the house was a large octagonal garden where grew both flowers and trees. My husband spoke of it as the forest, for in it grew a large olive tree; two orange trees; two oleanders, the one with red flowers and the other with white; a date tree; and for a time a banana tree, whose large leaves as they unfolded were a marvel to behold. Through the years it was restful and refreshing to sit in the evening by the octagonal garden, or as my husband would say, by "the forest in the house." Brightly green were the cannas, gay were the flowers, and varied were the trees. I especially loved to trace the waxy edges of the big canna leaves, which were almost transparent against the electric light of the entrance corridor of the court.

The house readily lent itself to special occasions and dramatic performances. Evenings when the moon filled the court with the light of day, or when Orion majestically hunted across it, the house became a Shakespearean theatre. The stage was under a balcony; the groundlings crowded the court; the balconies above filled; and expectantly we awaited the play to begin. Here plays both in Arabic and in English were given; here Russian refugees gave concerts; here, too, the first few commencements added luster to the imposing structure.

The imposing qasr has had a unique and interesting history. The British had occupied it as their high mess; and previous to that the German High Command, during World War I, had made it their headquarters. We were often warned that the ghost of General von der Goltz haunted the place. Dull days might have been enlivened had he put in an appearance, and listless students might have been shocked into studiousness had he materialized. Even prior to the German occupation it was the Italian consulate, and the flagstaff which they left on the roof was still there when we took over the house.

From the very beginning things went big, worthy of the house. Everything we did in those early days partook of romance. When we called, the houses seemed to us wonderful and the hospitality abounding. If we met officials who were shaping events, the events magnified the men. When these attended our social functions, or accepted the invitations to meet distinguished travelers in our big living room, with flushed cheeks and quickened heartbeats we welcomed and served them. Visiting the oil fields and seeing the hidden wealth of Iraq tapped, or making a trip to an irrigation project that was to reclaim the desert and make it fertile, we rejoiced in these economic assets for the country. When we received invitations to public functions, or to the dedication of new buildings, or to the opening of new enterprises, we accepted; and, what is more, felt as proud of these achievements as the people themselves. Even when the wind in a dust storm lifted the yellow sand of the desert and deposited it on the city, the particles as the sun shone on them looked to us as if they were gold.

We called on kings and queens, on Bedouin sheikhs; attended charming weddings; breakfasted or drank tea in lovely gardens; fervently greeted visitors on their arrival in Baghdad and showed them the sights; held school affairs to which we cordially invited the public; exulted in our work and found zest in it; and made plans to meet the needs of the day consonant with the seemingly growing greatness of the land. In these and other ways we launched out into the life of Baghdad, which was then so alluring because of its inspiriting hopefulness. These beginning days were great days for us when we lived, not, of course, in the city depicted in storybooks and in Arab history, but in the present Baghdad—a Baghdad, nevertheless, which to us at the time appeared equally great, since we saw it with our inner eye, and could through rose-colored glasses, as it were, behold the splendor that once was here.

So on the banks of the broad and noble Tigris which flows through the city, we made our home, and found life offering more than we had the capacity to grasp. This life in the earlier years drew us constantly on to explore, to enjoy, and to understand—with emphasis on the last as time advanced.

2

An Educational Adventure

Our appointed task was to be engaged in educational work in Baghdad, and to that end we at once addressed ourselves. It was an educational adventure in more ways than one, and was undertaken at a time when conditions for such a venture were favorable. This was shortly after the First World War, a time when the people of Iraq were hopefully looking forward to a Tomorrow while still clinging to a Yesterday.

We were commissioned to open and carry on educational work under the United Missions in Mesopotamia, a combined effort of the mission boards of three denominations. For nearly a dozen years we labored under mission supervision; but eventually, we undertook the carrying on of the work independently, having behind us no longer an organization giving financial support.[1] This was a heroic venture, breathtaking in its audacity. That we were able to balance our budget from year to year was a miracle, for in that budget had to be included all our living expenses and the rental

---

1. Staudt does not tell us why the Mission Board that commissioned them in 1924 decided to close the school in 1934. One possible reason: the Great Depression, at its most austere in the mid-1930s. It is possible also that the Staudts in Baghdad were much more ecumenically minded than the members of the Missionary Board in Philadelphia. After World War I, Christian missions began to reexamine their position vis-à-vis Islam. By the 1920s some of the assumptions of Western superiority, so characteristic of the nineteenth-century missions, were being abandoned in some quarters. Running a school in Baghdad whose students were "Sunni Muslims, Shiah Muslims, Wahhabis, Ismaelis, Bahais, Druses, Sikhs, Buddhists, Hindus, Confucianists, Yezides, Subbis, Jews of various slants, [in] addition to Protestant sects [and] Christian students [from] not less than a dozen religious groups," the Staudts could not but take into consideration the religious plurality of their world. For their ecumenicity, see chapter 21.

of the grounds and buildings we used. That we were able to do this for half of the twenty-three years we lived in Baghdad until we retired was nothing less than providential.[2] Calling upon the Ministry of Education soon after our arrival, my husband learned that the newly formed government had as yet made no laws or provisions for the regulation and supervision of foreign schools; and until such laws were passed enabling us to get a permit to open an American school, we were advised by the ministry to open and conduct a school for girls, a step which we were entitled to enter upon under an old Turkish permit that had been granted to a Protestant community.

Acting upon this advice, we opened a school for girls on a very small scale, for we had no appropriation as yet for a school, not even for equipment. This meant that we were obliged to use our private living rooms for classrooms. Twenty girls were all I felt I could receive and made an announcement to that effect. When the school was opened in fall, the twenty girls appeared and a waiting list was started. But on account of the constant pressure for admission, I was finally induced to fit up an empty room in the large house and admit twenty more.

How these girls had pushed to enter the school. There was not one among them who had come for any other purpose but to learn, and all drank in whatever was offered to them avidly. Their lessons were always well prepared, and all were eager to recite. The chief trouble a teacher had was to restrain those not called upon to recite from assisting the reciter. While studying a simple science book, I never needed to hunt for specimens or set up an apparatus. What was needed was brought by the girls. The morning devotions they learned to love sincerely, especially the singing of our choice hymns, even though their racial backgrounds and the religious beliefs of the families from which they came greatly differed.

---

2. With the assistance of a few prominent friends of Judge Harvey C. Bickel, the American School for Boys, Baghdad, was incorporated under the laws of the State of Maryland in the early 1940s. A Board of Trustees for the school was established that included, among others, the eminent broadcaster Lowell Thomas; Theodore Roosevelt Jr., son of President Theodore Roosevelt; and former U.S. president Herbert Hoover. For information on Judge Bickel, see the editor's foreword.

The girls fell in line with everything I proposed. When I suggested that it might be a fine thing to bring the families from which they came together one evening at the school and entertain them, the suggestion was at once acted upon, and a date was fixed. Excepting some Muslims, all the families came. Fathers, mothers, sisters, brothers—all were there. In entertaining the group the girls cooperated perfectly. Some were at the door to receive the guests; others led them to seats in the court and later to the balcony to see pictures thrown on a screen. Some brought the group down again into the court where sherbert and cake were served. Seeing her daughter ladling out sherbert and filling the glasses, a mother suddenly exclaimed, "Look at Naima; at home she does not lift her hand to do a stroke of work; but look at her now." In this school girls from high families had learned among other things that it is not dishonorable to work with one's hands. Inasmuch as this first effort of mine to bring divergent groups together was such a success, it opened up vistas of many possibilities along this line.

But this school which was such a joy to me, and which meant so much for the girls who were a part of it and for the families from which they came, suddenly came to an end: the school unexpectedly and abruptly was closed. In the spring of that year a woman was sent to the field to head the Girls School. Her plan was to start a simple primary school, but as the girls whom I had received and taught had had a primary education, there was no place for them anymore in the school the coming year.

The girls were heartbroken about it and so was I. The parents, too, were much concerned, and did everything they could to have the school continued. They drew up a petition, signed by every parent whether Muslim, Jew, Catholic, Orthodox, or Protestant, beseeching that the present school should be continued, and forwarded it to the proper authorities in America. They even proposed sending a communication to the State Department of the United States government. In my guest book is a touching sentiment opposite the name of a Canadian professor of Christian theology who was visiting Baghdad. Happening to call on us on a Sunday afternoon when a delegation of Jews had come to talk about the school, he wrote, "I have been deeply impressed by a deputation of prominent Hebrews begging that the higher school for their daughters should not be closed."

When fall came and schools opened, I was visited one day and a simple question was put to me, "What will you do for your girls?" I answered, "I can form them into a club, a study club." This I did. I could not bear the thought of having these bright and loveable girls to be frustrated in their desire to learn. Since they no longer had the chance to go on with their schooling, I resolutely determined that they should, at least, have some opportunity to improve themselves. Though they undoubtedly missed some things which a formal high school education might have given them, nevertheless in this club in which their interest was now centered and for which they lived from week to week, they acquired almost as much as a formal education would have given them. They received a great deal of valuable information, a rich cultural background, and a wholesome attitude toward life, all of which has been to them a source of mental and spiritual strength.

But since the Girls Club did not occupy all my time and strength as their school had done, I gave my services from then on largely to the American School for Boys which my husband founded. As the school was housed in the same building in which we lived, it was the natural thing for me to do under the circumstances. In this way I became a co-laborer with my husband, simply transferring my major interest and time from girls to boys.

The permit to open the American School for Boys, of both primary and high school grades, was granted and approved by the Council of State. The permit gave us a large measure of freedom in administration and in the working out of a curriculum. It also allowed us to teach our subjects in English. Arabic, Arab history, and Iraq geography, however, had to be taught. There was one interesting item in the permit which read, "The school should admit boys only and should not be coeducational, except in the kindergarten, where small girls may be admitted." Being aware of the fact that in America boys and girls are together in primary and high schools, the educational authorities possibly felt that we Americans might be foolish enough to introduce coeducation in the Muslim world.

Later we also secured a permit to open a four-year college course, though we never ventured beyond freshman. On several occasions the minister of education had intimated that when we really launched out to be a full-fledged college, we should specialize in agriculture, stating that as the University of Beirut specializes in medicine, and Robert College in Istanbul in engineering, so we should specialize in agriculture. Indeed, this we had hoped to do.

Nearly everyone in authority and position was favorably disposed to have an American school for boys in Baghdad. King Faisal was friendly to our plans and endeavors and had hoped we would be a help to make Baghdad a great educational center. Before our arrival he was reported to have said that if America wanted to do anything for this new nation, then the finest thing she could do would be to establish a university in Baghdad comparable to the American University of Beirut. More than once before he died, he had offered to donate government land for us should we be ready to build.

Jafar Pasha al-Askeri, who was prime minister at the time of our arrival in Iraq, also took an unusual interest in our work. A few weeks after our school was officially opened, he visited the school and inspected every phase of it, saying that he wanted to observe the school in action, so that he would be able to defend it if the occasion should ever arise. I take it that he also came for another purpose, a purpose which at the time he did not reveal. A few days later he returned, bringing with him his two little sons and a nephew, and placed them in our primary school.

The gradual growth and expansion of the American School for Boys in Baghdad are well illustrated by two questions which were sometimes asked. "Where is the American School for Boys?" was a question commonly repeated when our work began; and the answer was "In Sinak," Sinak being the name of the section in Baghdad in which the school was found. But in a few years the table was turned. The question then asked was "Where is Sinak?" And the answer invariably given was "Where the American School for Boys is located." As the enrollment increased, and as a boarding department was opened, and as an athletic field was added, the school was spread over a large area in this quarter of the city.

Eventually our big living room upstairs was turned first into a reading room and later into a classroom; our guest room became the high school library; and our dining room, which resembled a cloistered refectory, became a chemical laboratory. Finally we were reduced to a small bedroom and our spacious, cathedral-like *serdab*. The latter, which was not suitable for school purposes, we were obliged to occupy not only in summer for which it was intended but also in winter.

When I left my bedroom in the morning, I could never appear in negligee, for I was at once in the school. I rose early, and in stepping out on the balcony or going downstairs, I invariably encountered not only the boarders but some of the day students as well. I knew before I stepped out of the room that I would meet early comers, for I had heard our faithful janitor lift and let drop the strong iron bar that held the big and heavy double doors securely closed. This meant that the boys could enter.

Those from the outlying districts of the city and the suburbs had difficulty in getting transportation; and as we insisted upon punctuality and were rather severe with latecomers, many of the boys would try to get to school before the rush for the little, grey, dingy busses and the stampeding for seats began. One morning some of the boys who were late told me that at the bus terminus in their suburb an English officer was stationed for a time to line up the passengers and make them go into the busses in an orderly manner. Evidently the Britisher became weary of his thankless job, and as he failed to appear that morning the crowd hesitated to enter the busses, whereupon one of the bus drivers leaned out and shouted, "Politeness finished," with the result that the familiar scramble followed.

My day began with that stepping out of the bedroom fully panoplied for the day's encounters. It began early and came to no definite end. We lived among the boarders as well as among the day students, so that we were always surrounded by boys whether in the day or in the night. Even on a Sunday when from morning to early evening the house was blissfully quiet there were usually one or two punished by having their gate passes withheld.

For a long time the boarders were in the charge of a young man who had come to us from a peasant village near Mosul. He was a poor boy but his family through sacrifices and denials were able to get together enough money each year to pay for his schooling. He did not shine intellectually, but he had a winning way with boys; and after he was graduated, we thought he might make a good head for our boarding department. This was a difficult job due to differences in ages, in races, and in the surrounding conditions and influences from which these students had come. Among these boarders were the tent dwellers and the city dwellers, the refugees from the one-roomed huts and the children from the palatial house.

To this young man my mind turns in particular gratitude for his devotion and gifted power of leadership. The parents of the smaller boys marveled to see their quarrelsome and obstreperous sons become as docile as lambs, and the older boys were never irritated by an overemphasis of his authority. As he went about his duties quietly and unflinchingly, a peace descended upon the boarders. In the evening after the bell had rung for the lights to be out, he would tiptoe to me on the balcony, where we would whisper together about the incidents of the day, at the same time listening to be assured that all was well.

These whispered conferences followed a day of steady and varied tasks. Immediately after breakfast every boarder went to his room for inspection and stood by his well-made bed ready for my entrance. The local-made lockers were open and the rooms had to be in order. I could usually tell by their faces those who had done their work well and gladly gave them the deserved praise, but those whose beds and belongings were not in order were briskly set to work.

Teaching occupied most of the morning. My classes were usually English. How easily and quickly these boys mastered the English language. While I was struggling to learn Arabic, I often wished I could make the same progress. So correctly had some of our graduates mastered writing and speaking English that when they went away to England or America to study, they were often complimented for it. My greatest delight was to teach English literature. How I reveled in teaching Tennyson's *Idylls of the King!* The "Knights' Song" was our tour de force which we recited in unison, and for visitors we made it clang and clash. In studying Longfellow's *The Wayside Inn Tales,* we recited the "Challenge of Thor" in the same high spirit. We carefully studied one of the plays of Shakespeare, either *Julius Caesar* or *Macbeth,* and occasionally acted and recited scenes from them in the general assembly.

Our bedroom was so located that when I stood or sat in the doorway, I could survey the classrooms around the court, and as all teaching was done with open doors and windows the year round, I could see as well as hear. The office was downstairs and so were the laboratories, but all class-rooms were upstairs in my domain, so that the policing of the school fell largely upon me. Actually, my husband had conferred upon me the title of Police of the School, which he always claimed was higher than to be head of the English Department. Whether it was a higher title as he claimed is certainly debatable; one thing was sure: it was more onerous.

From my vantage ground of the bedroom door the least disturbance caught my eye and ear and found me swiftly on the spot. Two things were very characteristic about these boys. The one was that they soon gauged a new teacher's ability to teach, his knowledge of the subject, and his devotion to his profession. And woe to the teacher who did not make the grade! If a teacher went to his class and had not worked out a program before-hand as to how he was going to conduct the class, he would soon discover that while he hesitated or paused the class would take over; a dozen or more at the same time would suggest what to do next, and they were never at a loss to do this; confusion and noise would prevail.

In the second place, these students were endowed with limitless vital-ity. It was more than pep; my husband called it *sisu,* which is a Finnish word to describe endless energy and vitality, or a shot in the arm, as it were, giving one superhuman activity. Missionaries and educators from other countries also noticed this exuberant spirit and vitality in these boys. Once we had with us two lady teachers who were teaching their way around the world. They taught first in the Pacific Northwest of the United States; then in the Hawaiian Islands, in Japan, in China, in India; and finally they came to us. From their experiences in teaching these dif-ferent races, they discovered that the Iraqi students were the most active and energetic and that they required a greater presence of mind and a greater outlay of mental energy to teach than the students of any of the other nations. I still recall hearing one of these lady teachers sternly saying one day to a class that started to take things over, "I told you to open your books—not your mouths."

My constant visiting of the classes was not, however, solely for disci-plinary purposes—far from it. The two study periods, one in the middle of the morning and the other at the beginning of the afternoon session, was my time to range over the whole school and freely enter the classrooms. It was then that I talked matters over with the boys, commended individuals or a class for some outstanding accomplishments, or gave praise for things done that were pleasing. A class had won an athletic banner; a boy had recited well; someone had won in an oratorical contest; boys had spoken well in the Brotherhood Society meeting; a class had attempted to teach themselves in the absence of a teacher—there was no end of chances to encourage by praising.

Then there was the everlasting effort to keep the building clean and to chase away the vendors of seeds and cakes and sweets who were hanging around the buildings on the street. All kinds of seeds could be bought, and the hulls of the watermelon seeds which the boys liked were easily dropped on the floor; paper, too, was readily dropped. I had the boys so well trained that all I needed to do was to look on the floor when I saw on it seeds or paper or other litter, and immediately someone dived down to pick it up.

We hung good pictures in the classrooms, but so often they hung crooked. A glance at them sufficed to have someone get up and straighten them. I would often say, "Straight!" and then casually add, "Sit straight, walk straight, think straight, act straight." One of our graduates while visiting us here in America watched me bring orderliness to the living room before retiring. He began, "Straight! Sit straight, walk straight, think straight, act straight." I said, "Do you remember that?" He said, "That and many more things." This former student of ours wore a gold key somewhat similar to a Phi Beta Kappa key given to him by the University of Texas for having attained the highest grades in the freshman class in this big university.

One of my happiest recollections was the years when with my other duties I served as librarian and had oversight of the communicating reading room. On the reading room walls hung two bulletin boards, which for many years I kept covered with pictures and clippings to enlarge the interest of the students, changing them usually every week. Our library was our pride. We started it with books from our own collection. Then when we were home, we visited secondhand bookshops in both New York and Philadelphia and sent books out by the boxes. I recall a bookshop in New York where the head of it not only helped me to select sets of books, but was so thrilled at sending them to Baghdad that he personally attended to the packing and shipping. Knowing the students and knowing the books, I often suggested what would be of interest and benefit to a particular boy; and when a book was returned, I proceeded to ask a few questions in regard to the book to make sure that it was read.

In letters received from our graduates after they had entered a college or university where there were much larger libraries, they seldom failed to mention the benefit they had received from the reading of books in our library. An alumnus who at the time was a student in a university wrote, "Perhaps, the greatest contribution the school has made was to develop a love of reading. I have received limitless benefits from the reading of books in our old library, and that is why I am sending you a small sum for the purchase of more books." From a college in America another wrote, "I do wish to have once more those school days renewed when we used to sit in the library and read the fine magazines and good books."

In the middle of the afternoon I tried to get an hour's rest. But by four o'clock I was busy again drilling and whipping into shape a group of boys for the assembly or the Brotherhood meeting. Boys had to be trained to sing, to recite, to play in an orchestra, or to deliver a speech. In this I had always the help and cooperation of our teachers. Then at the first intimations of spring, which began the middle of February, the elaborate preparations for our public events began. The chorus had to buckle down to serious work, and so had the orchestra, the orators, the actors, and other performers. Then came the rehearsals, which were almost nightly. For whether the affair was great or small, we left nothing to chance.

Thursday afternoon was dedicated to the Girls Club. Here I met the girls who had been my first love and concern. I looked forward to this afternoon with the same eagerness as the girls. Both for me and for the girls it was the red-letter day of the week. If perchance a stranger appeared while we were having our meeting, she could not tell by the way the girls conducted the meeting whether they were Easterners or Westerners. We studied music from records prepared for the understanding and appreciation of music; we studied English literature; and one whole year was devoted to Shakespeare under the guidance of a gifted friend of ours who had given us a sabbatical year. We reviewed good books and studied history as in a class. Every now and then we devoted a meeting to current events—world events. Two of our lady teachers even met the group on another afternoon and gave them mathematics and science. One of the girls, who had studied in Paris, gave us an unforgettable afternoon with Ibsen's *Peer Gynt*, interspersing the story with the playing of the Grieg suite.

On a Saturday my program of activities was different from that of the other days of the week. In the morning there was either a general assembly where students recited poems in Arabic and English, and where they learned to sing all kinds of popular songs, or a meeting of the Arabic Literary Society, or the Brotherhood meeting. My services in the general assembly and in the Brotherhood were in demand; at the Arabic Society, which was sponsored by the head of the Arabic Department, my husband alone was present. The fortnightly Saturday evening meetings of the International Relations Club, at which I acted only as hostess, was to me most stimulating and informing; and the frequent Saturday evening parties, especially those for the boarders, were jolly and wholesome affairs.

At all our affairs, always and everywhere, we were there. Things never moved in a spirited way unless one or both of us were present. We purposely did this to keep up the morale, the level of standards that we had set, and to give an impetus for a high gear of teamwork. We believed that if a thing was worth doing at all, it was worth doing well. This principle we applied to the classrooms, to the study periods, to athletics, to our organizations, to our assemblies, to our public affairs, and to our many socials and parties for the students.

Sunday was my single day lent to leaven my spirits, and not a wavelet of it dared be squandered. I fairly attacked my reading material and did what I pleased until the evening, when school life began again with the vesper service. Before the service started our teachers, students, alumni, and young men from the city gathered, some on the balcony, some in the court, awaiting the hour. This Sunday evening service started at the suggestion, or rather request, of the teachers, who had asked for a simple service for themselves out of which grew this service for any who wished to attend. In the number attending, in the races and religions represented, and in the interest and spirit manifested, this has always been an amazement to visitors from abroad.

At first our summer recess was a real vacation, but as we became more and more integrated into the life of Baghdad, our vacations had to be shortened just as our living quarters had to be narrowed. There was no respite to the continuous calls for aid after the school year had ended. Numerous official letters had to be written for those who wanted to study abroad, to seek employment, to apply for Iraqi citizenship, to be exempt from military training, and scores of other requests. In many cases either my husband or I accompanied the student to his office or offices to intercede for him. There was a minister of the Interior who never failed to speak when he met me, of the time I stood by his desk until he signed the document granting a lad Iraqi citizenship. Then, after returning from a short summer vacation from Lebanon or Cyprus or Iran or Italy or the mountains of northern Iraq, preparations for the fall opening went into full swing.

All these activities were a drain on our own resources, but every now and then important people called giving us inspiration for our work, and by their assembly talks inspiring teachers and students. This was especially true during the first part of our residence in Baghdad when the country was still somewhat isolated, and when an address given by one from another country was a real treat. Some of these men and women were merely travelers passing through Baghdad; others had come to Iraq on a special mission as geologists, archaeologists, anthropologists, or journalists, or were interested in studying either the educational or the political or the social or the religious conditions of modern Iraq. For Iraqi students to listen to speakers from other lands was indeed a rare privilege. The ideas given and the statements made by these speakers, consciously and unconsciously, came to the surface later in the classrooms and were reflected in the speeches and essays of the older students.

Every speaker was surprised at the close attention given him from the time he began until he closed. A professor of an American college who later became its president afterwards wrote, "I never found a more attentive and appreciative and inspiring audience to speak to than the one that gathered on the balcony of your school." After Frances Parkinson Keyes had spoken, she later wrote an article for a magazine in which she said, "Never have I had more intelligent, more receptive and more responsive listeners. The handicap of language which I had dreaded raised no barriers;

there was immediate comprehension of every subject I discussed, swift and spontaneous laughter at every jest, and evidences of sincere and sympathetic feeling when I turned to serious topics. And I know they would bear favorable comparison with a similar group anywhere in the world."

Because of this educational adventure thousands of boys have been helped. These young men are today in every walk of life making their world a little better and the sum of good a little larger.

3

SCHOOL OF LIFE

As I was about to undertake the writing of this chapter, a letter came to us from one of our former students who is now enjoying a fellowship in a university in America where he is doing graduate work. In his letter he tells what the American School for Boys in Baghdad has meant to him. He says that the school had always been more than just a school; that it ought to be called "School of Life." This at once suggested to me the underlying thought of the chapter. Quoting from his letter in part, it reads, "During this Christmas season, I would very much like to acknowledge some of the things for which I am thankful, and many of these thanks go to you and the American School for Boys. . . . To it I owe the most important thing which I possess and that is my attitude toward life, my way of thinking . . . The American School for Boys may be called School of Life."

The letter expresses precisely what we had always wished the school to be. We were desirous that the boys under our tutelage should lack nothing which the best in education could bring them; but we were equally desirous, if not more so, that every boy should grow in wisdom as well as in knowledge, should respond to goodness as well as to instruction, and should acquire the right attitude toward life: an attitude of love and a love of service.

For a time we were unable to measure the academic standards and the general ability of our high school students, until we had the opportunity to judge them by their achievements as students abroad. Those who continued their education in colleges, universities, and technical schools in England, America, or the Near East really amazed us with their scholastic attainments. Many had become honor students and were already put on the dean's list at the end of the freshman year. In a university of 17,000

27

students one of our alumni received the highest grades in the freshman class. Another in his first year showed such outstanding ability that he won for himself a place in every important campus organization. Still another was awarded an annual prize for being the top student in character and leadership after he had been in his college for only a year and a half.

Teamwork was the key to much of our success. My husband and I worked cooperatively, and to a large extent complemented each other. One reason why our public functions were such a success and were so thoroughly enjoyed by everybody was in a measure due to this cooperation. But the credit did not belong to my husband and me alone. We always had teachers who entered into the spirit of the school, and who were efficient and devoted co-laborers. Possibly they had imbibed from us something of the joy and the zest for work. Not a few of our fine teachers were graduates of the American University of Beirut, mostly from Lebanon and Syria. We were never able to afford many Americans, though we usually had one or two.

The school pioneered in having lady teachers in a boys' school in this part of the world. And to the surprise of everybody they were a great success. It was indeed more or less an experiment to have women teachers in a school made up of adolescent boys; and this, too, at a time when it was generally taken for granted that women were mentally inferior to men.

I have such a fund of happy memories associated with these lady teachers. Some were regular teachers in high schools and colleges in America who gave us their sabbatical year; others were teaching their way around the world; while others came to stay with us for a few years. These were not only universally accepted but also honored, loved, and respected. What enthusiasm they created for study! What an inspiration they were in the classroom! They put on fine plays, trained boys to recite and orate, helped with the music, taught table manners, and assisted in entertaining people of the city and visitors from abroad. That they came to be generally recognized as having brains on a par with men was a step forward in the emancipation of women in this part of the world.

What really made this school to be more than just a school were the many activities and public affairs. The school was a veritable beehive of activities. In the big court of the commodious house and later on a portable stage erected on the playground, programs of various kinds were presented. There were plays in Arabic and in English, School Night, English and Arabic oratorical contests, Primary declamation contest, and other affairs which the public enjoyed and to which they came in large numbers.

The commencements were the climax of our many school affairs. But the one which remains most vividly in my mind was the first one. The guest speaker was none other than Jamil al-Zahawi, one of the great poets of the Arab world. He was known and honored not only in Iraq but also in Syria and Egypt. At the time of this commencement he was a member of the upper house of Parliament. It was an honor to have him on our program. His poems are read and recited in schools in all the Arab countries, and whenever our school had an assembly devoted to Arabic recitations, poems from Zahawi were invariably given. There was nothing about his appearance that was prepossessing; his frail body gave no indication of the fiery soul dwelling in it. When he read his poems he seemed to marshal hidden strength: his body vibrated, his hands gesticulated, and his voice rose and fell in accord with the sentiment.

Having written a special poem for the occasion, he read it with such fervor and poetic feeling that the audience swayed to the rhythm of the lines; and sensing the rhymed word at times, the audience repeated it ecstatically with him. They called out, "'Aal! 'Aal!" (Bravo! Bravo!) when the sentiment expressed profoundly appealed to them; and when he sat down they gave him a resounding applause. The entire poem was printed in the local newspapers. Freely translated, a few lines read, "Once Baghdad held the torch of learning, but the light was dimmed; and now you from the West have come to lead us again into the ways of knowledge."

In four ways, if not in five, did the school pioneer in Iraq. These were basketball, field day, commencement, and Alumni Association; and shall we add a fifth, the spirit of sportsmanship?

On an athletic field where the players were made up of different races and religions, and where raw players were for the first time trained, it was patent that trouble would arise while a game was being played. This happened once and only once, and that in an intramural basketball contest. The rivalry was keen, and as the play went on an ugly spirit developed.

Hands and feet were being used in an unsportsmanlike way; the game was called off. What were we to do?

The next day both teams were invited to a tea party in our large living room. The players were treated handsomely and given all the tea and cake they wanted. Then we spoke to them earnestly and straight, the word "straight" already being in their consciousness. We concluded our reproof by saying, "Let us now highly resolve that never again in the American School for Boys shall there be a repetition of the unsportsmanlike conduct we witnessed yesterday." Whereupon the boys gave three rousing cheers for the "Highly Resolve" that rang through the building. The resolution stuck.

We held three annual field days before the Ministry of Education took over and held an interscholastic one. Our field days were delightful and spectacular affairs for both the school and the citizens of Baghdad. The chief inspector of schools in Iraq at the time of our first field day said that for years he had been talking field day, but that he never could get it across. He congratulated us for what we had accomplished, saying, too, that our pioneering was an example and inspiration for other schools.

These first field days were held at the edge of the city where a large open space was prepared for the events. A person approaching the field on this great day, and seeing the flags flying, the colored tents, and the crowd of people, might have thought that here was a revival of a medieval tournament, so gay was the scene. Instead, it was the introduction of field and track events in this "new-old" land.

The students, grouped according to their classes, with their pennants, occupied the middle of the field within the oval track. Some of the spectators occupied the tents, but the large mass of people was standing around the field. To everyone entering a printed program listing nearly all the events of the Olympic Games was handed. The Iraq military band furnished music. To secure it, I myself interviewed the minister of Defense, asking only for half the members, since we felt we could not afford the full band. To our grateful surprise the whole band appeared, the minister backing this new venture of ours in a generous spirit. The prime minister, equally generous, appeared in person to distribute the prizes to the winning contestants and hand the cup to a representative of the winning class.

There is one more thing of importance and significance in this "School of Life," namely, its internationalism. In this sphere of activity the school made its greatest contribution. It created a league of hearts and minds, or as one of our alumni designated it, "a harmonious little league of nations."

Possibly there was no other educational institution in the world apart from the American University of Beirut where so many races and nationalities were thrown together. Students representing practically all the races and nationalities of Asia, except Japan and the countries of Southeastern Asia, were enrolled together with some from a dozen nations in Europe, mostly children of uprooted and displaced people, and a few from Egypt.

The school was also a veritable cross-section of society: every stratum of society was represented. The sons of the rich and the great were sitting side by side with the poor children of the refugee families. Relatives of the royal family and the favored sons of the ruling class, children of the feudal landlords and of the powerful merchants, sons of Bedouin sheikhs and of Kurdish chiefs, heirs of Afghan and Indian princes—these were sitting side by side with the needy and the underprivileged children from the Armenian and Assyrian refugee camps. It was a miniature world with its own racial and religious barriers. We tried to break down these barriers within the walls of the school and actually succeeded; they were replaced by a spirit of tolerance, mutual cooperation, and goodwill.

4

SIGNIFICANT OCCASIONS

No sooner had we arrived in Baghdad than we launched into a continuous stream of public events. These were significant occasions which introduced us to every phase of Baghdad's stirring and varied life. These occasions, too, were spectacular and dramatic in both setting and action.

The month of March in Baghdad and the early part of April make one forget all the discomforts of other months, for the weather can be so perfect. With the brief touch of spring the earth begins to break forth into an ecstasy of bloom. Gardens are in the height of their beauty; even the dead desert springs forth into a bright covering greenness. The short winter is forgotten; and the summer—but why think of summer? It is now spring, and spring perfection demands perfect delight.

It was during this period when the sun is friendly and the gardens are at their best, which in 1924 happened to be the first week of April, that the British high commissioner and his wife gave their annual garden party in the spacious grounds of the Residency by the side of the river. We had arrived in Baghdad a little more than a week before the occasion, and we undoubtedly owed our invitation to the thoughtfulness of an Englishman who had been a table companion on the boat from Bombay and who was destined for the high commissioner's office.

In the fairyland of the lawn of the Residency, with its high trees and gay flowers, we were in a Baghdad quite as romantic as if the garden had been that of Harun al-Rashid.[1] Here were ladies in dresses as many-hued

---

1. Harun al-Rashid was the most famous and powerful caliph-emperor of the Abbasid Empire.

as the flowers, vying with the bloom in attractiveness, and history-making gentlemen as variously costumed as a pageant of nations.

Sir Henry and Lady Dobbs were host and hostess to this large and distinguished company. Having so newly arrived in Iraq, we did not on that day know how important the people assembled in that garden were: British, Arabs, Kurds, Muslims, Christians, Jews; neither did we then understand the conflicting policies concerning the future of the country; nor were we aware of the crossing of British and Arab ambitions. Since the revolution in Iraq against the British in 1920, "the transformation of the facade of the existing administration from British to Arab" had been proceeding. Progress toward self-government had been made. The Constituent Assembly which was in session had been opened by King Faisal.[2] This was not only the first representative body under the new regime, but the first of its kind ever held in this old, old land. No wonder hearts thrilled; no wonder that this was an occasion for rejoicing!

Having left their lawmaking, the members of the Assembly attended the party. On that never-to-be-forgotten day they gave glamour to the garden by their costumes, which added color to an already colorful spectacle, just as the ladies had done with their many-hued dresses. These men who had come from every part of Iraq represented the many racial and religious groups of the land, and their clothes indicated to which of the many groups they belonged.

Very distinctive was the Kurdish 'agha, who had come down from the mountains of Kurdistan in the north: his big tasseled turban, embroidered jacket and trousers, and long white sleeves set him conspicuously apart. The great tribal sheikhs and the feudatory landlords, having come

---

2. In his speech to the Constituent Assembly, King Faisal referred to Islam once: to remind the assembly that Islamic law is based upon "consultation" (shura, 'ijma'), in accordance with the saying of the prophet Muhammad: "My community will never agree in an error." "In submission to this noble law," Faisal said, "and guided by the example of the civilized nations, and the will of the people of Iraq, we call upon you Members of the Assembly, to draft the constitution and to provide for the election of the Parliament." From the English newspaper Baghdad Times, Mar. 28, 1924, a copy of which Ida Staudt had saved.

from every section of the country, all of them Arabs and in Arab attire, formed a group by themselves. The dignitaries of the three great religions proclaimed by their robes and headdresses their particular adherences. Even the Europeans who were present had their classification, signifying whether civilian or military and to what rank they belonged by the braids and decorations that they wore.

I was tremendously impressed. The entire party was bewildering to a newcomer. It was as rich in setting and costume as any opera scene. I longed for a libretto to inform me as to what it was all about, and for a program to list the names of the actors and the parts they were playing. Could all these varied people be dwellers in one land? How could they work together if they were so intent on displaying their differences?

A stranger who comes to live in the land soon becomes conscious of something else than the everlasting sun, and that is the Wheel of Fortune which ceaselessly turns. At the garden party everyone appeared to be at the very top of the wheel, and it looked, too, as though he would remain there; yet, in the years that followed, many went down with the turning of the wheel; some fairly tumbled down and some remained down. But that tireless persistence that so exhausts the Westerner, that boundless patience of the East that waits and waits, were in many instances rewarded by a lift as the wheel turned upward.

One sighs as memory calls up the persons that so fascinated us that bright afternoon. Had I been able to look into a glass and read the future of these leaders in this newly born nation, how I would have recoiled in fright: Everything looked permanent and rosy that perfect day; and as most of the men were comparatively young, a long life of usefulness was the vista that opened fair prospects for the long stretch of years. Who foresaw death, assassination, suicide, exile, flight? No premonition of such fatalities on this day clouded the clear blue heavens.

In the confusions of the impressions of the day, one person stood out more prominently than even King Faisal and his retinue. She was introduced to me as Lady Surma. She spoke excellent English, and yet was not English. I was told that she was the aunt of the patriarch of the Nestorian Assyrians. Seemingly she was in high favor with Sir Henry and Lady Dobbs, for when she spoke of leaving, the private launch of the Residency was put at her disposal. She certainly had no presentiment of the fate awaiting her. That private launch docked at the landing steps had about it an enduring air, despite its light trimness. In it Lady Surma crossed the Tigris, while we, hailing an *'arabana,* drove to the little misnamed Palace Hotel with its characteristically high steps.

Many years have passed since we attended that garden party where we had seen practically all the notables of the land. It is almost incredible that only a few of these personages who had appeared that day so securely settled, so satisfied with their position in life, and so confident of the future are either alive or in Iraq today; I recall only a few. The change is overwhelming.

A few months later, in July, when the prediction in regard to the heat in Mesopotamia had reached complete fulfillment, there was held an extraordinary meeting in a girls' school, the first of its kind in the land. The newly formed government in Iraq at once began to open schools for girls as well as for boys. Simple primary schools these girls' schools at first certainly were, but it was a praiseworthy beginning. The largest of these, called the Girls Central School, was located in the densely populated Muslim quarter of the city; the girls attending were, with a few exceptions, Muslim. The course of studies covered four years, and twelve girls had completed it. The principal, an Armenian refugee from Mardin, Turkey, who had been educated in a Mission school, conceived the idea of preparing a school program and invited women to attend. It was the first real public function for women, and the memorable date of this meeting was July 19, 1924.

As I drove through the street to the school, about five o'clock in the afternoon, the heat seemed like the blasting breath of a prairie fire. Leaving the carriage at a narrow lane into which no vehicle could enter, I found myself mixed up with the black-*'aba*ed, closely covered Muslim women, shuffling along on slip-in slippers, one pair being edged with fur, all headed for the same place.

The gate leading into the school yard was guarded by three policemen, whose business, and business was brisk, was to keep out the mob of women who unfortunately had received no invitations. The policemen, however, had not added to their duty the collecting of invitations from the fortunate as they entered the gateway. These women, shrewder than the police, held on to their open-sesames; after having entered, they threw them over the wall to their friends, who, finding that the power of opening doors was not lost in the transfer, walked blithely into the school precincts. The audience was thus augmented by almost double the number anticipated. Six hundred invitations were sent out but almost a thousand attended.

This gathering of women was a cross-section of Baghdad's Muslim population. Under the black 'abas were all kinds of costumes, from the regulation dress of Muslim women, all being made according to one pattern, to the Parisian gown bought at the French store in Baghdad. The majority wore their hair in the customary two braids, one hanging over each shoulder, and the customary headdress consisting of a black kerchief folded like a breakfast shawl and held in place by a black satin band. I saw only two bobbed heads, but many henna-stained. The women who sat on the settees instead of chairs dropped their slippers and sat in their comfortable cross-legged way. No one felt constrained by convention.

The girls had had four years of study, and almost a thousand women had come out of seclusion to enjoy, for the first time, a program rendered largely by Muslim girls. I seriously pondered over the scene in the school yard: the eager, happy girls in a modern school, and the eager, excited women taking a first step toward their emancipation. The lives of the women in the Muslim world had been so barren, so limited, that it was not surprising that, with startling rudeness and force, they seized this dole offered them for a little wider living.

At this meeting the question was asked whether a group of women could have the use of a room in the building to organize a society, called a *nadi*. A letter had come from a woman's society in Egypt urging that a similar one be started in Baghdad, and plans were afoot to make an attempt. A very limited number of Christians were invited to these early discussions, and only three ever became active members, among whom I was honored to be included. After a time the club secured a house of its own, and hung a big sign above the door in order that the passersby, especially the men, might know that a woman's society was flourishing in Baghdad. Nevertheless, this strangely formless society was an expression of the aspirations of Muslim womanhood.

The president of the society was dear. In her home, where partridges walked about freely and companionably, guests were entertained by a parrot and by her victrola songs, known as laments, lovers' laments, for which, oddly enough, she had a special liking. She as well as the treasurer had never married, and this indicated an unusual independence of spirit. Though we liked our president very much, we could never win her over to like rules of order. Hence we never had an election because there was no constitution which called for one; and as no one wanted to offend her by suggesting that a rather lifeless body needed new blood, the group dwindled from less to less, until the society quietly and unobtrusively died.

Once a year the club held a public meeting, to which all contributors were invited, in order that they might inspect the house and listen to reports. The ladies would bring rugs from their homes, and not only covered the paved court but hung them from the balcony as well, thus making the place which ordinarily was most ordinary appear most elegant. Even a piano at times graced the occasion. One of these affairs was of unusual interest and to it the women came in goodly number. As the various ladies entered they were given the proper salutations. The "high-ups" were received standing: the right hand was lowered, then raised to the heart, to the lips, and to the forehead: a very lovely greeting. In the presence of the queen the earth was touched. The degree to which the hand was lowered usually indicated the degree of the rank of the individual; devastating to one's pride it must have been if the ladies receiving did not bother even to rise.

The meeting having been called to order, a place in the program was reached where the financial report was being read by a lady whose first public appearance had caused a nervousness that made the paper in her hand shake as though possessed. Just as I was wondering what might happen to the distressed lady, the attention of all was arrested by a high-pitched voice. All eyes were drawn from the shaking hand to the corridor, where we saw walking into the court none other than Miss Gertrude Bell, the legendary English lady, one of the pioneer-makers of Iraq (Stewart 2007). What happened to the report and the one reporting, no one recalls. Everybody at once rose; and Miss Bell, quite superior to such trifling matters as programs, passed from group to group salaaming and receiving in return the bows and salaams of the ladies. There was no haste on Miss Bell's part; her aplomb, her splendid assumption of priority, belonged to the best English tradition. Lady Dobbs, the British high commissioner's wife, was at the same meeting, but she had come on time and without ostentation. It took time for Miss Bell to greet all the ladies; and my only other recollection of the afternoon was that as the house was being inspected, she beckoned to me from the balcony to come upstairs at the request of Lady Dobbs, whose efforts to speak to me had been too interrupted to make progress.

I was present at another significant occasion. It was at a memorial service for Sir Sassoon Haskiel, held, as was the custom, forty days after his death. It took place in the large court of the Alliance School on the morning of September 7, 1932. He had died in Paris, and this memorial service was arranged to do honor to one who had rendered a fine service to his country, Iraq, and who had its welfare at heart.

Sir Sassoon had been a brilliant and distinguished citizen of Iraq and had taken a prominent and active part in the organization of the government consequent to the First World War. When Emir Faisal became king, he held the office of Minister of Finance in the king's first cabinet and was holding that same office, too, when we arrived in Baghdad. In forming the policy of the new government no man was wiser in counsel than he. His judgment was considered sane, and of his wisdom and moderation Gertrude Bell writes, "Among the men I met soon after my residence in Baghdad, he was one of them. I found him quiet in his manners, dignified in appearance and always commanded respect."[3]

Arriving at the Alliance School, I was conducted to the balcony where the women in a Jewish service sat. Not many women were present, and those in attendance were mostly relatives of the deceased, all wearing black 'abas in token of mourning, instead of the bright 'izars and 'abas. The balcony was a fine vantage point from which to observe the scene below, and assuredly nothing took place in the big court unnoticed by me.

3. Prior to World War I, Sassoon represented Baghdad in the Ottoman parliament in Istanbul. According to a source published at the time, Jews formed just over a third of the population of Baghdad, 53,000 out of 150,000 (Chiha 1908).

Just below me was a large platform for the speakers and the important personages; and in front of this were rows and rows of chairs and the customary straight-backed, hard-cushioned settees filling the court.

I watched in a quandary how unerringly the men were seated according to their station in society. How did the ushers know who should occupy the front seats below and to whom to relegate the rear benches? Apparently not a person protested against his assignment.

The space rapidly filled. In they came: *tarbush*ed gentlemen, hatted gentlemen, keffiyehed gentlemen, *sidar*ed gentlemen. Very conspicuous were the headdresses of the *hakamen* of the Jewish community, and there is no headgear more catching to the eye than theirs. Their short tarbushes are coiled about the edge with rolls of twisted cloth of a bright pattern. In this gathering there was a solid row of hakamen—they constituting the tribunal in their community. The round, black, velvet caps of the nawaba, the insignia of their princely rank, looked somber aside of the gay tarbushes; as did the black and grey *sidara*s of the officials and effendis in smart European clothes.

The Arabs had turned out in great numbers to show their sincere respect for a man who had worked wholeheartedly for the independence of Iraq. On the platform sat the king's representative, members of the cabinet, high-ranking officials, and the speakers. Sir Sassoon was a Jew, and the Jewish community was proud of him and of his fine record. Through the millenniums the Jews have lived in this land, and their ancestor, Abraham, from whom both Jews and Arabs claim descent, migrated from here. At a reception in honor of King Faisal before his coronation, which was held in the chief rabbi's official house, Faisal calmed the anxiety of the Jews, who had misgivings about being under an Arab government, by "his insistence on their being of one race with the Arab." To this land the Jews were brought again in the days of Nebuchadnezzar, and here many remained and became rooted in the soil from which they had originally sprung.

The memorial rites and speeches did not greatly interest me, absorbed as I was in the medley of races and religions sitting together so harmoniously. Arabs and Jews had been brought together by a common desire to render tribute to a man who had transcended border and breed and birth. It seemed to foreshadow a day of mutual understanding and appreciation. This I tried to believe as I was sitting on the balcony with the black-'abaed women.

Observing a scene like this, I became convinced that what I thought might happen would have happened had world conditions been different. At this memorial service there was an expression of genuine goodwill and a feeling of sincere friendship between Arab and Jew. Honor was given where honor was due regardless of race or creed. Here in this old, old land Arabs and Jews have lived together for millenniums, and what is more, largely in peace and contentment.

Why should they not continue to live in this relationship in the future? What might have been was upset by world problems, particularly the tragic struggle between the Arabs and the Jews in Palestine. This unfortunate situation did not remain confined to that historic land, but it had its repercussions in Iraq. Obviously, it might have been otherwise if historical events had been otherwise.

The heyday of stirring events, each of which was to me aura-crowned, was rapidly nearing an end. However, no one was aware of this at the ceremony of the unveiling of the fine equestrian statue of King Faisal, an affair which took place in 1933, a year of many calamities which are etched in my mind. The statue was erected in the center of a circle where the boulevard named after him intersects with another named after his brother, King Ali. The sculptor was an Italian, and this work was his masterpiece. It portrays the dignity and nobility of Iraq's first king. This imposing bronze statue placed on a high pedestal represents the king in Arab dress mounted on a royal steed.

Since the statue occupies a commanding position at the intersection of two busy thoroughfares, many people daily pass it. It faces the West, and persons coming to Baghdad either by train or by the desert route or by air must partly encircle it to reach the heart of the city. Indeed, this statue is a fine introduction to newcomers; and to the Iraqi citizen it is an ever-present reminder of the greatness of King Faisal.

Leaving the house early that morning, we soon fell in with the stream of automobiles crossing Maude Bridge, near which was the decorated circle where stood the veiled statue on its high marble pedestal. The seats assigned us at the unveiling were ideal from the standpoint of seeing and hearing. We faced the front of the statue; behind it stood the standard bearers with the many-colored flags. The military band in white and crimson entertained us during the time of waiting, and the busy servers of sherbert kept the crowd cool.

Punctually at a quarter of nine, the prime minister with the members of the cabinet arrived, and the ceremony began. While the prime minister was delivering his speech, he was interrupted by applause as one of Iraq's new airplanes zoomed back and forth over the festive-minded Baghdadis. At the conclusion of his speech, the canvas veil slowly parted to the accompaniment of the Iraq national anthem and the royal salute of the Guard of Honor. The covering then was to have dropped after the parting of the veil by an electric device, which in this case failed to operate as planned. The faulty link in the wire was over the horse's head, but "as the break caused flame and smoke to belch forth apparently from the steed's nostrils, the unrehearsed effect was striking in the extreme."

A special poem was written for the occasion by Jamil al-Zahawi. Because of his growing feebleness, he read his poem seated, but his ardor soon quickened energy in his weak frame, so that it often lifted him from his chair. The audience rewarded his enthusiasm with shouts and vigorous applause. This was the last public appearance of Iraq's greatest poet.

The band played; the cheerful crowd dispersed with many a backward look at Iraq's first great statue. That throng in holiday mood had no thought of disaster in the midst of their gaieties. Under the blue sky of the fateful year of 1933, which had opened without any signs of coming ill, they moved homeward feeling secure under the reign of the king for whose achievements they had erected this worthy memorial. Little did they dream that within four months the king's body would be carried past his statue on a black-draped gun carriage.

5

YESTERDAY AND TODAY IN BAGHDAD

I seldom went down the street in those earlier years without exclaiming at something new that had caught my eye: a new business establishment displaying new goods, the first large plate window installed by an automobile concern, a modern hotel modeled after a European, a cinema offering American films, a paved street. When I consider what Baghdad was when I arrived and how I found it when I left, I can scarcely believe it to have been the same city. The Baghdad of yesterday and the Baghdad of today appear as if they were two different cities.

In our American home during our retirement, a group of friends were sitting cozily before the fireplace. Fairy fuel on a log flashed rainbow colors as tea was served in Japanese black and gold lacquer cups from a Damascus tray standing on a Bukhara rug. It was in this Middle Eastern setting that a Christmas greeting was handed to me. When I read the name of the sender with her new address—Fine Arts Academy, Chicago—I gasped, "Nahida studying in Chicago!" The Christmas card flung open wide the door of memories associated with the girls of Baghdad.

The guests departed; I sat alone by the fire; my surroundings faded. I was no longer here, but on the great balcony of the old *qasr,* our home for so many years, welcoming two black-*'aba*ed women who in the privacy of our living room threw back their veils. A mother and daughter had come to talk about the classes I had planned to form. This was my first applicant, and if she was typical of others seeking admission, I felt I would have a rare group.

Soon other girls came who had learned from a simple typewritten announcement, circulated among a small group, of the prospective classes to be opened and the limited number to be admitted. The quota was soon filled. When work began I looked into the faces of girls who proved to be the most eager, intelligent, and responsive young people it was ever my privilege to contact.

The door that memory opened on these girls who had brought so much into my life would not close. I recalled a Valentine Day; the walls of the living room and the balconies around the court were decorated with cupids and arrow-piercing hearts in celebration of the day. Of course, Valentine Day had little meaning in a land where marriages among all the religious groups were arranged by the elders. But why not bring a touch of romance into these young lives? So, at least, I reasoned. Some of the girls asked to come in a particular costume, and an elderly photographer was engaged to take a picture of the group.

Naima came resplendent as Queen Esther, while Nahida wore a very attractive Turkish costume. The latter was so beguiling that she could not resist the temptation to have herself photographed. I looked at her questioningly. "Won't your mother disapprove?" "She won't care" was the answer. However, she did care. The next day I was warned that the mother would call on me, with the aside that she was very angry. Sensing her mission, I went to the photographer and begged for the plates, which he reluctantly turned over to me. The mother came. Showing the plates to her, I said, "Here are the three plates taken of the girls. Two I shall destroy in your presence, and the third I shall keep until you grant me permission to have prints made." I destroyed the two plates; the third I carefully hid. Today this first Muslim pupil of mine is in the advanced rank of modernity. It was from this girl who once was so strictly concealed behind the veil that the Christmas card came.

With this Christmas card in my hand, my thoughts ran on to other profound changes I had witnessed in Baghdad and Iraq during my long stay. This card as much as anything else "highlighted" these revolutionary changes. An obscure, isolated country was suddenly thrown into the world stream. For centuries Baghdad had little contact with the outside world. Then all at once, it was connected by air routes and land routes with the rest of the world, subjected to an unprecedented avalanche of influences. The West rushed in blindly and noisily over these airways and highways and deposited what the world had to offer, whether good or bad, whether desirable or undesirable.

For a time, when I tried to contrast the old Baghdad as I had found it upon my arrival with the newer Baghdad that I later knew, I just mentally limped. It was difficult for me to evaluate or appraise. There was so much in the old that I loved and appreciated which was lost in the new; and so much in the new that was of value that I had a hard time to come to a fixed conclusion. When I boldly launched an opinion, contradictory facts reared their heads and weakened my position to the point of retraction. The pros and cons just about came to blows, leaving me oscillating between two opinions.

Nevertheless, it was the old Baghdad, the Baghdad of yesterday, that eventually won me over and has held me enthralled ever since. It holds the first place in my heart, and my memory loves to linger on the things that gave a sparkle to those earlier years. There was so much fun and real joy in the old that is utterly lost in the new, and much of eternal and abiding value in the old that deserves to be, and should be, retained forever.

Materially, the East has been benefited by the Western inrush, and no one denies this. Yes, paved streets and highways lessened the dust and eased travel; electricity, which had been introduced before our arrival, surely has been a blessing; public waterworks, bringing water to houses by pipes instead of carrying it from the river, was an unspeakable gift, and when a filtering system was added that cleared the yellow, muddy water of the Tigris, words failed. Steel bridges offered better and quicker ways of transportation; home improvements and imported foods bettered living. Along these lines the country made great strides; but was it not at the expense of her great asset and attraction: "otherworldliness"?

For me it was a tragedy to see the old mode of life vanishing even though it lacked creature comforts. I loved the Old World courtesy, hospitality, love of leisure, respect for old age, and sense of honor. I liked the way youth gave a listening ear to counsel and honored religious tenets. "Was there not some way," I sometimes asked, "that this heritage of the East could be salvaged?"

Muddy streets were trying when my rubbers had to be tied on, but we laughed. To be carried on the back of a porter was certainly not as comfortable as to ride in an automobile, but it was fun. One day when the streets were a quagmire, I started out to make a call. Intent upon making this call by 'arabana and having my eyes fixed on a cloudless sky, I failed to notice the condition of the streets. The carriage was thoughtlessly dismissed when the house where I was making the call was reached.

When I was leaving my hostess walked with me to the door. We looked at the impassible street and then right and left for a carriage. Finally, we spied a husky porter. Calling him, he gladly took me for his load; and with my feet extended and dangling, stopping now and then for me to get a new grip, I was carried to the main street. How we often laughed to see variously dressed and variously sized individuals mounted on the backs of *hammals* as they were carried here and there through the miry streets and lanes!

These porters, who are largely Kurds, have always been numerous in the city. Impassable streets gave them a lucrative employment. Having an eye to business, they had discovered that it was to their profit to keep these streets as miry as possible for as long a time as possible in order to oblige pedestrians to be carried by them. After a rain they were known to plug up the small drainholes in the middle of the ways as an aid to business.

Since most of the streets and alleys have been paved, and since mud puddles are no more, there is no need any longer for the porter's tack. Ah! Baghdad now has fine boulevards, and in this respect it can compete with the cities of the West. In whatever direction one comes to Baghdad, he approaches the city on one of these splendid boulevards, artistically lighted, with lawns and flower plots between the driveways.

As you now pass through the narrow winding lanes or the wide avenues, whether in sunshine or in rain, it is just commonplace walking. Like in other places, the inhabitants of Baghdad have become standardized, and they walk sedately, decorously along the fine new streets—"rigid to the pattern." Civilization has come and spontaneous laughter has died.

What a boon electricity is! No normal person would want to live without it; but its light is very revealing. Dimness under the candle light covers so beneficently, makes the tawdry often lovely, and gives mysterious shapes and appearances to objects. In a dimly lighted street, I many a time mistook a Kurd in his ragged womanlike clothes and bobbed hair to be a lovely lady in her evening finery. Harun al-Rashid and Jafar the Barmecide never would have thought of making merry in these narrow *darbunas* (alleys) if brilliant electric lights had hung over their heads.[1]

It was actually possible for my husband and me to adventure in the spirit of Harun and Jafar during the first few years we lived in Baghdad. These winding canyons were a Moorish maze, where you lost yourself a dozen times, and often came to a standstill in a blind alley. At night the flickering oil lamps, placed at not too frequent intervals, showed faintly and dully through the dirty glasses; recessed doorways were darkly shadowed; the house with no downstairs windows and only one large nail-studded door looked formidable as if built to resist. Weird, shapeless, soft-footed figures, some enveloped in black 'abas, others with strange headgears, glided silently by, phantomlike. These lanes were ominously still, and the shadows were black.

It was easy to bring ourselves into the mood of believing that we had been whisked back into the days of the Abbassids. The two figures prowling about seemed to be none other than Harun al-Rashid and his wazir; and the sinister shapes lurking in the doorways looked ready to spring upon us with their swords. The gloomy, arid, and forbidding houses were so close on either side that you felt menaced. How eerie! We talked in whispers and hurried on.

All these streets under the brightness of the installed electric bulb are no longer interesting, though they may still be novel to the visitor. Shapes and appearances are now the same by night as by day; the tawdry does not become lovely, neither the ordinary magical. Evened and made firm underfoot, and lighted so well that the house number, another displeasing but necessary innovation, can be read, you pursue your way through the maze unattended by any flight of the imagination.

A pontoon bridge that rests on the water is certainly not as serviceable as a high, well-built steel bridge. The pontoons in Baghdad were so narrow that there could be only a one-way traffic for vehicles, and the walk for the pedestrians was only wide enough on either side for two abreast. When

1. Jafar the Barmecide was a member of a famous and powerful Persian family during the Abbasid period, known for their high lifestyle.

heavy vehicles went across, the bridge would curve up and down like the back of a dragon. In spite of this everyone seemed to enjoy crossing these primitive bridges. On a summer evening they were alive with people. In fact, they were the promenades for the Baghdadis; being close to the water they were much cooler than the baked streets.

At the beginning of every school year, I gave as a task for a composition in English to my students "How I Spent the Summer." Recording their doings, they would invariably include something like this: "And when evening came, I, either alone or with my friends, walked across Maude Bridge." Nine-tenths of the essays recorded this fact when the pontoons were being used, but when they were replaced by the steel bridges, the percentage fell to about two-tenths. It was one of my delights as well to cross and recross these old pontoons, so that I might feel the moist cool air from the river; but more so, that I might mingle with the throng who seemed to be unconscious as to their racial differences and who were unconcerned about their appearances in general.

The new steel bridges are high and wide, and there is no jostling of one another anymore. Most of the people that cross now have adopted modern clothes. That tilted hat on the young girls approaching me was likely bought in the French store of Baghdad; the dress is perhaps modeled from *Vogue;* the fabric probably came from Japan; and the shoes were possibly made in Czechoslovakia. These bridges that once were so gay with color when the ladies wore the 'izars and 'abas, and so fascinating because of the variety of costumes, bring no surprising sparkle to the eye anymore. People now cross trimly and staidly, as the world crosses bridges—all looking very much alike and uninteresting. The old pontoons I crossed when on pleasure bent; the new steel structures I never crossed except on business.

When we arrived in Baghdad, we noticed that many of the articles were handmade, and that they were sold in the same shop in which they were made. This was known as the guild system. It is still in vogue, though greatly reduced, and is even threatened to complete destruction by the manufactured goods from abroad which flood the market. A few local factories, especially for the weaving of cloth, have been established, but this so far has had little bearing on the economic life. The main problem has been the foreign manufactured goods. A pathetic petition was once addressed to the Ministry of Finance, alleging that the livelihood of 18,000 persons depended on the local shoe industry which was now at stake because of foreign competition.

Somehow the old bazaars at all times satisfied me; they brought me back to a healthy state of mind inasmuch as they, at least, remained unchanged, still breathing the atmosphere of the East. I loved to walk in the narrow covered streets which in summertime made for coolness and tempered the strong light and in winter kept the streets dry. I liked the shops, which were so tiny that squatting on the floor the shopkeeper could do most of his business without rising. The whole front opens up completely; the floor of the shop is raised above the level of the street just sufficiently for the customer to sit on the edge. It pleased me when a cushion was kindly provided while the progress of bargaining advanced. Little boys scampered about happily: one perhaps brought to me Persian tea served in slender-waisted little glasses if the merchant seemed hopeful; if I asked for something lacking in this shop, a little boy brought it from another; after I made my purchases others quarreled to carry my parcel, which I could easily carry myself.

There is such a fine spirit of camaraderie in the bazaar. Because the streets are narrow, and because the shops are against each other, the shopkeepers carry on active conversation among themselves when business is not pressing. There is no floorwalker to suppress sociability, or to goad the sluggard, or to appraise salesmanship. It is a common sight to see a merchant reading while waiting for customers, or drinking tea, or lounging on a cushion, exchanging with a friend the news of the day. Each spade in the bazaar has its own definite place. The cloth merchants are all in one section and the silk merchants in another. One knows exactly where to find the goldsmiths and the silversmiths, and the din of the coppersmiths locates them.

Many forces have been at work undermining this old order in the economic life, but it more or less simmers down to this: contact with the West. The people's wants have greatly increased as they imitate the Western ways of living. Because of growing expenditure the profit motive has come to the fore. Money had not primarily been an end in the old days.

Life had been reduced to simplicity; and even to live grandly, according to the accepted standard, required no great outlay of funds. The very moderately rich could live in ease since labor was cheap and servants plentiful. In the old days a man went to his shop, and after having earned enough for the day's needs he often closed it and went home or more likely to the coffeehouse. He went singing and happy in heart, but now that "civilization has come the song has died."

Now it is money—everywhere, much as it is in the Western world. Walking the streets, I listened to the talk, and the talk usually was of *dinars* or *fils* according to the currency in which each dealt. Money has become not only a medium of exchange, but also an instrument to expedite business. *Bakhsheesh* acts as a chemical that instantaneously changes the color of a solution. From rudeness a man's conduct can be changed by *bakhsheesh* to obsequious civility, and a bribe pushes dragging business transactions as if an electric current had been turned on. You ask to see somebody, and the *farrash* (janitor) at the door says, "Sayyid is not here"; but when a coin is dropped into his hand, the sayyid, as if by magic, materializes and is found at his desk.

The sudden impact of the West not only changed the physical, economic, and social conditions of Baghdad, but also the thought, life, and religious beliefs of the people. The current thoughts of our Western world were eagerly sought after, and books on philosophy and science were widely read. The impact of these ideas was so sudden and came in such large chunks that they could not be properly digested and assimilated. So revolutionary, too, were these ideas that no one could at the time rightly measure the consequences.

That there was an absorbing interest in the scientific and philosophic thinking of the West was very evident. Nowhere else had I found such an urge for modern scientific truth as I found in Baghdad upon my arrival. The effendi class became obsessed by it and was carried away with it to the detriment of their religious beliefs. Young men would proudly say, "I am no longer religious; I am scientific," as though science in the broader sense was the only thing that mattered. These men were strongly drawn to the materialistic thinking of the eighteenth century in Europe. It seemed that the last tidal wave of European skepticism had struck Baghdad.

Soon after our arrival in Baghdad, we were called upon by the president or secretary of what was called a scientific club. He told about this new club which was lately formed, and what its aims and purposes were. He asked my husband to interest himself in it. I could never make out whether he had thought that my husband might help to finance this new enterprise, or whether he had thought that he might contribute knowledge and ideas and ways of thinking: most probably both. This was in no way a social club. The club members came together to listen to the reading of papers and to discuss what to them was the truth. Soon I discovered that other communities were organizing clubs along the same line.

One Sunday afternoon one of these clubs had an open meeting, to which were invited among others the clergy of the city. The meeting was held in the open court of a large house. The religious dignitaries were given special seats of honor. Papers prepared for the occasion were read by some members of the club. In the midst of the reading of one of the papers, the men belonging to the clerical order who were occupying the seats of honor rose as one man; and silently and in protest walked out of the building. Most of the members of the club were undoubtedly sincere in their search for the truth; they believed they had found a truth and a wisdom higher and better and more realistic than what their religion had taught them. Neither were they afraid to express it.

Then, like most movements in Baghdad that started out so energetically and auspiciously, these clubs, after a few years, began to languish and finally disappear. In place of them sprang up the present clubs which each community supports. These, with the exception of the Armenian Club, where there was a program for athletics, dramatics, concerts, and lectures, were solely for recreation and sociability. In a certain sense, they were nothing more than high-class cafes, with sufficient space around a building for tennis and out-of-doors gatherings. To these clubs women also belonged.

The Baghdadi has had the feeling that he is nothing unless he belongs to a respectable club. Within four blocks of our house were four Jewish clubs. When the first club was founded its membership was united to a selective clientele. Then those who were left out founded another club, whose membership necessarily also had to be limited. The "leftovers" then undertook to organize a third club with a limited membership. In like manner a fourth club was started. So ingrained was this idea that one should belong to a club of good standing that our Alumni Association at three different times planned to start a club for themselves. Should they have been able to finance this project this club would have been different from those social clubs that are strictly confined to a religious group. The members of this club would have been a cross-section of the inhabitants of Baghdad, socially, religiously, and racially.

A tangible evidence of the interest of the people of Baghdad in modern ways of thinking is a bookshop in Baghdad carrying only English books. This remarkable store was opened before our arrival. It was said of Mackenzie's bookshop that it was the largest English bookshop east of Berlin. On its shelves were placed the latest and best books on history, literature, science, economies, philosophy, and religion. For a long time it carried not a single volume of modern fiction. From its size and still more from the kind of books that filled it, you could, as someone has said, "confidently assume that Baghdad's literary aptitude is critical and intelligent."

To all visitors as well as to myself, this bookshop was a great surprise. Once my husband went with some American tourists to Babylon as their guide. Looking at the foundations of the ruins of the Hanging Gardens, one of the seven wonders of the ancient world, these Americans seemed only slightly impressed. One remarked lackadaisically, "So this is one of the seven wonders of ancient times." Later he took them to Mackenzie's bookshop, and with almost one accord they exclaimed, "Wonderful! Wonderful!"

The bookshop became one of my haunts during the many years I lived in Baghdad. Whenever my mind became dull and I needed intellectual stimuli, I visited the store and turned the pages of the books; whenever I felt I was becoming a back number and was not keeping abreast with the times, I browsed for an hour or more trying to get knowledge through osmosis. I was never alone for there were always a number of Iraqis doing the same. This bookshop not only gauged the wide knowledge of English in Iraq, but also became an incentive for young men who did not know English to study it for the purpose of reading some of these thought-provoking books.

There were also other important changes that took place in the social structure of the nation, especially in Baghdad. These, too, have affected the people. There is an intense nationalism in Arab countries: the people are afraid of imperialism, communism, and economic exploitation; but they have not been equally sensitive to certain other outside influences and importations that have undermined the behavior patterns and social structure.

Drinking has crept into the land, and this also is due to the Westerner. It has become very common. In the market are liquors of all kinds which were not there when we first came to Baghdad. Small hotels sprang up overnight like mushrooms, the proprietors depending almost solely upon the sale of liquor for their income. Muhammad had forbidden the use of these intoxicants, and wisely so for a people living in a hot and trying climate. Europeans have made drinking in Iraq to appear respectable and the proper thing to do; and many have imitated them with the idea that in order to be up-to-date in social etiquette and to entertain in the proper style, it is necessary to serve liquor. Even the poor people are spending their hard-earned money for the cheaper, yet very intoxicating 'arak, which is made from grapes or dates.

There are now in Baghdad at least a dozen movie houses, and most of these have also open-air cinemas connected with them where films can be shown night after night for half the year. It is most enjoyable to sit in an open-air cinema in the cool of the evening, under the starry sky, and see a really good film. The best that the studios of Hollywood, England, and Egypt produce are sometimes brought to Baghdad; but as in the movie houses in America, the good films are in small proportion to the others sent out by Hollywood.

At first the films that were shown were largely of the gangster type and Wild West shows. From these the thief of Baghdad learned new tricks to add to his nefarious trade. Injurious as these films undoubtedly were, yet those of a more pernicious kind were introduced later, pernicious because they gave such a perverted view of life to a people innocent of such ways of living.

I often wished I could read the thoughts of the men and women, boys and girls who looked at the pictures which portrayed a way of life so antipodal to their own. When the Muslim would look at these American films, particularly the women, what do they think of the behavior of the movie star, of her indecent dress, luxurious living, unfaithfulness, the way she sails through her marital complications and her lovemaking? What to us in the West may be merely entertaining in a movie is to the Easterner, with a historical and social background so utterly at variance with ours, upsetting, to say the least. Old and young actually believe that what they see on the screen is the real America and the way Americans really live.

One of the large film-producing concerns in Hollywood once sent a representative to Baghdad and the whole Middle East to study the effect of different types of films on the people. Learning that certain films were very detrimental to the good of the community, he told us that hereafter his studio would select with the utmost care what they would send to this region. Whether this was ever carried out, I failed to follow up. Besides, it is sometimes difficult to evaluate a film. For instance, Romeo and Juliet drew overflowing crowds night after night for many weeks. I was surprised that the people's tastes had gone to Shakespeare, only to be told that the plebeians merely came to see the street brawls.

Modernity tumbled pell-mell into the land with no regard to the confusion in thought and living that it caused; neither did it care. The things of abiding value which the East possessed were too frequently exchanged for the tinseled baubles the West offered.

6

GARDENS, HOUSES, AND FEASTS

No one really knows the heart of Baghdad unless he has intimately entered into the exquisitely lovely customs that prevailed. It was my rare privilege while in Baghdad to enjoy many a garden party, to share the joys of the various feasts of the different communities, to be entertained with gracious hospitality in all kinds of houses, and to witness many a beautiful and charming wedding.

In this partly desert land a garden is sometimes described as *fardaws* (paradise). A garden means so much more in this part of the world where the desert almost engulfs us, and where the sun with open-faced fierceness glares down upon the parched earth throughout the long summer and the long summer days. A garden suggests the cool shadiness of trees: palm trees with waving fronds, orange trees with fragrant blossoms and golden fruits, ruddy pomegranates, apricots, banana and fig trees—a greenness healing to the eye and one that seems greener than in lands of ever-present beauty. A garden also suggests roses and flowers and leisure, that choice offering of the East, and a clean retreat from the dust and grime, from pressing duties and vexing problems. No wonder the voice sweetens when it utters the word "garden."

Before the recent expansion of Baghdad, the inhabitants were confined to a relatively small area. The houses were huddled together, one against the other; the streets were narrow, and the only breathing spaces were the open courts within the houses. Hence, a garden by the side of the Tigris or on the outskirts of the city was a delightful place to go to; and to it the people went frequently and joyously.

Some of my most vivid memories are of hours spent leisurely and carefree in one of these lovely gardens: sometimes enclosed within high mud walls which shut out the barren desert waste; sometimes by the side of the great river. Maybe I went to a garden to breakfast with a friend on a feast day, or to an afternoon tea, or to a meeting of the Girls Club. All of these I recall as I do a fairy tale: bewitchingly delightful.

Of all the gardens in which I was entertained, that of the minister of Education was possibly the most unique and enjoyable. We were very happy to go there because we liked not only the garden but the minister as well. We found Abdul Hussain Chalabi, with whom we had frequent communications, a kindly man; and as he held this portfolio a few times, our official relationship with him covered a number of years. He was a prominent Shiah Muslim, a status which also added to the popularity of his garden. Rarely, if ever, was he without guests in the cool of the evening.

"In the garden in the cool of the evening" is the biblical phrase. How natural and proper it is to use the Genesis expression! Was it hot in Mesopotamia then as now, and was everything outside the Garden of Eden desert? Did Adam and Eve realize only after they were driven out of it that it actually had been paradise, the land of bliss? Was the word for garden coined when the gates of Eden closed on the disobedient pair?

One evening we were sitting by the Persian pool in the garden of the minister of Education. A Persian pool is designed to mirror beauty. It is usually rectangular in shape, shallow, and often tiled; its smooth waters reflect the loveliness that surrounds it. To this rare garden—with its fountains and the pool reflecting beauty, with its many flowers, its glorious roses, its sunken beds, its symmetrical walks—came nightly the friends of the minister, most of whom being from the nearby holy city of the Shiah, Kadhimain.

This particular evening after we had sipped coffee from little *finjans* (glass cups), the men asked me about the women in America. I have often wondered how the conversation drifted in that direction, for these men presumably did not have the slightest intention of changing their attitude toward women. Anyway, there was a chance to shock them, and so I launched into the subject on a large scale and in high spirits. They enjoyed it as a diversion; and as I met different ones afterward, I was greeted with the question, "When will you lecture again?"

In this group was Sayyid Jafar, the mayor of Kadhimain, one of the four holy cities of the Shiah Muslims in Iraq, regarded as a suburb of Baghdad. Each of these four cities has a sacred mosque built over an 'imam, a descendant of Fatima, the daughter of Muhammad, and Ali Muhammad's cousin. From this line the Shiahs claim the caliph should have been chosen. The mosque in Kadhimain is one of the finest in the world. It is Persian in style and in decorations. The Iranians are Shiahs, and the people of the city are mostly Iranians.

Because two 'imams are buried here, the mosque has two domes, both of which are covered with gold; its four minarets are also tipped with gold. The burial place of these two 'imams makes both the mosque and the city holy. Pilgrims from all over the Muslim world visit it by thousands. Glittering and beautiful are these golden-crowned domes and minarets as they rise against the blue sky above the squalid city, and beautiful, too, are the delicate Persian tiles that adorn the great entrances to the mosque.

To be mayor of Kadhimain was something, but apparently Sayyid Jafar's official position was not uppermost in his mind that evening beside the Persian pool; neither did my dissertation on woman's freedom in America sink deep enough into his mind to divert his thoughts. He too had a garden, and most probably he was thinking of it as we praised the one we were in. As a consequence, he invited us on leaving to come and make an appraisement of his possessions.

The mayor's garden, which was enclosed by a high mud wall, was certainly reclaimed from the desert. It was entered by means of a crude wooden door, which we were glad to find open after crossing a desolate stretch of land under a pitiless sun. Inside it was cool and fragrant and green, a garden largely of orange and palm trees, and so different from the minister's garden that there was no basis for comparison. We walked up a shady, straight path toward a point of intersection with another straight path running at right angles. As we approached this point, we walked on Persian rugs; and looking to our right, our eyes opened with astonishment. A feast had been prepared for us! On long tables rose mounds of oranges alternating with bouquets of roses, and between these were dates of many varieties, pomegranates, sweets and biscuits of all sorts, marmalades, and half a dozen kinds of nuts.

While drinking tea from cups in silver holders, we so avowedly showed our appreciation and enjoyment in the mayor's efforts to eclipse the garden with the Persian pool that he took it as a high rating; and greatly pleased, he radiated satisfaction. He was a genial host, this Shiah Muslim mayor of the religious city of Kadhimain. Apparently he had grown tolerant enough not to follow the Shiah custom of breaking the cups and dishes which we had used after we were gone. He walked about trailing his 'aba slightly; his tarbush was tightly wound with the green cloth, the insignia of the lineage of the Prophet. When he looked at you his eyes were a bit roughish.

In this garden we did not feel what had already become so marked in the city, namely, the fading of the charm that belonged to Baghdad—a charm too sensitive to survive in an atmosphere of contending policies and the strong impact of the West. Here, away from the bustling city, in such a garden as this and with such a delightful host, charm's light and wonder-working touch remained as of old; while we were under the switching spell, we were at the same time aware that this was just about our last glimpse into a vanishing kind of world that was so inexpressibly lovely.

Though I was often entertained in a garden, yet more frequently did I share the generous Middle Eastern hospitality in a home. Soon after we were settled in Baghdad, I began to call, entering all kinds of homes.

Most of the region's cities were once alike in this respect, that they had much loveliness hidden behind walls. The reason for this was largely fear—the fear of the envious, the fear of taxation, and the fear of confiscation. A person's means could not be estimated by looking at the outside of his house. Besides, living in constant fear was also a determining factor in establishing quarters in the city, in which the inhabitants grouped themselves according to their religious and racial affiliations. This solidarity made the people feel more secure and gave them the chance for mutual aid and protection.

Concerns for safety and security also determined the style of the architecture of a house. A family had to be walled in. One strong door, and one only, gave entrance to the house. Windows on the first story were practically unknown, and all windows on the second story facing the street were barred; so were all the windows inside overlooking the court. Since air and sunlight were necessary, houses had to be built around an open space, an open court. This is a style of architecture going back to ancient times; a man's house had to be his fortress as well as his domicile.

Upon my arrival in Baghdad, I found that nearly all the people were living in the congested city and that nearly all the houses were in the narrow lanes. I had a little difficulty at first to know into which of the many slit-like openings on Rashid Street, the only thoroughfare then in the city, I should turn to reach the particular house I was after. Really, it did not so much matter which one I selected, inasmuch as the lanes had the oddest ways of meeting one another; and if I was puzzled, I asked the way and was kindly led to the very door. If these *darbunas* fascinated me and were full of surprises, how much more surprising were the houses which I entered from them. They simply took my breath. Possibly what so affected me was the sharp contrast between the dark, narrow streets on the one hand, and the roomy houses on the other. The courts of many of these houses were so great, the balconies so wide, and the rooms communicating so spacious that I stood in amazement upon entering from the hemmed-in lanes.

In a large traditional Middle Eastern house, there were the summer and winter quarters; the summer-house was downstairs, the winter one upstairs. The biblical statement "Now the king sat in the winter-house in the ninth month" has a new meaning to those who have lived in the Middle East. Twice a year we moved in our house: to the winter-quarter in fall and to its summer parts in the spring.

I remember taking to such a house the ladies of a stranded party who were dismayed at the prospects of spending a week in a city which externally had made no appeal to them. At the entrance to the court they stood in silence at this extraordinary assemblage of rooms, balconies, porticoes, pillars, and recesses. After the family had met us, they explained how this rambling house had grown as sons brought home their brides and the number of its occupants increased. Here was a typical example of a patriarchal home.

We were entertained in the spring *diwan,* a very imposing, deeply recessed, loftily arched, marble-floored guest room. The members of the household vied with one another in their efforts to please. Some offered sweets flavored with the essence of orange flower; others brought pastries artistically shaped; others served *laban* and tea. But of all the many things that were served, there was one that topped all. It was *manna min sama* (manna from heaven). This the ladies ate with overwhelming wonder, having thought of it solely as a miraculous food. They were told that the manna was gathered at different places, even in a Mount Sinai wadi, but that the manna they have in Baghdad came from Kurdistan; it fell in honeylike drops from the slender twigs of the oak when punctured by an insect. The most unique thing about manna is that when the thickened syrup is made into cakes, it must be carefully packed in flour. "Manna," it was said, "lives on flour, and without it, it quickly spoils."

Old-time dresses of beautiful fabrics were then brought out. In these the visiting ladies appareled themselves. Around them they draped the 'izars of heavy, creamy silk with borders that seemed gold-encrusted. Finally they were shown a high, harmless-looking window in an upper room. They were told that this was the entrance to a secret passageway which in time of peril could be used either to hide treasures or to conduct those in danger to a place of safety. The ladies stood amazed as if lost to this world. No wonder that after returning to the States, they said that Baghdad had been the high point of their travels.

There was another house in this congested quarter of the old city that I often visited. It, too, had a fortlike and unattractive front, but the inside was brightened by unusual decorations. The large court painted in various colors had a garden in the center where bulbuls in different cages sang to each other their tender songs. Fine Oriental rugs were in evidence everywhere.

The host was a unique person who had picked up a great fund of information on almost every subject. It was a delight to converse with him, and Baghdad had hundreds of others like him. If anyone should have told me before coming to Baghdad that when I called in this city, I could, as a rule, carry on a conversation on a high level, I would not have believed it. These men were surprisingly well informed and were doing a great deal of thinking. They read much, and what they read and heard they retained and assimilated. They also had a keen sense of humor and could see the funny side of things; their comments were at all times animated.

Incidentally, the host mentioned that he was about the first person in Baghdad who had learned to read, write, and speak English. "How did you learn English?" I asked. "When I was a young man," he answered, "I was bent upon learning English. One day I heard that a missionary on his way to Persia had stopped off in Baghdad. Secretly and by night, I went to the home where he was staying and told him of my desire. He gave me a New Testament having Arabic and English in parallel columns."

"Why did you go there secretly?" I inquired, knowing full well the reason but wanting the story from him. "In those days," he said, "had it become known that I had called on a missionary, my community would have severely censured me and my family would have been disgraced."

Refreshments in this house were usually served on the dining room table; as we ate the host would say in regard to the various articles of food: "This comes from Kurdistan, this from India, this from Iran, this from Syria, this from England or America." This geographic knowledge of the source of each article of food greatly added to the enjoyment of the eating.

In those earlier days there was a small coterie of congenial spirits in whose company the hard tasks were lightened and for a brief time forgotten. Nowhere did we meet more frequently than in a house that faced the river but which was entered from Rashid Street. In this house the father and son were hosts at many a feast in the Western connotation of the word, when we not only enjoyed the food but also reveled in lively talk, in quickness of wit, and in good fellowship.

I usually sat near the father at the table and talked in what he called *kitab* (book) Arabic. He tried to look understanding, but the ruse would not work: he needed to call for an interpreter to translate my Arabic into Arabic. There was so much good-humored raillery. When my project to continue the girls school that I had started failed, the men at a dinner party laughingly said, "If it will do any good, we'll walk the streets of Baghdad stripped to the waist like Gandhi."

We always wondered in which of the many rooms we would be entertained when we were invited; in summertime, in which of the gardens the table would be spread. By the river as the sun went down, big and with a lingering twilight, we often drank tea and basked in the courteous kindness that nowhere did we find surpassed. This hospitable home always remained open to us, even after the father had gently passed away and there had been a scattering of the friends we formerly met there.

As we left the place bouquets were always handed to us, and these for days continued to remind us of the happy time we had. Whether we just made a short call or had been invited to tea or attended a dinner party, a bouquet was given to each of us upon our departure: violets in the early spring grown in flowerpots that lined the garden paths, later roses, and as winter approached, chrysanthemums.

Whether in the great houses or in the one-roomed, mud-built huts of the Armenians and the Assyrian refugees, I found the same hospitality and the same friendliness. I was equally happy in both. Each, of course, had its own way of entertaining. The Assyrian refugees, no matter how poor the family or how meager the furnishings, invariably managed to have a Russian samovar. Around it we sat as we would sit in front of a hearth. As we drank tea, I listened to the often-repeated story of the terrible suffering endured in their flight during the First World War.

Probably no house offered more than this school-home of ours in interest and in the picturesqueness of the life that moved in and out of the big double door. If I wanted to see the race of men go by, I simply hung over the balcony and watched the costumed pageant. Throughout the years there came an almost endless stream—Muslims, Jews, Christians, Armenians, Assyrians, Arabs, Kurds, Yezedees, Syrians, Turks, Iranians, Indians, Eurasians, Egyptians, Palestinians, British, Americans, pashas, begs, effendis, refugees, advocates, judges, doctors, padres, merchants, archaeologists, geologists, educators, missionaries, globe-trotters, authors, diplomats, sheikhs, government officials, members of parliament, Bedouins, alumni—an assortment hard to duplicate.

Many of these came to make a social call, and as we had given formal notice that Friday afternoon was our "Day at Home," it was then that we received most of these guests. Special preparations were always made for this afternoon and evening: sometimes the big samovar steamed when we expected many guests; and sometimes tea was served from a Damascus tray. From week to week we looked forward to these hours of relaxation, when we could forget our pressing duties and when we could widen the scope of our acquaintance and have companionship with men and women of many minds and often, too, from many countries.

A few years we lived outside of the big house in a bungalow, which was hemmed in by a high wall. In front of the house was a grassy lawn bordered by a rose garden and shrubbery, behind which towered two immense mulberry trees which had the effect of the entrance to a stately forest. One year a flood came: the garden filled with water; the walls of the house built of sun-dried bricks became soaking wet; the foundations crumbled; the doors could no longer be closed, neither could the windows be opened and the woodwork sometimes cracked like a pistol. Yet, despite the fact that the building might collapse, we continued to cling to our attractive bungalow and lovely garden until the miserly owner came with a formal document asking us to sign on the dotted line. The paper was to the effect that he could in no wise be held responsible if anything should happen to us while in that house. Thereupon we concluded it was better to move at once than to sign our death warrant.

Many of the school functions were held on our grassy lawn. The International Relations Club conducted its fortnightly meetings there. Now it happened that a police station was on the opposite corner, and from the roof the police could look over our wall and observe what was going on on the lawn. At one of the meetings a student was reading his review of a book on world affairs, and for some reason or other he had written his comments on a deep pink paper. Seeing him read from this pink paper, which to them seemed red, the police became suspicious, thinking here was a meeting of Communists.

The sergeant of the police knocked at the garden door asking the purpose of this meeting. We explained and invited him to sit with us, which he did. Not understanding English, he asked to take with him the paper and the book that was reviewed, which happened to be one of the books annually sent to us by the Carnegie Endowment for International Peace. These he turned over to the British adviser to the police and Criminal Investigation Department. A few days later my husband was summoned to the police headquarters to meet the British adviser. Turning the book and paper over to him, the adviser brusquely said, "This is a splendid book you reviewed—good stuff. I read most of it, and it did my soul good. I want, too, to congratulate the young man for his excellent review and personal comments. But why under the sun did he use this colored paper?"

3. The International Relations Club at the American School for Boys, with Dr. Calvin Staudt at the center.

He laughingly added, "My advice to you is that hereafter you scrupulously avoid using colored paper at your meetings."

Even more interesting and important than the gardens and the houses were the feasts. A feast, called 'Id (feast), was with a few exceptions a joyous occasion, corresponding to our festival in the West. The feast days of Iraq are many: some are national feasts which all observe; others are religious feasts which each community celebrates. The need for a break in the monotony of living, which the feasts provide, was quite apparent in former years when the social life was simple. They turned the people out of the narrow rut of daily routine; gave them something to look forward to and prepare for; and quickened the slow pace of everyday life to a tempo more lively.

Feast days were celebrated in the past by calling, and this is still, to a great extent, in vogue, even though the substitution of sending cards has become common. The calling begins early in the morning and is continued throughout the day. What perplexed me at first was that since everybody appeared to be calling, who was home to receive? The lucid answer was that only the energetic did the running around; the older and feebler remained at home to welcome the well-wishers.

Calls were short, the aim being to make as many as possible the first day. The receiving room was so arranged as to accommodate many persons at one time: chairs and couches were placed stiffly around the wall or in a circle. When the places were filled and new guests arrived, the group longest in the room rose and departed. As soon as guests entered the room sweets were served, followed by small cups of Turkish coffee.

Christmas day was the great 'Id for us in our home. All hands were on deck to see to it that there would not be the slightest hitch in the day's demands. We rose early, for guests began to arrive at an early hour. The chairs were arranged in regulation style; candy and coffee ready, we were at our post to receive.

All day long they came, almost always in groups, from eight in the morning until nine in the evening. As each group entered they greeted us with the familiar "'Idkum mubarak" (May your feast be blessed). One year over two hundred guests were counted on Christmas Day; all types of people met for the first time in our living room. I recall how the chief rabbi of the city and the archdeacon of the Nestorian Church were introduced and learned to know each other. It was indeed a merry Christmas, though very exhausting.

The great Muslim feast 'Id al-Fitr follows the sacred month of Ramadan during which a good Muslim neither eats nor drinks nor smokes from early dawn until after sunset. The Qur'an calls for this fast, and this month was chosen because during it, it is believed, the Qur'an was revealed. The first sight of the new moon is the signal for this unique fast to begin, which interestingly reverses day and night; that is, the eating is done right after sunset and ends just before dawn. The end of Ramadan is uncertain, since it depends upon the sworn statement of several men that they had seen the new moon. The Muslims expectantly await the boom of the cannon which is the signal that fasting is to be turned into feasting.

There was always something infectiously festive about this feast. Baghdad turned out all spruced up in new clothes; the 'arabanas plied back and forth carrying smiling groups; busses and automobiles aided in transportation; the vendors of sweets and balloons drew a steady patronage; and the low, creaking Ferris wheels, which were set up on any unoccupied plot—sometimes the very edge of a dreary Muslim cemetery—became the very centers of hilarity. The swinging cars of the Ferris wheels were always loaded with deliriously happy and many-hued youngsters.

It was the children who made the feast so gay. We loved to walk around just to catch the exuberant joy. Such dabs of color, such overflowing gladness! Here comes a chubby youngster oozing joy. He wears the loved red slippers that make the shoe bazaar so bright. His stockings are purple, his little dress is rose satin, his little coat is of black velvet trimmed with gold, and his little cap is light green. Here come two heavenly visitants straight from the azure sky, who certainly have no intention to abide on this mundane sphere. They are dressed in cerulean blue; the little 'abas that hang from their heads, when the wind fills them, look as if they would lift and bring them back again to the realm from whence they came. Look at this chappie skipping along: his little black velvet cap is spangled with tiny gold discs, as is his little black velvet jacket; and how that orange satin dress glows. Where can you find anywhere such teeming colors and such abounding joy?

In the spirit of this feast, we would leave the house to make the feast calls. King Faisal may not always have received on other feast days, but he never failed to receive on 'Id al-Fitr, neither did the queen, nor did officialdom. Between making a certain number of calls and aimlessly walking about, we found these feast days exhilarating. Everybody was saying, "'Idkum mubarak." This custom of calling, however, is rapidly changing; even at the Royal Court those who wish to extend feast greetings inscribe their names in the royal register, then drive away.

Among the Christian feasts there were two minor celebrations quite novel. The one was the observance of a saint's day. If Saint Peter's or Saint Joseph's day came along, those whose names were Butrus (Peter) or Yusuf (Joseph) went early in the morning to a special mass which was read for them, and then remained at home the rest of the day to receive the congratulations of their friends, who greeted them with "'Idak mubarak." It so happened that the head of our primary school bore the name Yusuf, and as we were never blessed with more help than absolutely necessary, we saluted him on Saint Joseph's day with mixed feeling.

For those of her flock bearing names other than those of the saints, the church likewise had made some provision. For them it also arranged a holy day, in order that they, too, might have a day off when they could receive merit through a special service and later receive the congratulations in their homes. A feast was created known as the Feast for All the Saints; it was all-inclusive. Even a Billy or an Eddie can claim his holiday on this all-embracing feast day.

The second novel feast is called the Friday of the Dead. It is supposed to be a day spent in lamentation at the grave of the departed, and those who formerly went there wore the garments of mourning. But the crowd that gathers now has a gala air, more like an all-day picnic. The picnic spirit has so superseded the spirit of mourning that those who really grieve for their departed go to the cemetery either the day before the Friday of the Dead or the day after. Commenting on the festal attire of the young girls, I was told that they were exploiting the occasion for present and earthly advantage; that the girl's pluming is birdlike to attract an admirer in the hope that he may become a suitor, and that one day the father of the suitor may visit her home in search of a bride, and say in the flowery speech of the East, "Our bird has come to drink from your glass." The male, too, shares in this exploitation, and picnics in the cemetery on the Friday of the Dead for the same reason.

Sometimes it happens that two or three major feasts come together: the Muslims, the Jews, and the Christians may each have their own feast at the same time. This happened a few times while I lived in Baghdad. It is easy to understand how this is possible when we once realize that most feasts are moveable; that some communities reckon according to the sun; others according to the moon; that some follow the Julian calendar; others the Gregorian. To me, it seemed at first that every other day was some sort of an 'Id. Scarcely a week passed that some group in the school did not request to have the day off. Once a petition was presented by a group of students who wanted to observe a feast which read, "Our parents and our religion do not allow us to do our duty."

Although Easter is called the Great Feast by the Christians of the Middle East, Christmas is far more appealing in this part of the world. There is something winsomely lovely in whatever country Christmas is observed, but more so in the Near East where Christ was born. Christmas belongs to the East: the young mother, the first-born son, the shepherds keeping watch over their flocks, the brilliant star in a clear, desert atmosphere, and the Wise Men, riding on richly caparisoned camels, bringing gold and frankincense and myrrh, the precious gifts of the East. All these are typical of the Near East and belong to it.

7

WEDDINGS

Weddings in all countries are of ageless interest, and those in Baghdad were novel as well as interesting to us. This, in large measure, was attributed to the great variety of forms which stemmed from the many races and religions in the population and the desire of each group to hold on tenaciously to age-long customs. Then, too, in the same religious community there were often considerable differences: some remained old-fashioned; others tried to be modern. In not a few of these weddings, I also had a keen personal interest. Either the bride or the bridegroom or both were once under our guidance and instruction.

In the marriage of the girls of my club I was wholly engrossed. I knew before I attended that their weddings would be the best of their kind. As one of the objects of the club was to prepare the girls to become intelligent companions to their husbands, and to have them make their homes more attractive than the coffeehouses, I was concerned that the husband be the type who could and would respond to such efforts. I took a sly delight later in introducing these men as the husbands of my club girls, a reversal of order that not all Baghdadi men would have brooked. If, perchance, I should have felt inclined at any time to send regrets to a wedding invitation, in recalling the success of the first one, I would certainly have hesitated. The bride at that first wedding was one of my girls, a close relative to Sir Sassoon Heskiel in whose home the ceremony took place.[1]

The rather mean exterior of Sir Sassoon's house gave no clue to the impressiveness of the interior. It was this contrast that so enhanced the

---

1. For more on Sir Sassoon, see chapter 4.

stateliness of the house within. When my husband and I passed through the unpretentious doorway, which was lower than the level of the narrow and unpretentious street, we entered, as it were, into magic wonder. I gasped when the full light of the big court flashed on my eyes as I entered from the hemmed-in street. For a moment I stood still, trying to adjust to so extreme a change.

Then, when my eyes were accustomed to the brightness, I surveyed the whole scene. The court was filled with cushioned benches on which sat the men in white suits, wearing the red tarbush (fez), universally worn in those days, whose black silk tassels swung to the movements of the head as men greeted or conversed with one another. To the right on a raised dais sat the uniformed military band, which, incited by the sumptuous surroundings, frequently played with animation, setting the feelings, if not the feet, into motion.

Raising my eyes to the broad balconies surrounding the court, I noticed that these were brilliantly decorated with Oriental rugs. On them the ladies, garbed in colorful arrays, were sitting in groups. Lifting my eyes still higher to the flat roof, I saw a frieze of solid black, unrelieved by any other color; it formed a somber contrast to the bright colors on the balconies. These figures that were leaning over the railing of the balustrade of the roof were the black-'abaed uninvited guests. Knowing that their place was on the roof, they entered quietly and unobservedly to share in the joys of the occasion, remaining quiet through the ceremony and departing as they had come. (I now understood the biblical references to uninvited guests that so long had puzzled me.)

I left my husband in the court with the men; and to the music of the band, I tripped up the broad stairway to the broad, rug-covered balconies, the assigned place for the invited women. I was then with other women conducted into the large salon facing both the court and the river.

The bridal attire seemed to be in accordance with the latest mode. Once when I was on a furlough in the homeland, a dressmaker offered to send fashion magazines to Baghdad. This would have been like carrying coal to Newcastle. The fashion plates she wanted to send were already in Baghdad, and the bride looked as though she had stepped out of one of them.

On a grand scale like this in an American wedding there would have been elaborate floral decorations. Here, there were none. The decorations were not flowers but a lavish use of rugs of various makes, designs, sizes, and colors—a most satisfactory substitute. It is said that the Persians wove flowers and birds in their rugs that they might have gardens in winter. No greenhouse could have made these balconies and the rooms that opened out to them more gardenlike.

On the balcony a canopy had been erected to which very soon the bride walked, attended by her family, and to which the groom came from the court below, attended by his family. The rabbi intoned, the choir of boys answered antiphonally. Then from a silver cup the rabbi poured wine into a small cup, took a sip, and then passed it to the groom, who handed it to the bride; taking a sip she returned it to the groom, who, after drinking the remainder, dashed the cup against the wall with such vigor that it broke into bits.

The bride told me later that the significance of the act was to subdue the joy of the day by bringing to their remembrance Jerusalem and the lost greatness of the race. She said, however, that she thought few brides at their marriage lamented the past; at least, she did not. Now that Israel is a nation one wonders what will happen to this symbolic act.

Immediately after the marriage rites were concluded, the *hilhal* or joy-cry was trilled. This high-pitched sound is made in the throat, and as the lips are swiftly patted with the hand the sound escapes in quavers. Whenever a group gave the hilhal it always aroused my emotions, and others had the same experience. This joyous cry is given not only at the wedding ceremony but also at the engagement and at other functions connected with the bride or groom. Then while the band played, best wishes were extended by the women to the bride under the canopy, and congratulations by the men to the groom, who after the ceremony had returned to the court below. Unlike the American custom, the bride and groom were not standing together to receive the felicitations. The men quickly cleared the court below, but the women lingered on the decorated balcony which was so inviting to sociability.

In the Jewish community the largest number of weddings took place before the Passover in spring, a reason being that it is the lovely season of the year; but since the good weather continues until May, why should there be no weddings after Passover? Because the interval between Passover and Pentecost is considered unlucky; when this answer is given, the shoulders are shrugged, the hands are spread out open, indicating utter helplessness as to why this period is fated. But ill-fated it is believed to be. Then, after Pentecost, summer starts with a vengeance, and who cares to be married then?

Two synagogue weddings followed this home wedding, and in both of them I took a particular delight and interest because of the impression these two lovely brides had made upon me when I first came to know them. They were brought to my school for girls by their mothers. They wore the handsome 'izars; one daughter wore a beautiful 'abaya and the other a hat. The mothers asked to have their daughters admitted into the school. I replied, "I cannot take your daughters because the rooms will hold no more; they are full"; and I added, "You know when a tumbler is full, you can pour no more water into it." "Yes!" was the swift reply of one of the mothers, "but you can place two rosebuds on top." I needed no more persuasion; I made room for the rosebuds. These girls who had blossomed into beautiful womanhood were now being married.

Both weddings were different from those I had previously attended. It was at the first of these two that the differences were conspicuous and striking. It took place in a synagogue where there were no uninvited; neither was there any music. It was very quiet, almost solemn; one had no desire even to talk. Looking around, I was surprised to see all the ladies sitting downstairs with the men, with heads uncovered. Looking around to find the bride, I espied her sitting apart, surrounded by fairylike little girls. They lifted her veil as she left her seat to ascend the steps to the place where the rolls of the law and the Prophets are kept and where the bridegroom was awaiting her.

When the ceremony was over, the bride turned to resume her seat as was the custom; but again to my utter surprise the groom restrained her, keeping her at his side to receive the good wishes with him. I watched with inward elation to see what would happen. Not a young man failed to avail himself of the privilege of shaking hands with the bride, and a blue-eyed bride at that. But eyes could not seduce the older men; they never deigned to give her even a glance. I am sure they were saying to themselves, "A woman rising to the height of man? Not yet, *al-hamdu lillah*" (thanks be to God).

For millenniums this part of the world has been man's grand preserve, and these innovations must have been disturbing for they challenged what he considered his inalienable rights. As the groom was a prominent figure in the community, it must have been galling that no one dared to protest.

Other club girls of mine were being married, and I was growing inordinately proud. I took far more credit for their eligibility than I in anywise deserved. This pride was augmented by an Armenian mother of five sons. She so loved the three daughters-in-law of my club that she declared, "I want no other daughters-in-law but girls of your club for my other two sons."

About the time of these unusual weddings, another took place that had not one touch of modernity in it. The bride was young and pretty, another one of my girls. When I had inquired why this haste to marry her so young, the answer was given that such a proffer was not so common as to be rejected.

This old-fashioned wedding was held in the Alliance School where the meeting in honor of Sir Sassoon Haskiel had taken place. Instead of orderliness and dignity, there was an uncontrollable cramming and jamming. The uninvited guests who had quietly witnessed a wedding from the roof and who had been deterred from entrance at the synagogue weddings here became a rabble, pushing into the court and forcing their way onto the balcony. Through this sea of unfamiliar faces a young man piloted me, and by using force led me to the room where the bride with her female relatives was sitting in solemn state.

Following the old custom of appearing absolutely joyless, the wedding seemed more like a funeral. Not a smile flickered across the face of any woman sitting in that room, and all except the bride were dressed in the old Jewish costumes. Entirely ignorant of the custom of showing no happiness at a wedding, I seated myself beside the bride, who sat alone on a settee, and began talking to her so cheerfully that she smiled. I wondered why all those women scowled, sitting on benches placed at right angle to the bride's. One does such a lot of blundering in a strange land, but with charity the people excuse unwitting mistakes by saying, "*franji*." I am not so sure, however, that those women excused me, because they may have had the superstitious fear that the smile would bring ill luck.

The bride was in modern attire. But out of what storybook had these ancient-looking dames stepped? They wore on their heads tiny hat crowns, decorated in gold; the richer the family, the more the gold. This crown was fastened to an embroidered head-covering that was tied under the chin and draped with artificial braids of hair attached to the little crown. This old costuming, plus the heavy solemnity, made me feel like Rip Van Winkle among the dwarfs.

We heard in the room the Jewish band, with the drums booming and the horns blaring. Thinking that the scene would be worth viewing, the bride and I walked out upon the balcony. To make room for us, a boy had to push back the women. We leaned over the balcony; directly below us was the vociferous band, and to the right a choir of boys, who attempted to outdo the band. On the other side sat the bridegroom on a raised platform with a little boy on each side of him. The men guests filled the rest of the court. The bride said to me, "You don't like this; neither do I, but it is the custom." Then, as the women began to press heavily against us, we hastily retraced our steps to the room.

When the call came for the bride to meet the bridegroom under the canopy, she in her nervousness took my hand, and together we walked to the passing place where the rites were performed. Then back through the same crowd, after the ceremony, we returned to the room—the bride, the women, and I. We shut the door, leaving the bridegroom to receive the congratulations as best he could.

One day an invitation came inviting my husband to the marriage of another of my club girls. The invitation did not include me. For a moment I thought that was rather strange, but I soon understood when I became aware of the fact that both the bride and the bridegroom were Muslims. This was to be only a man's affair. Custom did not allow the bride to be present even at her own wedding. Likewise the women, mothers, grand-mothers, aunts, who undoubtedly took a major part in arranging this match, were debarred; of course, I also had no business to be present.

Since I could not be present at the marriage of this member of my club I had to depend upon my husband's eyes and ears to know what was done.

About fifty or more men had gathered. A mullah intoned a prayer, after which the bridegroom and the person who represented the bride faced each other; and holding each other's hand over which a handkerchief was placed, they answered questions put to them. Then the contract was signed, and that sealed the marriage.

A social hour followed, during which all were refreshed by a delicious sherbert. Then as the guests quietly left after having congratulated the bridegroom, each received a silk handkerchief in which mixed candies were tied. My husband had started to make a collection of differently colored and variously designed handkerchiefs which he received at weddings. Then the war came on, and as silks were no longer imported, his collection, to his dismay, ceased to grow.

Sometimes the bride and groom entertain their friends separately before coming together. The daughter of the family to whom I was indebted for many kindnesses celebrated her marriage the day the Muslim bridegroom was coming briefly to the house of his bride to meet her, and later in the day to claim her. The house was filled with guests, all women. The bride was seated at the end of a large room on a dais with the bridal veil enfolding her. She was an unusually pretty girl and beautifully dressed. Entering the room with the other ladies, I seated myself and surfeited my eyes with the loveliness of the dark-haired, dark-eyed young girl. Then we moved into another room to give place for new guests, but not until her father had entered to perform the symbolic act of tying a ribbon about the daughter's waist, which signified the new bond that was uniting her to another, and which it was hoped would be enduring. After the ribbon was tied, the bride knelt and kissed her father's hand, who then retired. Coming in and going out, he looked at no one.

Suddenly, the word went about: "The bridegroom has come!" and in a rather unseemly haste everybody hurried to the balcony. It was a false alarm. But when some women gave the joy-cry, and the equally lovely sister led the bride out of the room and downstairs, his coming was certain. The two sisters stood in the center of the court waiting; the bridegroom hurried in; approached his bride briskly; kissed her hand; and, offering her his arm, they ascended the stairs and walked into the daised-room alone, where it was supposed that for the first time they met face to face.

He remained in the room only a short time and left as briskly as he had come, looking at no one. If this was the first time they met, what did they think of each other?

This meeting of the bride and groom was the climax of the afternoon's festivities. But before leaving, we were entertained by a Turkish dancer from Istanbul, whose many pleasing costumes were more gratifying to the eye than the movements of her torso.

As to the weddings of Christians, they vary greatly, because each of the many Christian sects has a ceremony of its own. These ceremonies ran the gamut from the simple Protestant rite to the elaborate Armenian ritual, the length of which, being regulated by the amount of money paid, could run as long as two hours.

One summer when the hope of cooler weather was still too far removed to raise the spirits and little was happening, my life suddenly flared with interest. Daud, our Assyrian and faithful helper, had received a letter from his brother at the British air base at Habbaniyah, some sixty miles west of Baghdad, informing him that his brother had become engaged. Daud was requisitioned to do the buying and to hasten since the wedding was to take place as soon as possible. The buying included all that the brother had assumed as his share of the expenses and was meticulously itemized. The business would have been simple had Daud gone to the market alone, but the letter stated that a party would come from Habbaniyah who would companion him in the purchasing. Daud was eager to please his brother and anticipated a good time. Alas for human hopes: the party consisted of domineering, dictating relatives who were out to please themselves, and to make a display of squandering money.

Of course, all people have a certain amount of pride, whether rich or poor, high or low. The bare struggle of existence does not root this trait out of the heart. Then, too, an uprooted and dispirited people who have known better days long particularly for moments of exaltation and elevation of spirit. They grope for the fullness of life of which they once had had a taste. Weddings offer this release from the humdrum and the perpetual skimping. That, undoubtedly, is why weddings occupy such an important place in the lives of these people and why they are so lavishly planned.

The height of feeling seems to be measured by the amount of money spent for the occasion. The boastings of money spent continues long after the ceremony, even though the debts incurred mortgage the couple almost for life. The feel that for once the purchasing can be done without regard to the purse, just as if the spender owned a mint, is an experience that tones up life whenever it is recalled. The future even without a debt brings many cares as one settles down; so why not have this one grand fling!

A certain father in Habbaniyah had four daughters and no sons, "Wherefrom do I get money to marry my girls?" he said; "the young men must pay me well for them." One hundred *dinars*—a dinar having the value of an English pound—were offered for one of the damsels, but her heart inclined towards Daud's brother. The two families finally agreed on forty dinars. When the bargaining reached a conclusion the forty dinars were paid at once in order to insure the girl against the temptation of higher bidders. Then began the friendly discussion as to what portion of the expenses of the wedding should be borne by each family.

Knowing well the relatives who would accompany the bride to Baghdad, the bridegroom wisely closed his letter to Daud with the injunction that when the party came to Baghdad, he was to be the leader and the purchaser. Six came from Habbaniyah, and were augmented by six more relatives from the city, so that the party led by Daud numbered, inauspiciously, thirteen when they went to the bazaar. The bride's relatives urged large spending, the open hand, with a male leader of the fighting sort; the relatives of the bridegroom parried the urgency of the greedy with the resolute spirit of thrift. The gap between the two groups could not be breached, and as a result the party was neither congenial nor happy.

The first day was concentrated on gold ornaments for the bride and dresses for the bride's aunts and cousins. The first balk came with the purchase of a wristwatch. A European lady purchased, in the presence of the thirteen, a watch for a dinar, thereby setting a noble example, which, however, fell on the stony soil of vain and selfish hearts into which no roots could penetrate. The bellicose champion of the bride's party said loudly, "Buy this," pointing to an eleven-dinar watch; and when Daud indignantly refused, he swung off in high dudgeon, and the party was reduced to twelve, a luckier number, with still the same amount of covetousness but less boisterous. A friend of Daud's happening to pass by, and sensing the predicament the latter was in, whispered to the jeweler as a ring was being admired that he should say eight dinars instead of three, which was the cost. This he obligingly did, returning unobservedly later five dinars; and the ruse brought a temporary brightening of the atmosphere.

The aunts and cousins, to the number of seven, had to receive the gift of a dress. As Daud narrated this to me, I said, "That at least was simple and cheap," for the market was flooded with cheap Japanese silks.

Daud answered, "Do you think they were satisfied with anything cheap? No, indeed, they went in for the expensive materials, 250 *fils* a meter."

"But," I said, "where do they go to wear such extravagant clothes? Habbaniyah is out in the desert."

"That isn't the matter," he retorted; "it's to say how much it cost."

It was a grueling day for Daud, and he came out of the skirmishes looking battered and exhausted, but was held up by the thought that he, at least, had prevented a landslide in expenditures.

The next day the bride's trousseau was on the docket. It was Daud's duty to go to the house where the bride's party from Habbaniyah was reposing, and most likely imposing, in order to lead them again to the bazaar. It went against the grain, for the injuries sustained the day before were still raw and hurt. "Never mind," he said, "it won't last much longer," and swallowing hard, he went. Noon came when shopping ceased, and Daud's wife, weary of the whole business and of the burden of feeding this delegation, hailed carriages, paid a fare to each driver, omitting to name a destination!

The third day three hundred invitations were purchased besides sweets and sundries; and as this took only a part of the morning, it left ample time for the Habbaniyah members of the war-torn party to return. Those three hundred invitations would in all likelihood be accepted, and all, including the children, would remain for the meal. It was calculated, however, that the food bill would in a measure be covered by the gifts. Alas again, for the frailty of human hopes.

Having given Daud a week off to celebrate with his brother, I anticipated a beaming countenance on his return. Disappointedly, I looked
at his dejected mien. He had labored and sweated to please everybody,
and now he had to go to the market at once. "Wherefore?" I asked. Then
came the most unkind cut of all. Not only had the wedding guests been
miserly in their gifts, but when the rented tumblers and cutlery were to be
returned there was considerable shortage. The hurried rush to the bazaar
was to reimburse the lenders. For several days we ruminated on the way-
wardness and thoughtlessness of the human race.

In a discussion in the Girls Club one day as to which marriages are to
be preferred, those arranged by elders or those by personal choice, one of
the girls now happily married advanced the argument that affection grows
after marriage and is less likely to cool than that ardor in the wooing time
which is intensified by idealization. "There is no rude awakening," she
said, "in our way, because less is expected and hoped for; and when marriage proves more romantic than anticipated, happiness is increased." So
she said, and as all the weddings I had attended were "arranged" and had
proven to be "more romantic than anticipated," I felt that her argument
had substance and weight.

Very unexpectedly, however, I became involved in a wedding of the
"personal-choice" kind, to which even the word "romantic" seemed a pale
word to use. This appeared weighty, too. One day there came to the house,
during the summer vacation, a message from the American consulate asking whether my husband would marry two Americans that evening. He was
ill, and no definite answer could be given until the doctor had paid his visit.
The doctor gave a blunt and unqualified "No" to the question, which was
relayed to the consul, and the matter dismissed from the mind. When evening had come and my patient was on the roof, for in summer everybody
sleeps on the roof under a protecting net, I descended into the cool *serdab*
to read. Hearing persons entering the court, I emerged to meet them; and
there was the consul with the wedding party, saying that no one could be
found to perform the rites. We descended into the serdab for a conference.

What an exquisite bride and what a manly groom! They had met on
shipboard and fallen deeply in love. In love, an expression I had not heard

for many a day and a phrase not much used in the East. It is not an item primarily to be considered in the marriage arrangement. In my absorption in the ways of marriage, the trappings and not the subtle essence of union had occupied my mind. These young people belonged to my world, which I suddenly realized was, after all, a different world from the one in which we were living; they led me back into it as if into a fragrant garden like one I had seen at home where Easter lilies and larkspur grew together.

The consul and the bridegroom went out again at my suggestion on what proved to be a fruitless quest and returned disconsolate. A thought flashed into my mind. "Would you object to being married on the roof?" "Oh, no!" was the immediate response. "Would you object to my husband's wearing a dressing gown?" "Oh, no!"

Going on the roof, I explained to my husband the urgency of the marriage, stating that the young man had to push on at once into Iran and that it would take only a brief time. He consented. The party then climbed the long flight of stairs to the roof, lighted by a lantern carried by the vice-consul and a Persian *lala,* a tall, slender lamp burning a candle, by another member of the party.

"Here comes the bride," we sang. There was something ethereal as we emerged upon the high roof, with Baghdad sparkling on one side, the dark-fronded palms lifted in air on the other, and the vast desert beyond. Above us was the Milky Way, which made a path of radiance in the heavens; and Scorpion, a magnificent constellation in an Eastern sky, hung low on the horizon.

My husband was ready; the lantern made the printed page legible. We stood in the calm presence of the night, listening to a ritual very simple yet so profound, very brief yet so enduring, in a language very human, yet carrying the spirit to noble heights. We stood rapt in the wonder of the night and the wonder of the words, each one deep in thought. In the hearts of the two taking the vows, there was exalted happiness; it radiated to us and made our hearts glow. As for myself, there was a gratitude beyond utterance for the Christian ceremony and its inspiring motifs; its liberation of womanhood; its sanctification of marriage and the home; its teaching of the Truth that makes men free.

There were no flowers at this wedding, no decorations, no attendants, no altar, no music: only the night, love, sincerity, the chastity of the shining stars, and the uplifting and abiding words. These never sounded holier than when stripped of all accessories; they fell on the ear in their untrammeled strength and sublimity that matchless night, when in Baghdad, the Christian marriage service was read under God's lighted dome.

8

LITTLE JOURNEYS ABOUT THE CITY

How long the summer days in Baghdad are. The sun rises early and greets the sleepers on the roof with a heated and vehement call: "Arise, arise." And it is the part of wisdom to heed this fervid call. For the sluggard who continues to doze after Phoebus has given the call there is no mercy. He shoots his fiery darts into the loiterer's head with such sureness of aim and with such force that the wound is felt all day.

The effort of the sun to rout folks out of bed is forestalled by multitudinous noises. Baghdad is filled with noises that are jarring, incessant, and insistent. They begin early, some even before dawn. The street vendors—on how many hours of sleep do they exist?—call out their foodstuff in the early hours of the morning. The garbage collector, loud and persistent, hammers at the door and shouts, "*zibil*" (garbage), as if to wake the dead. The pestiferous sparrows rise at the first streak of dawn; and when they begin their morning jubilation, or a single one overflowing with joy sits on the pole of your mosquito net, you do not need the sun to rouse you. To have a day open with this kind of a program once in awhile might be tolerable, but when it is a daily occurrence, it is exceedingly exasperating.

All these noises that awaken one at dawn have a competitor in a nearby church bell. The bell-ringer begins his job before the first intimations of the coming day, and continues to ring at close intervals for some time thereafter, preventing anyone from falling off into the last, sweet, healing sleep. He rings rather rapidly, pausing occasionally to tap in groups of three, which you simply must count. I groan and say, "Is there no consideration?" It has always been a difficult problem for me to make out whether the bell-ringer's motive is primarily to call worshippers to the house of God, or whether, like the pompous cock Chanticleer, he thinks the sun's rising each morning awaits his summons, or whether the bell ringing is done in rivalry to the muezzin's call from the mosque across the street.

Indeed, when both are calling and urging the faithful to devotions at the same time, one surmises that in the hearts of neither are devotional thoughts uppermost. Rivalry, as we know, is not conducive to generous feeling; and aside from the irritation of the bells which drown the human voice, this particular church had also aroused the envy of this neighboring mosque by raising the two spires in which the bells were hung higher than the minaret of the mosque. Church bells in this part of the world have often been a source of discord between Christians and Muslims. The Muslim believes that the faithful should be called to prayer by the human voice and not by the metal tongue of a metallic bell. When Jerusalem was taken by the Muslim conquerors, the Christians were allowed to continue their worship but were required to give up their bells.

Since I was compelled to rise early, the problem was what to do with the long vacation days and how to divert the mind to something other than the everlasting heat. During this particular summer, because of the World War, it was both difficult and inadvisable to leave Iraq. The problem was solved when the idea popped into my mind that to prowl about the city in the early morning hours, in order that I might make new discoveries and renew old interests, would not only occupy a part of the day, but also furnish enough interests to enliven the rest of the day.

Acting upon this idea, I made an energetic start. I had become interested in the letter writers when their place of business was the narrow, short street that divided the *serai* (municipal building) from the law courts. As there was always a crowd at the law courts, the letter writers did a flourishing business. They wrote all kinds of letters—personal, business, petitions, applications, testimonials, and all kinds of documents required by the government. They squatted on the traffic-less street beside the little, low wooden tables on which were their necessary supplies.

With these letter writers in mind, I drove to the serai, only to find the street in which they were accustomed to sit unoccupied. What had happened? "They have moved," I was told, "but not far away." The Wheel of Fortune had certainly turned upward for the letter writers. I found them on an island in a square between crisscross streets, each seated in a little booth, with just enough space to accommodate a table and two benches; business as always was in full swing.

I observed that one of the scribes had an Arabic typewriter. I asked to look at it, and to my surprise, I read that it was made in the state of New York; and wasn't that *katib* proud of it! A veiled woman in another booth was dictating a letter, while nondescript men were in other booths.

After returning home, I began talking to friends about the women who had their private letters written in this place by public letter writers. I said, "These women certainly have secret matters to write about—love letters, family affairs, personal troubles, secret information. Does the scribe protect their confidences?" The question was greeted with derisive laughter. "Confidence?" one said. "You know how the people of Baghdad chatter. Anyone with secret matters goes either to a letter writer who knows nothing about the person at all, or to one who knows everything." As very little that was going on in the city was kept secret, it did not much matter who wrote the letter.

The plan worked so well the first day that I cast about to decide where to go the next. "Why not visit the market near us where I do most of my bargaining and buying and see for yourself your food source?" said Daud. I think the suggestion was a sly one, for he knew only too well that the market, which had been built according to modern standards of cleanliness, had lapsed, and that I would likely open my eyes and mouth when I saw it.

When the new market was finished, an ordinance was passed forbidding the sale of vegetables and meats in the neighborhood except in these new shops. This meant that the squatting on the street to sell vegetables from wicker trays was to cease, and that the butchers were no longer to string their carcasses and chunks of meat like flags before their dingy old shops to draw flies and dirt as well as customers. They were to occupy the clean, new stalls in the municipal market where the floors were tiled and where there was running water to encourage its use.

I set out with keen anticipation to see this new, modern, clean market, but when I reached it my eyes fairly bulged out. "What had happened?" I asked. I learned that change was against the grain, that reforms were at first carried out forcibly, but that gradually there was a return to the old ways. The meat hung again flag-like before the new shops, which were now dirty and splashed with blood, and the squatters were again sitting on the street, fingering their vegetables and bread with their dirty hands. The reversion to type was complete.

This reversion illustrates more than almost anything else the accumulated lethargies of centuries and the age-long inherited habits. One cannot blame the government or the municipality for this lapse from forced cleanliness. Hygiene is taught in all the schools, but it is another thing to put it into practice and form health habits.

In the interest of health and cleanliness, an order was given that on a certain day all butchers were to wear white aprons and white caps. This came like a bombshell among the butchers. No one had bothered about cleanliness before, and the people survived; why begin now? However, on the day appointed the butchers appeared in white caps and aprons. When the time seemed auspicious, and the zeal for health and cleanliness ebbed, aprons and caps were neatly folded and quietly laid away against the evil day when there might be the renewal of health interest focused on the butchers.

In this part of the city, which is in the old part of Baghdad, life moved along much as it had done for centuries. Seemingly, in this quarter nobody cares about anybody. In the street where I continued to saunter, which was narrow and without a pavement yet wide enough for vehicles, loaded wagons drawn by two horses, who were whipped to speed, came dashing along, making everybody scamper for his life. At a corner, a lorry that could not make the turn almost collided with a small wagon that could; and there was pell-mell flight on the part of the pedestrians as the horses reared and the lorry backed. Donkeys loaded with bricks were goaded to run, caring for no one either. Pack horses acted as though the whole street belonged to them. Porters carrying heavy burdens shouted loudly, "*Balek. Balek*" (take care. take care). In this melee I could make little progress. Sightseeing was interrupted by lifesaving leaps from one side of the street to another; and woe unto him who is pressed against the wall by a wagon or a loaded donkey or a heavy-laden porter!

In this process of dodging to save my life, I finally jumped up into a candy shop, where, after having recovered my breath, I saw the interesting process of making Eastern candies. What the various ingredients were that went into the making of these sweets, I did not learn, but one thing was evident: in this quarter the trade catered to the level of the people's tastes, which were emphatically for color and shape. The colors were not the delicate pastel shades, but autumnal purples, deep reds, all gradations of green, yellows mingled with orange, and indigo blues. Besides the enticements of color, the candymaker was wise also in the molds he chose. These were animals, fish, guns, airplanes, dishes, and tiny boys: the things children love the world over.

It had been a trying morning. The market had so disappointed me that not even the shrilling of the *hilhal* to attract my attention by a seller of watermelons who was lazily reclining on his pile could get from me more than a momentary laugh. The lifesaving activities had so wearied me that, upon my return, I had no energy left to express as explosively as was expected my feelings about the market. It took me several days to recuperate before starting out for that which I knew would not disappoint: the Shorja, a bazaar consisting largely of Jewish shops.

The Shorja is a covered bazaar that runs at right angles from Rashid Street, winding through the heart of the Jewish quarter. The shops are prevailingly small, mere cubbyholes which hug one another the whole length of the long, irregular street, with here and there large khan-like stores where grain is sold in quantity. Here, as on the pontoon bridges, I mixed with men and women of all stages of affluence and poverty: clean people and dirty people, pestiferous basket-boys, laden porters, and the everywhere-present donkeys that run straight ahead regardless. Strange to say, no camels are seen in the city except at the far end of the Shorja where bags of grain are delivered. In all the years I lived in Baghdad I saw camels in the city only at this place, and no one could tell me why.

My object in going to the Shorja this particular day was to buy those charms which were commonly used by the people. I wanted especially the blue beads which are a charm against the evil eye, and which are everywhere in evidence. I wanted, too, the cowries, which are small shells, also much used to counteract the "eye of envy," and the flat, blue, buttonlike *dehasha*s with five or seven holes which are sewed on garments or caps for the same purpose. I could not however find the tiny metallic Abbas's hands, sometimes called Fatima's hands, which have the power of protecting a person against ill luck. So very cheap are these magical charms that the poorest can possess them, and the frowziest tot has dangling from a lock of his hair a short string to which is attached one or more of these amulets.

The evil eye is an eye that has the power to injure another, to inflict blight by merely looking at a person. Sickness, misfortune, and a host of other evils are often attributed to the influence of the evil eye. In this malign power the illiterates believe, and to ward it off they resort to magical rites and charms. To this end the blue beads are most commonly used and are everywhere to be seen. Not only do children wear them, but horses are necklaced with them and donkeys wear them; sometimes the radiator cap of an automobile is circled with them, and harnesses and saddles are decorated with them. Even my shepherd's pipe has tiny ones pressed in the bitumen, and the *guffa*s used to be generously decorated with designs of beads and cowries. Most unfortunate, indeed, is the person to whom this power of the evil eye is attributed. "His neighbors dread and shun him; his family looks upon him as an affliction; he is an unwelcome guest at any social function."

An English lady in Baghdad, who had made a study of the persistence of the use of charms and magic formulae and the ways of warding off the evil eye, found that on the old Babylonian cuneiform tablets are inscribed the very formulae and methods employed today. A superstitious practice that still persists is to start floating down the Tigris on a Thursday evening a tiny boat made of a piece of date cluster with one or more votive candles alight on it. Whenever I saw this bit of the date tree on the river, I knew a woman was watching with her heart as well as her eyes to see whether the little craft will pass out of her sight aglow. If the candle continues to burn, she returns to her house with a light step for her prayer will be answered; if the candle is puffed out, she returns with a hopeless heart.

Having made my purchases, I continued to linger in this covered bazaar for it was cool in comparison to the unprotected street. I watched the motley throng; I watched the buying and selling and the bargaining. To keep up the mood, I ventured home through unknown *darbuna*s.

Another interesting day I spent in the Great Bazaar. Unlike the Shorja, this bazaar spreads out over a large area and runs parallel to the river. This, too, is covered and could be explored in comfort. It receives its customers, its friends, its loiterers, and its sightseers through many entrances. At these entrances and exits the hungry and the thirsty can get refreshments. The old fancy *lemonata* container, with its brass ornamentation and clinking of brass dishes to arrest attention, is vanishing; in its place is a white enameled pail from the West, with a ladle to serve the thinned *laban*, or dark mulberry sherbert or lemonade. The quick-lunch tray provided with tomatoes, hard-boiled eggs, ladyfingers, or coarse beans, radishes, and cucumbers—carried on the head and set down anywhere on a light metal stand—still provides a popular eating counter.

This particular morning I began to wander slowly through the Great Bazaar. Passing by the small bookshops, I turned off into a doorway opening into the goldsmiths' bazaar. Here, by the most primitive of methods, the standardized jewelry is hammered out. Nothing in centuries has changed in this bazaar, neither in tools nor in designs. Little charcoal fires were burning on little clay stands fed with air through a pipe from curious bellows. With practiced hands the goldsmith placed the gold nugget in the fire, lifted it out, hammered it partly into shape, heated and hammered again, and finally dropped it into water.

This bazaar caters a great deal to Bedouin trade and handles mostly bracelets, anklets, ornamental ankle rings with tiny bells for children, nose rings, finger rings, and earrings. With one of the goldsmiths, Bedouin women were bargaining for little anklets that make music wherever the child goes. They were insisting that one of the pair was larger than the other. This was not true as the goldsmith proved by measurement. The women fairly screamed, and the goldsmith shouted, "*Ruh*," which is rather a brusque way of saying "Go." All went but one. She stayed behind to spout out all the abuse she knew, the cursing gushing forth in a powerful stream. "What did she say?" I asked the goldsmith after she had gone. "She said I wasn't a gentleman," was the answer, and that answer was the supreme art of soft-pedaling.

Going on, I soon turned into another lane where a great din was heard. It was where the coppersmiths hammer all day long. They work in a wide, covered street; the hammering goes on outside their shops, while inside are the fires and the bellows. The noise is deafening. Here, too, ancient methods are used, and the conventional forms are hammered out by hand with no desire for change or improvement. There seems to be no measuring. A coppersmith who made a plate for me determined the width with his elbow as he turned the flat piece of copper, producing something very pleasing. Here the big trays are made for the handy-lunch vendors, the utensils for the kitchens, the ewers and basins, water jugs, coffeepots with their long spouts, and other articles in common use.

My ramblings brought me to a few rug shops. To pass these by is absolutely impossible. They just draw me like a magnet. A rug dealer soon gauges your taste and pocketbook; and though his stock today does not come up to that of former years, yet he has a few "luscious" treasures. An unusually lovely Bukhara and a silk rug highly valued made me lament the flatness of my purse. During the days of the mandate, when the British were many and the tourists many, these Eastern shops were quite large, well stocked and prominently located. They were filled not only with rugs but also with Persian vases, wondrous bowls, plates of rich designs, brass trays, and fabrics woven with silk and much gold.

These shops have since fallen upon hard times, and the chorus of lament is strong when the decrease of American tourists is dwelt upon. These were the most easily victimized, being the most gullible. What tales are told of those balmy, money-pocketing days when before an American group a lovely rug was held under the proper light, and in just the proper way to make the sheen glisten, the hand gently stroking the pile in the right way until the glow in the faces of the prospective buyers gave confidence. Then, with meekly bent head, eyes innocent, and voice soft and bland, the dealer pronounced the price as though the rug at that price was a gift. As the buyer counted out his money, feeling mean at the advantage he thought he had taken of the dealer's generosity, the latter received the lucre with a favor-bestowing smile and repressed the chuckle over the fat profit.

Another morning of sightseeing took me to the Mustansir, or River Street. What makes this street so well known is that the Amara silversmiths, familiarly known as Subbis, have their little shops strung out along here. They have a secret process of decorating their silver with a curious inlay of antimony, the scenes in black on the silver articles being taken from the land. They call themselves Mandeans or Gnostics. Muslims thought them to be Sabeans, a people mentioned in the Qur'an, and because of this they have been singularly free from persecution. They sit cross-legged on the floor in the small shops in which they work beside a charcoal fire, which little boys fan into a flame by means of goatskin bellows. Their wares are displayed in glass cases on low stands from which they draw out their silver articles as you indicate your choice. Just as their wares are unlike anything else seen in Baghdad, so the men are strikingly different from the people daily seen on the streets.

A Subbi can be recognized anywhere on earth. A few worked in the Iraq pavilion at the World's Fair in New York. His hair and beard are black, and all the darker because of the contrast with a pale skin. He dresses in white, but wears a red and white checkered *kaffiyah,* which contrasts with his black hair and beard. He is slender and fine-featured; always appearing friendly, he calls the European lady that passes his shop "Sister." Stranger even than his appearance is his religion. It consists largely in ablutions; the ceremony of purification is lengthy. For this reason the Subbis have also been called "The Followers of John the Baptist," whom they greatly revere.

My morning rambles were soon interfered with by a spell of withering heat. Not a breath of air stirred, and the camel-thorn screen at the bedroom window facing the north, and kept wet by means of a perforated tube above it, could give no relief since the north wind had withdrawn. The nights, too, were hot, and an oversized moon leered at suffering humanity which had sought the roof in the hope of finding comfort.

What was even more exasperating than the heat were the pests. They were unusually numerous this summer on account of the spring floods, and the rise in temperature incited them to activity. We were afflicted with more plagues than there were in Egypt. There was the everlasting dust and dirt, and the occasional dust storm when the wind whistled the fine particles through the cracks and crevices of the old house. Into these same crevices slithered the bats, spotting our furniture and swooping down upon us when we sought rest in the court. The big roaches, which I always missed when jumping at them, sucked all the lovely colors from the books, leaving them palely mottled. Then the grasshoppers, working in full collaboration with the roaches, came along and pretty well finished the books, and with appetites unsatiated, they advanced on my cushions and best dresses.

The rats, driven out of their lairs at the river, appropriated the house. The *zanburs*, a heavy and hardy variety of wasps, in spite of all vigilance were bound to nest somewhere in the building. Sparrows by the hundreds took a special fancy for the trees in the court, causing us to wage perpetual war against them. The mosquitoes were never weary of pestering me, and the ability of the dainty sandfly to annoy me was beyond telling. Last, but not least, were the dreaded scorpions with their sharp spears in their curved tails ready instantly to strike.

When I first came into this part of the world, fresh and in fine fettle, I boldly marched to the fray in the battle spirit to exterminate the pests and thus stop this endless contention. Should I allow life to be reduced to an everlasting struggle with these plagues with humiliating defeat hanging over my head? It durst not be! Then something happened, suddenly and strangely. A bat just missed me, a zanbur knocked against me, a roach ran across my path, the grasshoppers chirped shrilly in the serdab, the house needed more cleaning, and a sandfly squeezed into the net and bit me just as I was falling asleep. Balked efforts to cope with the pests had brought a collapse of spirit and broke down my morale so completely that, like everybody else, I just sat doing nothing about it!

In this part of the world, the word "sit" has acquired a new connotation. A student asks to sit in the school, not to study in it; he asks to sit for an examination, not to take it; a parent comes to sit with a boarder, not to visit him; a person asks for the privilege of sitting with you, not of calling on you. People can sit all day, day after day, aimlessly, and enjoy it. When my will ceased to function and I just sat, then I knew the East had done something to me.

After the intense heat wave had passed, and I had recovered from the collapse which defeated struggle with the pests had caused, I resumed my morning jaunts. The urge of adventure led me to make a few more explorations. I was, in particular, desirous again to see and to study the great finds and relics that were deposited in the museums. Since my coming to Baghdad, three museums had been opened, each of which represented a distinct period in the history of the land. I am of the opinion, however, that this was not thought of at the time these museums were planned and formally opened; yet, in reality, this is the case.

One museum contained the remains of the ancient world, and this, of course, is the largest and most important; another had the finds of the golden age of the Arab period, which was during medieval times; and the third had the exhibits of modern Iraq.

My first jaunt was to the Museum of Antiquities, a museum which had been created by the initiative of Miss Gertrude Bell. In this museum are deposited priceless treasures which the spade uncovered since the First World War. It can be said that there were three periods in the history of excavating in Iraq. The first work was done before World War I. This is when Ninevah, Ashur, and Babylon were excavated, mainly by the English and the Germans. The finds were mostly taken to Europe and Istanbul, where I saw many of them. Consequently, the Iraq museum is deprived of nearly all these early remains of excavations.

During the second period, which began after the First World War, Mesopotamia became a paradise for archaeologists. As many as twenty-five sites were excavated, and always with important results, by sixteen foreign institutions of five different nationalities. It was also the period when the American School of Oriental Research was incorporated and began to send to Iraq annually a visiting professor.

In accordance with a law which had been enacted, the finds of foreign excavators had to be divided between the excavator or institution financing the project and the Iraq museum. Obviously, the most spectacular and most precious articles found their way to the Iraq museum, whereas tablets and objects throwing light on the history of the past, as a rule, were taken out of the country for further study.

It was a thrilling experience to live in Baghdad during this period when startling finds were made, and to see the "digs," and to handle some of the articles that had just come out of the earth. Simple finds as well as those of great historic significance sometimes dumbfounded me, as, for example, when at Kish the excavator allowed me to handle a little clay sheep, which when shaken, rattled. It was the plaything of a child about six thousand years ago. It was a delight, too, to meet, to learn to know, and to entertain these scholars who had come from institutions such as Yale, Harvard, Johns Hopkins, Oxford, and the universities of Chicago, California, Michigan, Pennsylvania, and London.

Again, on account of the archaeological activities so pronounced during this period, we were led to adventure in the realm of the past with as much enthusiasm as we were adventuring in the present. Before the reports of the season's excavations were made public, we who were living in Iraq had the coveted privilege of hearing a lecture on these important finds before anyone else was so privileged. Before the people of New York, London, or Paris or the scholars of the world knew what was unearthed, we who were living in Baghdad knew all about it.

The lectures on the season's "dig" were, as a rule, illustrated with projected pictures, and to this absorbingly interested audience the most precious and valuable articles were also exhibited. This was especially true of Sir Leonard Woolley's excavations at Ur, where the most important relics during this period were found. Indeed, his annual lectures during the dozen or more seasons he dug became a great occasion, keenly anticipated and eagerly attended. In like manner, other excavators also reported on their labors and rewards during these hectic days of digging activities.

What a light the excavations during this period have thrown upon history. The uncovering of ancient sites has contributed to a better understanding of the ancient world, and because of these discoveries ancient history must be revised. We know now that there was the flood mentioned in the Bible by the discovery of heavy deposits of clean clay with evidences of human occupation both above and beneath. We know more than we ever knew of the earliest inhabitants of the Tigris and the Euphrates Valley. We know, too, that when God called Abraham to go forth from Ur of the Chaldees to the land of Canaan, he left behind no "mean" city—probably the most civilized city of his day. Twenty-five years ago there was not a single book on the city of Ur; today there is a whole shelf-full.

Equally important in the history of excavating has become the third period. This began with the outbreak of the Second World War, an event that for a time had put an end to foreign expeditions, leaving the work of excavating entirely in the hands of the Iraq government. All the finds now became the property of the Iraq Museum of Antiquities. Foreign archaeological expeditions, however, are at work again in the land, and the excavations as before are still energetically pushed. The finds have been surprisingly rewarding, much as they had been in the preceding period. A code of laws has been found which is dated earlier than the famous code of Hammurabi. The oldest agricultural community in this part of the world has been uncovered.

One of the greatest surprises was to find school tablets which give clear evidences of an understanding of the basic principles of algebra and geometry, 1,700 years before Euclid lived, who has been popularly reputed as the father of geometry and a pioneer in mathematics. These tablets also contain an outline of the scientific knowledge of the age which will force us to change our ideas about these ancients. Again, in the dark, twisting mountain caves, relics have been discovered of "what may be history's first man, estimated to have lived 20,000 years ago." Archaeologists of the Directorate of Antiquities of the Iraq government must be credited for most of these recent, valuable finds. The rewards of their "digs" are published every quarter, and the finds are so numerous that almost every year a new section in the museum had to be opened, usually with an impressive ceremony. A new building for the museum is planned, and when erected it will be, hopefully, on a par with the great museums of the world.

The Museum of Antiquities occupied me one whole morning, and so rich and marvelous were the exhibits that I returned to it the next day. To tell and describe all I saw would read like an official guide and would sound exceedingly boring; nevertheless a few of these finds have universal interest.

The first case that overawed me by its golden splendor had the rich treasures taken from the royal tombs of the Sumerian city of Ur. As I feasted my eyes upon the exhibit, my attention for the moment was diffused, not knowing on which of the glittering objects to focus. In front of me was a woman's head, heavily adorned. She wore a "Spanish comb" of gold with flowers made of gold attached to stems that bent forward toward the face. These decorations, which were very showy, partly obscured the golden ribbon festooned in loops upon the head. In connection with such a ribbon there is a story with a very human touch. One of the ladies hurrying to the tomb for the burial ritual had no time to arrange the ribbon on her hair. She thrust the coil, wound just as ribbon is today, into the pocket of her dress where it was found by the excavators five thousand years later.

These bodies were discovered in the royal tombs, in the gruesome "death-pits." Like in ancient Egypt, there were buried with the dead many articles the departed might require for a journey to or in another world. A royal person required the same servants and attendants that were serving him during his earthly life. These followed the dead body into the "death-pit," where they were sacrificed as a part of the burial rites; and by all appearances from the position of the skeletons, they must have voluntarily laid down their lives. There were twenty-five in the tomb of Queen Shub-ab, nine of whom were court ladies; and in the largest "death-pit" unearthed, there were the bodies of six menservants and at least sixty-eight women.

The victims placed themselves in rows on the ground, attired in their best, to journey with their sovereign, whom they regarded as a god, into the unknown where they believed they would serve him or her as on earth. It must have been a gaily dressed crowd assembled in the open pit for the royal obsequies, persons who willingly and voluntarily allowed themselves to be sacrificed, believing that in so doing they would pass from one world into another, "from the service of a god on earth to that of the same god in another."

I next came upon the famous helmet of beaten gold, sometimes referred to as a gold wig. It was worn by a prince in whose tomb it was found. It is delicately modeled to resemble hair and is a piece of exquisite workmanship of the ancient Sumerian art. Nothing like this relic was ever before unearthed in Mesopotamia, neither since. In this tomb were also found the prince's belongings: jewels of gold, bracelets, and amulets. In the same case were wonderful gold daggers, which were among the most precious finds. One of these has a handle of lapis lazuli and gold. These ancient craftsmen were masters of their art. It used to be said that the goldsmiths of London were unable to reproduce these daggers, so exquisitely fine were they wrought.

Much more could be said of other important finds that came to light at Ur, and much also could be said of other treasures that were unearthed at Nineveh, Babylon, Ashur, Khorsabad, Nimrud, Warka, Nippur, Ubaid, Lagash, Opis, Fara, Taklan, Tape Rawra, Tell Asmar, Khafaje, Jemdet Nasr, Agar Quf, Tell Hasuna, Tell Harmel, Tell Muhammad, and a dozen or more other sites which yielded their hidden treasures and thereby enriched our knowledge of the past.

In the other two museums that I later visited, my interest was more in the buildings that housed the exhibits than in the objects themselves. One morning found me at Khan Ortmah, now the Museum of Islamic Art. I felt at once its symmetry, its spaciousness, its harmony, and its simplicity. Outside were the loud noises of the turbulent street; inside were serenity, stillness, space—a blessed retreat from the cramped thoroughfare. All the exhibits at the time had been placed in the small rooms communicating with the great hall; the only decoration in the hall was a large granite basin in the center, taken from the caliph's palace at Samarra. It, too, had the same superb simplicity as the stately hall. The third museum contained the memorials exhibition of King Faisal I; here my mind was occupied with the architecture of the restored building, an Abbassid palace, making the museum especially important.

With this visit my summer ramblings ceased. The city of the *Thousand and One Nights* had had for me, not a thousand and one adventures, but enough to transform what would otherwise have been a tedious and weary summer into one that was filled with lively and engrossing interests.

9

Baghdad from the Tigris

It is the Tigris that draws you in Baghdad; at least, it did draw me. The river is so accessible, so near to every part of the city, flowing almost through the middle of it, that one would suppose much use would be made of it for recreation and enjoyment. But we did not find this to be so, though when we first came motor launches ran back and forth between the city and the suburbs. Later when boulevards, smoothly asphalted, were constructed and automobiles and busses appeared, they superseded the launches. Like the *guffas*, the launches disappeared, leaving only the *balams* (boats) to take people across the river who preferred to be rowed rather than walk or drive over the bridges.

Yet, when the caliphs ruled in Baghdad, the river was alive with crafts. It was said that in the days of Amin, the son of Harun al-Rashid, thousands of gondolas were on the river, and that the people so enjoyed crossing in balams that the number of these boats was 30,000. This caliph also arranged gorgeous fetes, with five royal gondolas in the center, constructed in the shape of a horse, an elephant, an eagle, a serpent, and a lion. The river today is much the same as it was then and has the same possibilities.

To row down the river through Baghdad today is to row through history. Therefore, in order to understand, appreciate, and evaluate Iraq's glorious past and her present achievements, I deliberately rowed one evening from one end of the city to the other. The history of Baghdad from the time it was founded until the present day moved before me like a moving picture. Along the shores of both sides of the river were the "leftovers" of a bygone age and the achievements of today. Baghdad's checkered life for me became real.

Rowing down the river through the whole length of the city is the best, and possibly the only, way to relive that "pulsating life that built here a great city, and from it ruled such an enlightened empire that it gave the lamp of learning to Europe; and so stimulated and fertilized the minds of our ancestors that it led directly to the dawn of the modern world." Besides, it is a good way of bringing one face to face with the Baghdad of today, as it is striving and struggling to regain its former greatness.

I had a somewhat similar experience years before when I strolled along the Seine in Paris. Paris was founded only a few centuries before Baghdad; and every boy and girl in Iraq who has gone to school knows that Charlemagne and Harun al-Rashid had exchanged gifts. I took a delight in walking along the historic Seine and observing what both shores had to reveal. I had then walked through history, just as now I was rowing through it.

It was on a summer day when I rowed through the whole length of the city. It was an unforgettable evening, when the sky was glorifying the earth, and a silver-grey mystic light flooded the city. The rays of the setting sun were reflected from glazed domes and minarets; and as twilight deepened, the stars began to peep out one by one, and later burned brilliantly in the heavens. As I now launched out upon my river trip, and passed lovely gardens at the edge of the city, these words of Tennyson flashed upon my mind:

> By Tigris' shrines of fretted gold,
> High-walled gardens, green and old.

On both sides were green gardens, and some of them indeed were old. The sunken Persian garden of the minister of Education, in which we occasionally spent a delightful evening, was just a little further up the stream; and beyond that was a shrine of fretted gold, the golden domes and minarets of Kadhimain. Had Tennyson been fortunate enough to visit this spot, he might have said, "Not only have I written what is beautiful, but also what is really true."

It seemed most gratifying that shore and river should have conspired to bring me first to the royal palace. Here the new Iraq began, while across the river is the supposed site of the first beginnings of Baghdad.

In a well-kept garden that slopes down to the river are two one-story buildings. In the one are the royal offices, and in the other the king or regent has his suite of rooms where he works and receives. For a time these two unpretentious buildings were entirely separated, but now they are connected by a closed corridor, giving a rather stately approach to the king's quarters. The palace grounds appeared this evening unusually beautiful as the slanting rays of the sun fell upon trees and shrubbery and flowers.

I recalled a summer when the garden was a desolation. Just above the palace grounds the river in flood-time decided to change its course. It broke the bund and scooped out a deep, wide channel that encircled the entire city, leaving a flooded area that lasted for four months. This turbulent river had no more regard for the palace than for the Arab huts nearby. Both were equally flooded, and the occupants of both were obliged to flee with their belongings. The floors of the palace were covered with the yellow water, leaving behind in the royal rooms a heavy deposit of mud when the water had receded; the garden was a sight to behold.

The city which Caliph Mansur built with the help of 100,000 craftsmen from Syria, Mosul, and Persia is so completely wiped out that not one stone or one brick is left upon another. The city which was so novel in its day, which had four famous gates from which roads radiated to the four corners of the earth, and which in fifty years had spread beyond the bounds of the Round City with a reputed population of two million—this city has not a single trace left of its beginnings.

Time, floods, and man's destructiveness have ruined remains of walls, houses, and public buildings that once stood so proudly here. How can it be that the famous Round City which was built less than 1,200 years ago could have been so completely obliterated? Archaeologists in Mesopotamia have been able to spot sites that go back in history six thousand years, and even to the prehistoric and the antediluvian period; yet the exact place of this Round City and its beautiful palace cannot be found; it is completely destroyed and lost.

By this time my boat had come in sight of the Royal Hospital. As I looked at this medical compound with its wards, clinics, medical school, and nurses' home, I recalled the many, many times I was here, not for myself but in the interest of others. To this hospital I took many of our students and helpers and always received kindness and consideration. Whether I came with the patient or sent a note with him, it was like an open sesame that opened the door at once.

What impressed me always at this hospital was the fact that the people in Baghdad, and to a lesser degree in all Iraq, could have much the same care and treatment as the sick in the West. The hospital is well equipped with all the important instruments used in diagnosing and in treating diseases and has access to the same medicines used in other countries. Many of the doctors are highly specialized, having taken advanced courses in Europe or America. This also is true in regard to a few private and community hospitals. The Jewish hospitals and clinics have had the help of highly trained German physicians who had fled from Germany during the Nazi regime.

On the other hand, there are local people who never were in a medical school, who never read a book on anatomy and physiology, and yet have an uncanny skill that verges on the miraculous, especially the bonesetters. These bonesetters acquired their art and skill by inheritance, by intuition, and by watching and helping their fathers and grandfathers in this art. The practice comes down through the same families. They do not know the names of the bones they set, though they set them right. Their fingertips serve them in diagnosis the way the X-ray serves the professional surgeon.

One day I had a severe fall down the steps from our balcony. I fell upon my hand and I thought my wrist was broken, which later X-ray photographs confirmed. A professional doctor put my hand in a cast, and when the cast was removed the bones had not been set right. I was persuaded to get a bonesetter who was recommended. He found what was wrong by his sensitive fingers, and then began to pull and twist the wrist to get it in shape. It was exceedingly painful, for these bonesetters are not allowed to give an anesthetic; but the hand is right today.

All this happened shortly before my return to America, and as I had not yet the full use of my hand, I feared that the job might not, after all, have been properly done. I went to a specialist at the Medical Center in New York after my arrival. He carefully examined the wrist, and then to my relief said, "The hand is as good as any doctor can set it; all it needs now is exercise."

My husband, too, had an experience with a bonesetter. Coming down the same steps he had his knee wrenched. A professional doctor looked at it and prescribed fomentations. This did not help; the knee swelled, and walking was painful and difficult. The same bonesetter came, and moving his sensitive fingers up and down the knee, he located the position of muscles and tendons. He then gave the limb some twists and jerks. All at once there was a crack. The tendon which had slipped out of place sprang back, and all was right again.

About two blocks below the Royal Hospital, there is a large house on the east bank, which for a time was the residence of the king and queen, a house where I often called. It is now the Parliament building. In this house the laws for the new nation are made, for Iraq is a constitutional monarchy, modeled after our Western democratic governments: a legislative body of two houses, a prime minister, and ministers of state.

The legislative body is a varied assembly: of effendis, who appear in European clothes wearing the *sidara;* of Sayyids, the descendants of the Prophet, indicated by the green band wound around the tarbush; of mullahs or religious sheikhs, wearing either a turban or a red tarbush which is wound around with a white spotless cloth; of Jewish and Christian dignitaries, who appear in robes of solid black or flashing scarlet or rainbow colors. I am afraid that whenever I attended a session, my interest was more in the assemblage than in the business procedure or in the debate on hand.

Parliamentary procedures, in those early days, were new and strange to the land. It was a new experience for senators and deputies, and to some it was a tedious process. The sheikhs naturally grew weary of the long sessions in which they had no particular interest or leading part, and the impulse often moved them to saunter out for a cup of coffee and a chat on lighter subjects. Sometimes they had to be recalled to their immediate duties, business of national importance, though their major interest may have been, like that of some congressmen in Washington, only in pleasing their own constituency—their tribe. This is just a little aside. On the contrary, I was always impressed with the orderly procedure and the careful consideration of vital matters.

Close to the Parliament building was the *serai,* the municipal building, which had been erected during the Turkish regime. The old serai I always greeted with pleasure. It is unique in its architectural design, a style which unfortunately was not adhered to in the newly built additions. The ample grounds facing the river are laid out in grass and flowerbeds with a tall clock-tower near the river.

Very frequently I drove with my husband to the serai; and while he was attending to business, I lazily watched the "goings-on" in the serai court, which was as good as watching a drama. Here were sellers of food and drinks; automobile washers, often too near the sleepers on the grassplots; couriers with messages in their hands; effendis clutching their briefcases as tightly and carefully as if they contained the most precious documents; Bedouin sheikhs, either singly or in groups, who had come to air their grievances because a centralized government was curtailing some of their traditional rights and privileges.

Most of those there were heading for some office in the serai, looking as though they had business of major importance. There were scenes where men were vehemently arguing, more volubly with their hands than with their mouths. Though I had never learned the language of the deaf and dumb, yet I could invariably get the gist of their story without hearing one word that was said. Their facial expressions and their expressive gestures sufficed. What greatly helped me in this was that certain gestures are so commonly used to express the particular thought or emotion that one can learn them as he does the letters of the alphabet. Many of these stereotyped gestures I knew; and when they were made with the corresponding facial expression, which I also had learned, I found the meaning conveyed quite apparent and more forceful than words.

At other times, I had come to the serai to do business myself, and then the tables were turned. I no longer posed as a spectator but was an actor myself. My business often led me to different departments of the government; whether my business was important or not, at least I was a kind of liaison officer between the school and the government. Nearly all the ministries were either in the old Turkish serai building or in the buildings adjoining them. Here were the offices of the prime minister; the central police; the ministries of Defense, Education, Interior, Finance, Communications, and Works; the Ministry of Justice; and the law courts.

By this time my boat had drifted to a low pontoon bridge known in those days as the Kotah Bridge, but later, when replaced by a high steel structure, as King Ali Bridge. On this narrow pontoon bridge, more so than on Maude Bridge, the old and the new jostled together cheek and jowl. At close quarters commingled modish ladies and veiled women, well-groomed effendis and coolies in rags, Europeans bent on business and Bedouins with 'abas touching the ground, luxurious motor cars and worn carriages, heavy lorries and local wagons drawn by horses, fine Arab steeds and trotting donkeys, aimless pedestrians and children of all sizes—in fact, everybody and everything that could move.

At the bridge ends are the coffeehouses, offering the men who had found crossing the bridge a bit fatiguing a place to rest on the hard benches. The whole male population of Baghdad from homes, offices, and shops appears to empty itself in the evening into the everywhere handy coffee shops. Baghdad seems to have more coffeehouses to the square mile than any other city in the world. They are of every description, from the small dismal hole into which a few benches can be cramped to the new and spacious pavilions along the river or the boulevards. These coffeehouses are so typical of Baghdad that one cannot think of Baghdad without them. Some men seem to live permanently in them. They are there summer and winter, coming before daylight and sitting there all day; and for all I know sleeping there on the hard benches. As the coffee shops are of all sorts, so are the habitués. Here the male inhabitants of Baghdad sit: some talk, some drink coffee or tea, some smoke the *narghile,* some play backgammon, some transact business, but most of them just sit doing nothing. All these coffeehouses have blaring phonographs and most of them also radios, both of which are usually turned on as loud as possible. One time in coming down King Ghazi Street, we tried to ascertain, as we slowly drove along, whether we could hear an exciting speech that came over the radio from beginning to end without a break. So close were these coffeehouses that we lost it only once.

After passing beneath the pontoon bridge, I rowed past a long edifice along the waterfront. It was erected by Caliph Al-Mustansir bi-Allah as a college, and is the only intact building of the Abbassid period remaining in Baghdad. It contains a law school, a magnificent library, a hospital, and a famous medical school. That which at the time made the greatest impression was a large timepiece, which enabled students to know the appointed hours for lectures and prayer. This long building with its broad, inscribed frieze in decorative Arabic and its designed brickwork impresses one in its neglected state even today.

About the middle of the seventeenth century, business encroached upon the building, and a bazaar was built near it, which now almost surrounds it. Today the riverfront is used as a wharf, and the building as a depository for goods arriving by riverboats.

It happened that during my summer rambles about the city I came one day to the old Mustansiriyah. I walked along the waterfront in order to study again the large Arabic inscription that runs along the full length of the building. Arabic letters lend themselves easily to decorative purposes, and the art of Arabic calligraphy is beautiful. Letters spreading harmoniously from right to left "whirl on their own axis, sometimes in intricate shapes, sometimes in pure forms." I was always captivated by the beauty of this frieze, its flourishes and proud perpendicular letters moving in long parade.

I had scarcely made a start when I discovered that I was not welcome. War materials were being unloaded, and the customs official plainly did not want me there. When I became aware of it, I withdrew in a cloud of cement dust. If that visit received a cold reception, a warmer one was given us once by the Kurdish coolies employed on the wharf. These *hammals* entertained quite an audience on the landing in front of the old Mustansiriyah with a five-act play depicting their Kurdish life. The play was given in the Kurdish language, and as few if any could read and write, the actors had to learn their part by word of mouth. The stage setting was very familiar to us for it was borrowed from our school. The players performed with such a realistic faithfulness to actualities that it raised these coolies to the status of genuine actors. This one night, when the "poor things" were transformed into a theatrical cast and performed before an audience in formal dress, gave them other matters to talk about than the boastings of the heavy weights they carried; and gave them something else to do than pool their meager earnings to buy 'arak, so as to forget their hard lot in life. The play was certainly not along the line of the Mustansiriyah tradition, but the college would have had no reason to despise the efforts of these Kurdish laborers.

It is fortunate that when the Mongol hordes, who left little behind when they took Baghdad but ruins and the dead, should for some reason or another have spared this building which is nearly a thousand years old. What Hulagu had left of the city, Tamerlane later altogether destroyed, so that when all was over there was little remaining of buildings, gardens, and inhabitants. How and why this building survived will forever remain a mystery. Historians say that a million and a half people were slain, and the city that had been "the abode of learning, the seat of culture, the eye and center of the Saracenic world" was no more.

I wish I knew where the other great colleges and universities were located. In particular, I should like to know where the famous Dar al-Hikmah (House of Wisdom) once stood. It was a research center, an academy, and a museum. All we know is that it was on the banks of the Tigris.

To this House of Wisdom, founded by Caliph Ma'mun, came the great scholars of many lands. To it were also brought manuscripts in Greek, Hebrew, Syriac, and Persian to be translated with commentaries into Arabic. Hundreds of camels it was said used to file into Baghdad with no other freight than volumes of manuscripts. Valuable contributions were made in physics, chemistry, astronomy, mathematics, medicine, and agriculture. At the same time, men with the gift of imagination and with creative powers enriched the literature of the world.

While meditating upon the wonders and achievement of the past, my mind was suddenly jerked into the present when I rowed past the British Residency on the opposite shore. The Residency was surrounded by a spacious garden with trees and flowers. The garden party which I attended upon my arrival in Baghdad at once flashed into my mind, and the unalloyed happiness of the afternoon was recalled. But this was soon displaced in my mind by the pressing thoughts of the political situation which the scenes from the Tigris disclosed.

It so happens that nearly all the buildings in which both the British and the Iraq governments function are along the river. The imposing British

Residency, now the embassy, stood more or less by itself on the west bank; opposite it were the buildings of the Iraq government on the east bank— very symbolic. The two political forces pitted against each other in this reborn land were separated, not intentionally but opportunely, by a wide and swiftly flowing stream. On the one side was the British seat of power, which during the period of the mandate was the ruling power in Iraq; and after the mandate, which had ceased in 1932, it, to all intents and purposes, still remained the unseen ruling force behind Iraq's independent facade.

Between the east and the west bank there were, during my stay in Baghdad, many occasions for differences, open opposition, and political tussles. Soon after the Iraq government was formed under the British mandate, the Iraqis began to agitate for more rights and greater freedom. This was slow in coming and was grudgingly given; promises were usually postponed until a crisis arose that looked desperate. Then when Iraq secured more of what she believed were her inherent rights, she began to agitate and demand that the mandate cease, and that she be admitted into the League of Nations. After considerable pressure this was granted, surprisingly soon, perhaps too soon.

A bipartite treaty now took the place of the mandate, by which Britain was able to retain much of the authority and privilege which she had enjoyed under the mandate. The treaty provided that the advisers to the ministries and the foreign, technically trained men were to be Britishers; that the British be allowed to build two air bases in Iraq; that Britain be permitted to bring troops into the country when necessary; and other privileges and concessions. In order to gain her independence, Iraq had to yield to the British pressure, and in signing the treaty conceded more than she wanted to. Therefore, constant dissatisfaction and irritation remained between the east and the west bank. Eventually, the east bank took matters into its own hands, which resulted in a clash of arms, commonly known as the May Revolution, or the Blind Revolt inasmuch as the revolt was not successful.

My boat now passed beneath the lower pontoon bridge which we had crossed for the first time upon our arrival in Baghdad. By this time night had come on, and not only the stars in the heavens sparkled, but the electric lights along the shore as well. To the left of me were the brightly lighted hotels, grouped closely together. They looked very inviting with their open-air dining services on the lawn or on platforms built out over the water and with smartly dressed waiters moving about.

Then passing South Gate, which was once the lower limits of the city, I came to Baghdad's recreational river bund, where the row ended. Here provision has been made for the people to come and enjoy themselves in the evening, or, as they in their flowery language say, "To smell the air." All along the river for about three miles there is a delightful promenade; and between it and the river is a space for flowers and benches where one can sit all evening and be refreshed by the coolness of the river and the open spaces. Or a person may choose to saunter all evening on the promenade, where he will have a chance to meet nearly all his friends and exchange a few words with them.

To this haven of rest and tranquility, my husband and I frequently resorted. No matter how hot or trying or monotonous the day may have been, and how depleted our energies, we were always refreshed and re-created here. To do nothing else but just to sit in the evening quietly on a bench facing the river sufficed. The cool air, the calmness of the night, and the healing virtues of wondrous beauty atoned for the hardships of the day.

On the shore and on the small islands, we watched the many fires, boxed in by four halves of fish to be grilled, the faces of the men being lighted up by the fires they were feeding on the river. We often dimly perceived fishermen's boats quietly creeping along the shore homeward. Looking to the opposite shore, we saw the river fringed with tassels of reflected light. Turning toward the great bend of the river, we noticed the lights of Karradah flashing like a jeweled necklace; gazing into the heavens, we beheld the stars which seemed so near in their constellations. Wherever the eyes turned, there was beauty, tranquility, and peace.

10

To Basrah on the Tigris

Having learned to know the Tigris as it flows through the heart of Baghdad, I bestirred myself to follow its course also from Baghdad to Basrah. Henry Van Dyke once wrote that every river has its own quality and that it is the part of wisdom to know and love as many as you can.

It has been my privilege to learn to know intimately and to love dearly the twin rivers of Iraq: the Tigris and the Euphrates. No other rivers do I know so well. Rising in the mountains of Central Turkey, both flow south through Iraq, almost parallel to each other. On the latitude of Baghdad the two rivers are as close as thirty-five miles. Here the Euphrates seems to be headed to join the Tigris but suddenly makes up its mind to turn south again and away from its companion. About one hundred miles from the Persian Gulf the two, however, do unite.

Both, more or less, have the same qualities and the same personalities. The life and character and voice of each are the same, so that, if you have learned to know the one, you will also know the other. Both rivers carry about the same amount of water; both are usually flooded in the spring when the snow melts on the mountains in the north; both are navigable for riverboats in the lower plain; and both have changed their course often. Along the banks of each river sprung up the great cities of the plain, ancient and modern. When the rivers decided to make new channels for themselves, these cities declined and finally died. Nowhere else on the surface of the earth do we have rivers so much alike.

Should it not have been for these rivers, the lower part of Iraq would today not be land but water; and should it not be for these two rivers, nothing worthwhile would grow on the plain. There would be no green fields and no flourishing cities: all would be a vast desert. In fact, the whole plain was built up by the sediments of the rivers. In historic times, we know that such cities as Ur were on the Persian Gulf; today, they are 150 miles inland. In prehistoric times, the same buildup of land went on. Every now and then a bar was formed at the mouth of the river; then between the bar and the land already formed the muddy waters carrying deposits became quiescent, whereupon the particles of earth carried by the water were released and went to the bottom. When this area between the bar and the land was filled up, the river sought a new channel to the side. The same process continued until, through the ages, the entire plain called Iraq was formed.

The boat trip we took gave me exactly what I wanted, and I learned in this leisurely sailing that the Tigris has a distinct quality of its own. There is no other river comparable to it except its twin sister, the Euphrates. The physical features of the river, its varied shoreline, its serpentine course, its historic associations, the changing scenery, the *dhows* and the *mahailahs* on the water, and the race of men contiguous to it—all these combine to give to the Tigris a compelling charm.

There is no trip in Iraq I should so like to repeat as this river trip, which we were able to take one spring vacation. Good fortune was with us: the river was high, spring was in its beauty, and the moon was full. We were on the river three days and three nights. There was only one drawback: we had no choice of a boat but had to take what was sailing at the time, which happened to be the second best on the river. The *Majidiyah* was all right theoretically and had pretty much what was to be expected on such a boat, but in actual practice nothing worked.

To make this trip required some planning and preparation beforehand. Our bedding had to be taken as well as some food. The two deck chairs we carried with us had been subject to the intense heat of several summers, and soon after the boat had started, while we were sitting in a state of bliss watching the shore life, my husband and I found ourselves almost simultaneously sitting on the floor. The chairs had collapsed. Someone of the crew patched them up, and they lasted exactly until within an hour of reaching Basrah.

Looking at a large map of Iraq, and giving particular attention to the Tigris, you find that possibly no other river makes so many turns and has so many loops as this river from Baghdad to Basrah. It winds in serpentine fashion across the flat country, and by the many abrupt curvings it produces strange effects. Sometimes I lost my bearings completely and imagined that the boat had turned back toward Baghdad.

Just outside of Baghdad where the river makes a great bend, almost in the form of a horseshoe, we saw what Iraq can be one day if properly irrigated and cultivated and what abundant fruits and vegetables and grain a plot of ground can produce. Almost every year we drove out here to see the almond blossoms in February and later, to get a real touch of spring, to see the apricot and peach trees in prodigious bloom.

On this river trip, I observed what the soil can bring forth and visualized from this abundantly fruitful area what the whole plain of the Tigris and the Euphrates was like once upon a time. In the days of the Babylonians, Mesopotamia was the granary of the world. Herodotus, who had traveled in many countries, testifies to this when he says, "Of all the countries we know there is none so fruitful in grain." But this vast irrigation system, with its numerous canals, which had been constructed with much toil and skill, was completely destroyed; the desert marched over the soil, and a lesser people, not able to cope with the situation, lapsed into indifference and apathy; a period of stagnation followed.

Our next object of interest was Ctesiphon. It did not loom in the horizon until evening came on. By automobile it is reached in a short time, but because of the many bends in the river and a slower motion, it took us several hours to get there. We had been told repeatedly that Ctesiphon should be seen by moonlight. Fortunately, the *Majidiyah* was so timed that it brought us to this remarkable ruin when the moon was in full radiance.

We had driven to Ctesiphon often, and to us it was a familiar landmark, but never did the great White Palace, once resplendent in its outer covering of polished marble, appear so grand as it did this night as we approached it on the river. There it stood, solitary and alone, a huge pile of bricks—now denuded of all ornamentation—still majestic. At a certain angle in the river, we could see through the huge throne room, this being possible because the front of it is entirely open while the back wall is partly broken down. This mighty arch of the throne room has a span of over eighty feet wide and a height of 120 feet. It is said to be the widest span of masonry in existence, ancient or modern.

If this White Palace at Ctesiphon where the Sasanian kings held their regal court was so magnificent in its ruins and denuded state, what must it have been before it was stripped of its polished marble? And what must its interior have been like before its walls were stripped of their gold, silver, jasper, lapis lazuli, onyx, and every other precious stone the East could produce? The riches of this palace stagger the imagination. Gibbon writes that when the Arabs took Ctesiphon in the seventh century of the Christian era, the naked robbers of the desert were suddenly enriched beyond the measure of their hope or knowledge. In the throne room hung a priceless carpet of silk and pearls which depicted a garden with flowers, fruits, and shrubs. This carpet, sixty cubits in length and the same in width, was taken to the caliph Umar, who cut it into pieces and distributed them among his brethren in Medina.

At the same time the site of another ancient city which was famous in its day was visible. Almost directly opposite Ctesiphon stood the Greek city of Seleucia. This Hellenistic city was founded, or at least embellished, shortly after the death of Alexander the Great. It marked the high tide of Greek culture and civilization in Mesopotamia. To build this beautiful city Seleucus Nicator tore down the palaces of Babylon and thereby ruined that historic city.

In the moonlight the tell, or mound, which marks the site of the ancient city was visible. I recalled a visit we had made to it while it was being excavated. Two American tourists drove with us to Ctesiphon, and the only craft we could find to take us across the river was a *guffa*. As the guffa could not come close to the shore, each one of us had to be carried to it on the back of a coolie. It was such a funny sight to see these frightened ladies of goodly size hanging on the back of a man and trying to keep their feet above water. This looked funny, but it was no fun to get down from the coolie's back into the unsteady guffa out in the river.

The archaeologist occupied a small house along the side of the river. What enthusiasm and zest for their work these excavators have. It must be the continual hopefulness of lighting upon some valuable find that causes it. The smallest thing is cherished as of value. This archaeologist kept a lot of these finds in boxes right in his own house, and the most precious of them under his bed.

Not much remains of the loveliness that once was here except mounds, "a little more dust in a region of dust." It is almost as necessary here as at Nineveh to have a knowledge beforehand of what the city was like, in order that the mind may project the mental pictures of "the golden ceilings, the jeweled panels, the silver tiles and the bronze gates" that were brought here from Babylon. All that one knows of the life of a Greek city can be transferred to Seleucia: the races in the stadium, the plays of Sophocles in the theatre, the athletics in the gymnasium.

The founding of Seleucia was the death-knell to Babylon. The Tigris, having been found to be a more navigable river than the Euphrates, was henceforth chosen for the site of the future capital of the land. Of the two, the Euphrates has been a much more inconsistent river and more fickle. It had deserted many a city that was built along its shores. Mercilessly, the river left such great cities like Ur, Kish, and Erech to wither away in a waterless land.

After passing the impressive ruins of the White Palace and the dreary mound of Seleucia, we leaned back in our chairs and tried to forget both the past glories and the present decay in the healing of the night, under the clear shining of the moon and the long reaches of the solitary desert. How silent and peaceful it was on the boat. The air was clean and cool, and the water was so calm that we scarcely felt any motion. We lolled in our chairs and listened to the singsong drones of the two Arabs who sat in little booths on the floats affixed to the boat on both sides. They plumbed the depths of the river with long rods, and the captain steered his course by this monotonous announcing of how far the rod measured.

The next morning the sun sprang again into a clear and cloudless sky, such as are nearly all the 365 days of the year in lower Iraq. In these early morning hours the river was at its best. Sometimes the dark green fields of wheat and barley extended on both sides as far as the eye could see. At times there were only ribbons of green with the drab desert beyond. Sometimes the green altogether disappeared awaiting irrigation and cultivation. At times we passed through stately palm groves where the lofty trees formed a beautiful avenue for the boat. Sometimes the river was narrow and then again it was broad. But whether narrow or broad, wind it always would.

It has been rightly said that Iraq's wealth lies in its rich soil as well as in its stored-away oil. On a trip like this one, one becomes aware of the richness of the soil and how little is under cultivation. Mr. Herbert Hoover, while studying the world food crisis, had come to Baghdad. It was at a time when we had a great flood, so that we had to entertain him and his party in the big court of our house for our living room was flooded.

Mr. Hoover became convinced that what the country needed was not only an extensive scheme for irrigation but also flood control. He made an aerial survey of the land. As a result of his observations, he later charted the proposed Tigris and Euphrates River Authority, which would enable four or five times more acres to be put under the plow, and at the same time would keep in control destructive floods. The scheme, and it is one of six or seven more, if ever carried out will make the valley of the twin rivers again become a granary of the world.[1]

The possibilities of the land and its returns when properly farmed grew increasingly upon me. But what startled me and vividly arrested my attention was an anomaly, and for the moment, I could not bring myself to the point of believing that it was really so. Over against great fertility were bedraggled and poverty-stricken inhabitants. Seeing this situation, and the sharp contrast between the wealth-producing land and the poverty of the people, I asked myself, How can it really be that in the midst of this rich soil and abundant growth, human beings should dwell in misery and abject poverty? How is this subhuman condition of living possible in a region on God's earth where you have His copious gifts? Is it due to ignorance, stagnation, primitiveness, the accumulated lethargies of the past,

---

1. One of the most ambitious such schemes was initiated by Sultan Abdul Hamid II, not long before he was overthrown by the Young Turks in 1908. The prominent British irrigation engineer Sir William Willcox was engaged by the Young Turks in 1908 to draw up his plan for the development of Mesopotamia. His glowing report proposed how the country would be protected from floods and how, through irrigation, some three million acres of land could produce one million tons of wheat and two million "hundredweights" of cotton, etc. But not much could be accomplished by Sir William; the Young Turks became preoccupied in the Balkans. They fought two wars there in 1912–13, followed by the Great War of 1914, which they entered in support of Germany (Great Britain 1905).

the dead weight of centuries, the feudal or semifeudal system that still prevails? These are questions that have haunted me ever since.

At four o'clock in the afternoon of the second day, we approached Kut, which, lying in the bend of the river, is surrounded on three sides by water. During World War I, the British forces were bottled up here and after much suffering were obliged to surrender. The fall of Kut had brought the Mesopotamian campaign against the Turks before the world for the first time, and had had in England a profoundly depressing effect. It was after the fall of Kut that General Maude then took charge of the British forces in Iraq and later took Baghdad.

Kut also had another interest for us at the time. Here a barrage was being constructed by the British across the Tigris, one of the major irrigation schemes undertaken by the Iraqi government. This was built to divert part of the waters of the Tigris into the Hai channel, a canal which in the summer became dry when the Tigris was low. The barrage, by raising the level of the river, ensured a continuous flow of water into the Hai all the year round, thus enabling the land between the Tigris and the Euphrates to be extensively cultivated.

Landing, we were told that we had an hour-and-a-half stay at Kut and at once sallied forth to see the sights, particularly the barrage. We had just accepted an invitation to be carried across the river in a cage on a cable used to transport material and the workmen, when we heard the whistle of the boat. We hesitated, for we had been on the shore only a very short time. But when the whistle blew the second time, and then most vigorously, we realized that it was the boat's signal to start. We scampered back in a hurry and breathlessly got on the boat just as it was moving away from the shore. The captain consoled us by saying that he had left word with an official of the steamship company that he should find us and take us to a place around the bend of the river where the boat would pick us up.

As evening came on, this large construction plant was flooded with light, and as we looped around the town on the bend, the plant appeared exceptionally bright against the dark background of the desert. I could not help but contrast the primitiveness of the desert dwellers with the developed modern technical mind that can build so powerfully and use nature so commandingly. The wandering Bedouin and the poor fellah live within the radius of this bright light yet have none of its benefits. The sterilities of centuries were symbolized by the one; modern ingenuity and enterprise by the other.

The next day brought us to Amara, a rather large town, where we docked right against the front street where other boats were moored. This place had no special interest for us save that it was the home of the Subbis, the so-called Disciples of John the Baptist, whose shops in Baghdad always drew me.

When I became aware that Amara was situated at the head of the marshlands, I became curious for I wanted to see the people who live in these marshes and the way they live. Did you ever ask yourself the question what had become of the Sumerians and Babylonians and other ancient peoples of lower Mesopotamia when these cities were conquered and their empires and kingdoms overthrown? Do these races still exist or were they all amalgamated and racially mixed with the conquerors?

In these marshes, according to many scholars, is the answer. The people who live here are called Marsh Arabs, but in reality they are not Arabs. The limited vocabulary of the language they speak is hardly Arabic, and their visage clearly shows that they are not of Arab descent. The boats they use are like a model found in the Ur tombs. Is it not, then, highly probable that these people of the marshes are a remnant of the Sumerians or the Babylonians or both who for safety fled to these marshes when the country was invaded? Was I looking into the faces of the descendants of an ancient people that had lived and flourished in this land four or five millenniums ago?

The people who live in these marshes of shallow water, often with high reeds growing in them, on plots of elevated land here and there, are said to be descendants of the most ancient people of Iraq. They live in tubelike reed huts, eking out a bare existence. If they are the remnants of a bygone civilization, what a mighty fall it has been for a people who once had built beautiful temples and palaces, produced works of art that can scarcely be reproduced today, had a literature, organized society into a government, made laws that are still used, and contributed to the welfare of future generations in many ways! This fall of man's mind and spirit was immeasurably greater in its consequences than the destruction of Ur and Babylon.

At eight o'clock that evening our quiet on the boat was broken by an unusual hubbub. We had stopped at a town to load cattle, and everybody had come out either to help or to tell others how to help. Everybody shouted this or that at the same time. The Arabic word, borrowed from Turkish, is *qalabaaligh,* and no English word exactly conveys the meaning—just general confusion. Some planks were raised to the boat for the cattle to be pulled up, pushed up, cajoled up, but every cow objected to each one of the three methods.

The men pushed and pulled, hollered and sweated. Two cows being pushed too far fell on the canvas which covered the hold and landed somewhere in the bottom of the boat in the grain pit. Another slipped on the canvas but was rescued before it could join its companions below; another fell into the river. But a fourth, evidently with some brains and a high IQ, deliberately jumped into the river and swam across, disappearing in a palm grove, where it could not be found. We sailed without that cow. The calm that follows a qalabaaligh has in it a quietness deeper than ordinary calm. Added to this calmness was the serenity of the night as the Tigris flowed through the marshland with no sight or sound of human habitation.

Before reaching Basrah, we passed two traditional biblical sites. These were Ezra's tomb and the Garden of Eden. Mesopotamia is rich not only in oil and soil but in biblical sites as well, real and traditional. Ezra was a citizen of the land and had made two journeys to Jerusalem in the interest of the rebuilding of the temple. We were in hopes all along that we would pass the tomb in the daytime, but to our sorrow we passed it about three o'clock in the morning. We were called as the boat was approaching the tomb, and we did our best to discern its shadowy outlines. The building facing the river is large and impressive and is a favorite subject of the Subbis in decorating their silver.[2]

The other biblical site was the traditional location of the Garden of Eden. Here is where the Euphrates eventually joins the Tigris, forming the Shatt-al-Arab, a wide, deep, tidal river on which the ocean liners come

2. See chapter 8.

to Basrah, the port of Iraq. In the fork of these two rivers lies Qurnah, which is supposed to have been the biblical Eden. This is often referred to as a barren place, yet, as I saw it in the spring of the year with its stately palms lifting high their fronds, and the Euphrates pouring a large volume of water at right angles into the Tigris, I found the place by no means a bad replica of the idyllic Eden.

Qurnah also figured very much in World War I. The British Tommies who were stationed here used to say that if this was the biblical site of the Garden of Eden, then Adam and Eve should not have lamented the fact that they were driven from it. In this region is also an *abra sec* (a dry tree), which is said to have been the Tree of Knowledge from which Eve received the apple from the serpent. The Garden of Eden is no mere metaphor. For whether here or elsewhere in the land is of no great consequence; and as gardens always held a special place in the affections of the people of Mesopotamia, it was natural that the first man and woman known by name should have been placed in a garden of overwhelming beauty and unspeakable fertility.

Basrah, where we disembarked, has been called the Venice of the East because of the many creeks and canals that run through it. The boats that are in them are long and narrow, on the gondola style. Sitting in one of these cushioned and decorated gondolas, in holiday spirit, we were leisurely rowed up and down the largest of these creeks. It was most unfortunate for this Venice of the East that we had formerly visited Venice itself. But as this was our spring outing to be enjoyed in its own way, we waived marring comparisons.

If the Ashur Creek is not the Grand Canal, Basrah has a claim to fame along another line. It is her dates, the best in the world, a fact which Marco Polo in the thirteenth century had already noted. Three-quarters of the date palms of the world are in Iraq and most of them along the Shatt-al-Arab. Before the last world war 80 percent of the dates entering the international market left from the port of Basrah.

The date is a simple tree to cultivate. What the date palm needs is plenty of water for its roots, a rich alluvial soil, and a long, hot summer. All these conditions are found in lower Iraq. There are 350 different kinds of dates that grow in Iraq, though only five of these are cultivated for export.

On our table in Baghdad were served many of these varieties not exported to America. They were of different sizes, shapes, and colors, and different degrees of sweetness. Many of these dates were very delicious, but they could not be preserved for shipment. The date has great food value, and the Bedouin and the *fallahin* live largely on them.

Reliefs found in the Assyrian Royal Palace at Khorsabad portray the king carrying in his hand the symbol of the date fertilization. On the coat of arms of Iraq are placed date trees. In the center of our school seal is a date tree. All this is as it should be, for the date tree is indigenous to the land; and much of the wealth, the occupation, and the food of the land depends upon the date culture.

Our stay in "Sinbad's Bassorah" was brief. The height of enjoyment there was not the native life, but the comfort of a modern rest house, screened in from pestiferous flies that had tormented us at times on the boat; the exchange of a small cabin for an expansive bedroom; and a bathroom that worked. In these comfortable surroundings we concocted a scheme for the return journey that would allow us to see Ur and at the same time get home on schedule.

The plan was to take the evening express train to Ur, see the ruins by moonlight, and before dawn take another train for Babylon. The plan was perfect, but when we came to Ur Junction, the police and others with them would not cooperate. They said we could not go over to the ruins by night even though we had found a chauffeur willing to take us; they said robbers, wolves, and jackals inhabit and haunt the holes and ditches in Ur. The stationmaster astonishingly declared that such a request had never been made before. To our pleadings all were adamant. We would have tried to steal away and walk the two miles, but it had just rained and the mud did not allow us to venture. Besides, they watched us like hawks.

On the train we tried to console ourselves on our disappointment in not getting to Ur by saying that the marvelous finds are nearly all in the museum in Baghdad, and that we had repeatedly seen them; that we had heard all of Professor Woolley's lectures at the close of each year's work; that we were living in the same kind of a house in which Abraham had lived nearly four thousand years ago; and that we were really within sight of Ur. This philosophizing was not bad, but after all it was not satisfying.

We knew we had not seen Ur. Then, suddenly, our depressed mood vanished when we came in sight of Babylon.

It is not an ordinary thing to visit mighty Babylon, "the glory of kingdoms and the beauty of Chaldean's pride." Although I had visited Babylon many times before, I was again emotionally stirred. I recall how on our first journey from Basrah to Baghdad, we scrutinized the country eagerly as we approached Babylon for some glimpse that would identify it. I recall, too, the undertone of suppressed excitement, soon after our arrival in Iraq, when we started out on our first visit to see the ruins.

Yet, what do you see when you come to Babylon? Nothing of the city of Hammurabi, the great lawgiver, remains. What we see are the remains of the city of Nebuchadnezzar. Fortunately, the foundations of this city have withstood the ravages of time; and happily, the excavators who uncovered the city left these walls intact.

Having heard that many people had found these ruins disappointing because they had gone there without first having acquired a knowledge of the city, I attempted to recreate in my mind the splendor that once was by comprehensive reading. Babylon must be erected on its foundations by the imagination; otherwise, the mass of ruins on the palace mound will seem hopelessly chaotic. The traveler who comes with no interest in history or no zeal for memorials of the long-buried past might better stay at home.

But if you see Babylon, "the great city," in your mind's eye before you ascend the palace mound, you will thrill when, on top, you survey this city center of Nebuchadnezzar and the temple mound across a rather wide depression. In his reign of forty years, this king ruled with power, and built as the giants had built for the gods. You see the foundations of his great palace with its banquet hall, where Belshazzar feasted the night he saw the handwriting on the wall. You see the vaultings of the Hanging Garden, "the greatest marvel in a palace of marvels," where green and flowering terraces made it one of the seven wonders of the ancient world—built for a princess who loved gardens.

Standing on the palace mound, I lifted my eyes to see the remnants of the thick wall that surrounded this mound. I lifted my eyes farther trying to trace the outer wall of the city, which had been eleven miles in circumference. Looking to the south across a lower stretch of ground, I beheld the temple mound where the great temple of Marduk, the patron-god of the city, once stood. I saw where the Tower of Babel, which was the city's ziggurat, once was reared to a lofty height, and lamented the fact that the bricks of this famous temple mound, including the foundation, were removed to build the city of Hillah nearby. Turning to the west, I saw the Euphrates, which once flowed through the midst of the city.

The *serdab* part of the famous Ishtar Gate, named after the goddess, is the best preserved of all the structures and is the only impressive survival in Babylon. A newly constructed stairway now descends to the very base. On this lower gateway are animal figures in relief on the bricks—perfectly matched; on the upper gateway, which was on a level with the Festival Way, the walls and figures were enameled in brilliant colors: yellow, blue, and white. These were removed to Berlin, where I saw them carefully reconstructed.

On the Festival Way or Procession Street, I walked not alone but moved, so I thought, with a gorgeous throng on this sacred avenue that ran along the front of the public buildings; then descending from the mound and crossing the depression to the temple precincts, I entered the great court of the temple of Marduk. With pomp and grandeur the religious processions used to pass along this Royal Way, between the walls deco-rated with the same yellow, blue, and white enameling that had made the Ishtar Gate so brilliant. Over this way the priests, clothed in rich raiments, carried the images of the great gods, passing the stately magnificence of the vast imperial palace and the offices of the government, to the temple mound where rose the lofty platform of the great ziggurat, which in the Bible is known as the Tower of Babel.

Taking the train again, it brought us back to Baghdad. The region we had traversed in going down the Tigris by boat and coming back along the Euphrates by train is only a little speck of the earth; yet, within this small area most of the foundation stones of civilization were laid.

Just as the priceless revelations of monotheism and of a righteous and fatherly God were discovered in Palestine in an area of only about seventy-five miles long and twenty miles wide, and just as the highest reaches in art, literature, and philosophy were confined to a single city in Greece, so the outbursts of greatness in the Mesopotamia valley were limited to a small area of the twin rivers. Here contributions to humanity were made by the Sumerians, the Babylonians, the Chaldeans, the Persians, and the Abbassid Arabs. Like the Hebrews and the Greeks, these Mesopotamians lived vigorously and creatively, each in their own way making a contribution along the lines that have advanced the world.[3]

3. For the heyday of the archaeological discoveries noted here, see the editor's foreword.

11

VISITING THE SHIAH HOLY CITIES

The rug below the table on which I am writing was bought from an Iranian pilgrim. As I look down and see the intricate design, and turn the rug over to see the many knots to the square inch, I am touched with a profound thought. This pilgrim came with very little money in his possession, but he had this beautiful rug, which was possibly woven in his own home; and into it he wove the hopes and prayers for the longed-for pilgrimage to the holy cities of Iraq. I am also touched with the thought that he parted with it willingly, gaining thereby something of far greater value, for in making this pilgrimage to the holy cities and worshiping in their sacred mosques, he will, as he believed, be spiritually rewarded and receive merit in heaven.

One evening on the playground of the school after the boys had left, we lingered for a time. The pilgrim carrying the rug on his shoulder saw us and entered. He offered to sell the rug to us. After some negotiations we bought it at a price that was satisfactory to him, and which to us likewise seemed reasonable. As he received the money, I sensed the joy and happiness that radiated through his whole being, for now he knew that he could not merely visit the sacred cities of Iraq but also linger for some time in each. The pilgrim also told us that the next morning he would have the satisfaction of seeing Kadhimain, the shrine where two 'imams are buried, for the first time.

I knew perfectly well how he would go; I had gone this way many times before. There is a tramway between Baghdad and Kadhimain, built originally for the convenience of pilgrims. The tram cars are double-deckers and are drawn by horses. Most probably the pilgrim will take a seat on the unroofed upper deck. As the tram moves slowly on toward Kadhimain, he will suddenly behold the golden domes and minarets reflecting the rays of the sun in the early morning. What a thrill this will give him. The greatest thrill and joy in his life! For this day he has lived for many years, and now his dream is being realized.

This pilgrim was a Shiah Muslim, who had come to visit the shrines where the 'imams are buried. The two main sects of the Muslims are Sunnis and Shiahs, a division that corresponds somewhat to Protestants and Catholics in the Christian religion. The division took place shortly after the death of Muhammad, and it came about because of a difference of opinion in regard to Muhammad's successor. One party claimed that the succession should come through Abu Bekr, Muhammad's father-in-law and friend; the other that the succession should be through Ali, a cousin of Muhammad and married to his daughter, Fatima.

Muslims of both sects look to Mecca as their holy city, and to it they are enjoined to make a pilgrimage at least once in a lifetime. When the pilgrim returns from Mecca, he is called a *hajji,* which at once raises his status. In addition to visiting Mecca, Shiahs are also supposed to visit their own holy cities, of which four are in Iraq and one in Iran. The Iranians are altogether Shiahs. Iraq and Bahrain are the only Islamic countries where the two major groups are almost equally divided. (The Sunnis of Iraq are equally divided between two ethnic groups: the Arabs and the Kurds.) Shiah minorities are found in Syria, Lebanon, Kuwait, Afghanistan, Pakistan, and India.

I could conceive the pilgrim's staying in Kadhimain for a week or ten days, going to the great mosque every day to pray. Passing into the court of the mosque he would not fail to kiss the heavy brass chain that hung across the entrance. Then entering into the mosque itself, he would be found going through the stated prayers at the stated times for prayers when the muezzin from one or more of the minarets would give the call. Most likely, too, he would be engaged in prayer at other times, and some of the most earnest and fervent prayers undoubtedly were made here.

From Kadhimain I could see the pilgrim go to Samarra, another holy city along the Tigris, but seventy-five miles farther north. Approaching this shrine, he is again impressed with the glittering gold on dome and minaret as he sees it afar off. Visiting this holy city and praying in its sacred precincts will give him added merit in heaven. Pilgrimage is considered a solemn duty in Islam.

Inside the mosque at Samarra he finds something else to interest him besides just going through his prayers.[1] It is said that under the beautiful golden-domed mosque is a cave. When the Twelfth 'Imam disappeared in the ninth century, God hid him in that cave; from it the Hidden 'Imam will return at the end of time to establish justice and peace. As the early Christians had looked for the Second Coming of Christ in the clouds, so the orthodox Shiah Muslims have looked, and are still looking, for the second coming of their Messiah, al-Mahdi, glorified and deified. From time to time Muslim zealots have risen in Syria, Persia, Turkey, and Egypt, each claiming to be al-Mahdi; of these the most spectacular was Muhammad Ahmad, who had desperately fought against the Egyptians and the English in the Sudan in the late nineteenth century.[2]

When my husband and I visited Samarra, we too found something of unusual interest to us. The remains of a curiously shaped minaret of a demolished mosque stand outside the city wall. I recognized it at once as the picture I had occasionally seen in my childhood, illustrating the Tower of Babel. I greeted it with surprised pleasure as an old acquaintance. I had then wondered how anyone could ascend and descend safely that spiral stairway on the outside that had no railing. Standing now before it, I was quite willing to watch someone else make an attempt to climb it, and found that the man whom I was watching gave up his efforts soon after he had begun.

The pilgrim whom we have followed so far was only one of thousands of devoted Shiah Muslims that annually visit these holy cities. Yearly, tens

1. In the recent war, infuriated Shiah militia attacks against the Sunnis soared in 2006 after Sunni insurgents destroyed part of this Samarra shrine, most recently in June 2007.

2. Since the establishment of the Islamic Republic of Iran, especially during the last decade—viewed as a period of crisis and persecution of the Muslims—there has been a resurgence of interest in the Twelfth 'Imam's imminent coming. The president of Iran, Mahmoud Ahmadinejad, has often referred to the approaching apocalypse in his public speeches. At the end of his speech at the United Nations in 2005, he called upon God to bring about the speedy return of The Expected One (al-Muntazar) (Ruthven 2009).

of thousands visit them in order to worship in their sacred mosques. The inhabitants of these cities are almost altogether supported by the constant influx of pilgrims. Because of the trade they brought, a city sprang up around each one of these tomb-mosques. Should pilgrimage cease, these cities could no longer exist. When the shah of Iran had forbidden his people from making a pilgrimage to Iraq and had ordered them to go to Meshed only, the shrine in their own country, the income of these Iraqi cities was greatly reduced.

Once when my husband and I had stopped at Speyer in Germany to see the tombs of the earliest kings in the vaults of a church, the guide incidentally remarked, "This city would be dead, were it not for these dead kings." So one might say of the holy cities of Iraq: Were it not for the dead 'imams buried beneath these golden domes, these cities would not only be dead but most likely would not exist.

At one time we had a lad from Karbala in our school by the name of Jawad, who had cordially invited us to his home during our spring vacation, an invitation that was later reinforced by his father. The family evidently was so desirous to have us come that Jawad came all the way from Karbala to help my husband, if necessary, drive the automobile. A lucky stroke for us. It had rained the night before, and the newly repaired road had become so slippery that even with the most careful driving, we skidded into a ditch that required the help of some *fallahin* to get us out.

Jawad then asked to drive, and by taking no care at all, he delivered us safely before his father's door. The father proved a most genial host, and Jawad, who excelled in the art of entertaining more than in his studies, showed us Karbala and its surroundings in gay and gallant fashion.

Karbala is a pilgrim city of first importance; its two great mosques are built with the same delicate and beautiful Persian tiles, and according to the same Persian architecture, as is the mosque in Kadhimain. The one was built over the spot where Hussain was treacherously killed by the people of Kufah. To this sacred shrine many come from all over the Muslim world; we were especially interested in this mosque because of the annual observance of Muharram, a period of ten days of mourning for Hussain, grandson of the prophet Muhammad.

The other mosque enshrined the body of Abbas, a half-brother of Hussain, who was killed at the same time. Abbas is greatly feared, having been a brave soldier, a stern disciplinarian, and a man of hot temper. One way, and often the best way, to make a man keep his promises or tell the truth is to make him swear by Abbas. Everybody knows that the head "embedded in the ceiling of his mosque" was blown there when the person swore falsely on Abbas's name. Ask a man to swear by Abbas, and he hesitates when the lie comes to his lip: he remembers the head of his fellow countryman. The tiny metal hands which I sometimes bought in the bazaars of Baghdad were named after this Abbas.

Many Muslims from India visit these sacred cities in Iraq, bringing with them many treasures. Opposite our host's residence, Muslim Indians had built a pilgrim house. From it we watched a constant stream of men and women and children either entering or coming out an open door. The women were curiously covered. A light cream material which had been gathered on the top of the head showered down to the feet, enveloping them completely. For eye-peeps square holes were cut out of the material, and then covered with a black woven screening. Twice a day these pilgrims made the rounds of the mosques to pray. We, too, made the rounds of the mosques, but could not enter; neither were we allowed to linger at the entrances, nor go alone: we were always attended.

Climbing the steep stairs of Jawad's home on our arrival, I observed a screen on the landing and marked it with my eyes. It was a screen of some size which might be needed when night came on. Each time I passed it I found relief in seeing it there. In the evening when the clean, good beds were spread out on the floor of the big receiving room, it was certain that our small party was to occupy this one room. This was no surprise to us since we had had much of this before. The screen, however, caused my spirits to rise, and I said ingratiatingly, "Jawad, on the landing of the stairs is a screen. Is anybody using it?"

Opening his eyes, he said, "No."

"Will you please bring it to us?" I said. It divided the room and gave the privacy we wanted. Thereupon, in quietness of mind and tranquility of spirit, we all went to sleep.

Hajji Hassan, a friend of the family, had found exceptional favor in my eyes. He understood my limited *kitab* (book, bookish) Arabic, and I understood his simple and clear colloquial. He informed me that he lived on the oasis of Shifatha, an oasis copiously watered and abounding in date trees, being only about two hours' run from Karbala. On the day of our arrival he announced that he would return on the morrow, and that we should accompany him; and, as a further inducement, he added that he would take us not only to Shifatha but also to Ukhaidir, a ruined fortress-palace in the desert. He assured us that the whole trip was worth taking, which we could later certainly testify.

On the morrow, two automobiles were solidly packed, Jawad's relatives having decided to join the party, and off we started for Ukhaidir with Hajji Hassan as our guide. No one really knows much about this astonishing landmark in the waterless desert except that it was built in the early years of Islam. Once it was supposed to have been a caravan stop on the way from the frankincense groves along the wadi Hadhramut to Mesopotamia. But most likely it was built by some eccentric Arab potentate. The buttressed enclosure wall that surrounds the palace is almost intact, and so are the stone-vaulted chambers. The inside is really palatial. Some of the rooms that are ornamented looked like places of worship. The wonder is that in the heart of the desert there should have been erected a structure so royal.

Leaving the ruined fortress-palace from which today no caravan roads lead, no road of any kind, we had to zigzag here and there because of the sand to find firm earth to get to Shifatha. Eventually, a belt of green appeared that gradually increased in size as we drew nearer. Water began to ooze out of the earth, making the ground marshy as we neared the palm trees that thickly covered this desert isle. In what way and by what means the hajji had sent word ahead that we were coming is a mystery, but the lunch was ready upon our arrival and was served at once to hungry guests. Low tables were loaded with meat, rice, *laban*, flat bread, Bedouin cheese, nuts, tea, and the very best dates from Shifatha—deliciously sweet.

We walked out to see the pools fed by underground springs. The inhabitants say that the water is cold in summer and warm in winter. These pools looked like circular swimming pools, with the water as blue as that of the Mediterranean, and crystal clear. These springs are the lifeblood of the oasis, and from them little channels carry water into the gardens and palm groves. As the hajji's house was pleasant and the oasis offered a quiet retreat, entirely isolated from the rest of the world, we were loath to leave; but time was pressing. We said good-bye to the simple, dignified, gentle hajji and turned our backs on this fertile oasis with its blue pools and crowded palms to traverse the uninhabited desert back to Karbala, skirting on the way the big salt lake of Abu Dibis.

The next morning when we were planning to go to Najaf, our host said, "I do not accept your leaving." We thanked him and said, "We must go." For this family to have entertained us was a very advanced and brave act. We spoke our parting words of genuine gratitude for a most pleasant visit in our best style. This was done inside the house with all the men of the household present, except an uncle who had faithfully guarded us and been particularly thoughtful. He was waiting for us by the side of the car.

As we drove on leisurely, we reviewed our Karbala visit and were astonished that in this pilgrim city, where solemnity characterizes the deportment of the pilgrims, we had been unusually mirthful. Even the women, and there were quite a number in the harem—Jawad's father had three wives, and there were the wives of sons, besides the unmarried daughters—appeared happier than women I had met elsewhere. This genial spirit showed itself not only in the home but in the city as well. Streets were wider and therefore brighter; one had an outlook and felt freer. There was even a park where every plant exulted in blooming.

Najaf, toward which we were driving, is the holiest of the holy cities of the Shiahs, the city where Ali, the first 'imam, is believed to be buried. To enter this walled city and see it satisfactorily, one had to be well fortified with letters. These we had secured from friends in Kadhimain.

Soon after leaving Karbala, a strong wind arose, filling the air with dust, so that Najaf did not become visible until we had come upon it. On a clear day the golden dome, it is said, can be seen at a distance of forty miles. Suddenly, through the curling mist of dust the walls of the city and the dome loomed spectral. At times, the gold flashed; sometimes the walls "prick'd thro" the mist; and sometimes when the wind blew with a gust, the "whole city disappear'd." Like Camelot, it seemed a city of enchanters.

The story of the founding of Najaf, a city that sprung up in the desert, has the same unreal touch as had our approach. According to the legend, Ali was slain at Kufah, and the body, having been placed on a camel, was buried where the camel had finally knelt to rest. The place was kept secret. The story goes that on a hunting expedition Harun al-Rashid was pursuing a gazelle which suddenly stopped on a mound and stood there quite unafraid; neither had the caliph the strength to shoot it. Then an old man told him that if he would dig, he would find the body of Ali under an alabaster slab. Over this spot Harun raised a mosque, and around it a walled city sprung up.

We were favored in having a letter of introduction to Sayyid Abbas, the *killidar* of the great mosque—keeper of the treasures. These treasures, it is asserted, are enormous. When Nasr al-Din, shah of Persia (1848–96), visited Karbala and Najaf, the treasures were opened, and the weight of gold and silver alone reached a total of seven tons, not to mention the other precious gifts. On our way to the killidar's house we were met by a relative of his, who by some magic means had learned of our coming and who conducted us to the house. We were kindly received, and as time was limited, we plunged at once into matters of interest.

We had heard that Najaf was not only a city of houses above the ground but even a greater city underground, and that this *serdab*-city communicated, so that it was easy for a fugitive from justice to make his escape. I broached this subject, and one of the young sayyids with alacrity volunteered to take us down into these subterranean cellars. Unlike the serdabs in Baghdad, these are the genuine thing, and are not just a few steps below the street level. We descended the first cellar, then down into the second, and in some houses there is even a third and a fourth. We were told that the air down there in summer is as cool as on Mount Lebanon, but one wonders about its freshness.

Sayyid Abbas measured in girth more than any man I had ever seen, yet, despite his gluttonous appearance, he was unusually entertaining, and so were the other sayyids who had come to greet us. Each had the green cloth, the color of the Prophet, neatly and tightly wound about his tarbush. We wondered why we could not see the treasures in the mosque, saying that in America everything of this kind is displayed. He tactfully said,

"Become a Muslim, and you shall see." Our host invited us to dine with him—a real surprise. He ate with his hands, and the food rapidly vanished. A big, long platter of rice, shaped into a mound, with small pieces of meat on top was on our table. He dug in on his side and came half way before we had made a dent on our side. After observing our dainty eating, he remarked that in twenty days we would not eat as much as he does in one. This statement was only a slight exaggeration.

Sayyid Abbas wanted me to meet the new wife of his nephew, who had recently married a cousin of the deposed shah of Iran and resided in a house nearby. I was guided there by a relative and had the surprise of my life. Such a dazzling room in colorless Najaf! It was ablaze with red: red satin hangings, red velvet upholstered furniture embroidered with gold threads—red everywhere. I was impressed even more so with the sweet little bride, who wore her hair bobbed and was dressed according to the newest fashion. This contrast of an inside scene of Najaf with the outside left me speechless. Such contrasting cheer in this room, when without, the atmosphere was that of melancholy mourning; such an emulation of royalty, when without, everything looked drab and forlorn; and such an up-to-date little maid in this walled city on the edge of the desert where the dead are forever being brought to be buried, in the hope that paradise will be the reward of those lying in this sacred soil.

Our host was pleased with my account of what I had seen. In that happy frame of mind we made our salaams and departed from the city. Driving from Najaf, we met corpses all the time in crude, unpainted boxes that stuck out of automobiles or were balanced on horses or donkeys or conveyed in a cart. The occupants of a car may be having a rather good time with a box on their knees. The surprising thing, however, is that the cemeteries in Najaf seem just the size for the inhabitants thereof, and one wonders what has happened to the vast number of bodies brought here through the centuries. The same is true everywhere in the land: cemeteries are not numerous. Of course, there is a profit in this burial business to the citizens of these holy cities, and the ground is deep.

Returning, we directed our car toward Kufah, which is on the Euphrates, and which once had played such a false role in the annals of Islam. The city is older than Baghdad, but its former grandeur has altogether disappeared. I recall little that I saw, for the storm that had been brewing all day was gathering force, and it behooved us to move on to Hillah. Only once had I experienced a dust storm worse than the one that burst upon us in fury that afternoon. The worst sandstorm within living memory occurred in 1935, when "an opaque ball of dust several thousand feet high, swept across Iraq at seventy-eight miles an hour in the spring." People lost their way on the streets as in a dense fog, and the nomads had their tents lifted and their flocks almost buried in the sand.

This, too, was a terrible storm that came upon us on our return. The land seemed strangled. Past us swept the wind, howling and whirling dust in forms that looked like wraiths of the departed. All the dead of all the millenniums seemed to have risen from their graves in tumultuous wrath; and, driven fiercely by this tempest, the mighty throng tossed their arms impotently as if goaded on to some fateful destiny. Yet there was at times something grandly glorious about it when the sun pierced through the density of the yellow sand, turning it into gold.

That storm was the fitting high peak of the journey: the driving wind and the ghosts of the numberless dead who fled by us in an agony of distress. Probably the visit to Najaf, notwithstanding the gay room, had left me depressed and susceptible to gloomy and ghostly impressions. How long people have lived in mourning for these early martyrs. The sufferings of these centuries seemed to weigh on me.

The unfortunate death of Ali, and the brutal butchery of Hussain under the cruel and treacherous Yazid, had been vividly kept alive in the hearts and minds of the people throughout the centuries, by the Muharram processions and the passion play. For nine successive nights these processions moved through the streets of Baghdad until they were suppressed some years ago.

The first time I saw one of these nightly processions was in a narrow and dim *darbuna*. Torches made of tin cans stuffed with petroleum-soaked rags and fastened to a wide crosspiece flared and smoked, and in the fitful light became unearthly. Through the smoke and light of the flaming torches passed black-dressed chain-beaters, horses and riders; black-'abaed women wailed on the roofs of houses or at the latticed windows, and there was incessant drumming and the sharp cries of "Ali," "Hussain."

The passion play was usually given in a home in the afternoon of the tenth day of Muharram. In Baghdad the play was given in the house of a *nawab,* an Indian prince whose family had been brought to Baghdad by the British. Twice my husband and I were honored guests at one of these afternoon renditions in the nawab's house, with privileged places with the family to view all that went on. The first time, the stage broke down during the performance, and as it tipped, the actors rolled off, turning tragedy into comedy. But the second time there was no trusting to luck; we had the satisfaction of seeing a strong and energetic performance.[3]

The story of the passion play gathers round the central figure of Hussain, son of Ali. The Umayyad Caliph Muawiyah chose his notoriously wicked son Yazid as his successor to the caliphal throne. Hussain never recognized Yazid's right to the caliphate, and when the Iraqi Kufans sought Hussain's help to release them from the curse of the Umayyad rule, he felt it his duty to respond to their appeal. Yet, in spite of all persuasion not to trust them, Hussain started for Iraq. He was accompanied only by a few kinsmen, a few devoted followers, and a retinue of women and children. Suspecting treachery, Hussain put up his tent at Karbala, where the Sunni Umayyads heartlessly killed him and his followers. This, in brief, is the history on which the passion play is based.

The play lasted about three hours. A part of the tragic scene was played on the stage, while the more spectacular pageantry took place on the floor of the unusually big court. A mass of people crowded into the house to see this spectacle. Because of the crowd, there was scarcely room in the court for the passage of the procession of horses, riders, banners, breast-beaters, soldiers, drummers, trumpet-blowers, bloody corpses—all moving endlessly in and out the doorway. The balconies could hold no more guests, and the roof held more people than it could. So realistic and dramatic were some of the scenes that the murderer of Hussain, and those who took the

3. Note that the Muharram passion play witnessed by the Staudts is according to the traditions of the Shiah Muslims of India, elaborately staged in Baghdad by an Indian Muslim prince. These commemorations are practiced differently in different countries, varying according to the ethnic group and its social and cultural background.

part of the deceivers, were in such danger that policemen were on special guard lest these actors should be injured or killed by an infuriated mob.

As the horses and riders were many, it was a miracle alone that saved the crowd in the court from being trampled down. At last the dying and the bloody dead; the horses and riders; the lacerated chain-beaters; the swollen chest-beaters; the armored soldiers; the bare-footed, ragged urchins that barely escaped imminent death; the black-enveloped women on the balconies and their poorer sisters on the roof, all went out through a common doorway.

Figuratively speaking, the curtain was dropped on the passion play; the mourning for Ali and Hussain had come to an end; and the tragic scenes in the nawab's house were over for another year. Sobered and considerably shaken, we followed the crowd out of the door into the narrow, cheerless lane, crossed the river on a boat, and hurried to our home where, in spite of its busy life, there was an air of calming quiet.

12

In the Land of the Kurds

When you are in Baghdad you certainly are confined to it. Are there pleasant drives in the environs, or a variety of scenes nearby, or hills with a cooler air within a reasonable distance? None. The plain of southern Iraq, throughout most of the year, is a hot, parched desert, with towns not especially attractive and villages of unmitigated dreariness. There are no hills in sight except the artificial "tells" of ruined cities. So flat is the plain that I needed to look at a map to be assured that hills and mountains were really in Iraq. The map gave me a feeling of hopefulness for a summer vacation in the north.

Others besides us were prospecting in Iraq, not for oil but for a recuperating change. They returned to Baghdad to speak in tones of wonder about their finds. They described a new road that had recently been built through two gorges by a New Zealand engineer. One of these gorges, the Rawanduz, had been deemed beyond the power of man to make available for traffic because of the precipitous cliffs and the torrential streams. They also told of the grandeur of scenery farther north near the Turkish border. "In these regions," they said, "are high mountains, lofty passes, gushing streams, mountain torrents and alpine meadows."

This was rather difficult to believe. But being told to go and marvel, we went to see the Switzerland of Iraq, and returning, joined the chorus of extravagant praise. The automobile, loaded as on the previous year, started northward again, traveling the familiar Kirkuk-Arbil-Shaqlawa road. At Kirkuk we turned eastward toward Sulaimania, the city which was the center of the political and national life of the Kurds. Here, too, dwell the most powerful and influential of the tribes, such as the Barzinji, the Jaf, the Baban, and the Auroman. The city lies at the foot of the Azmir

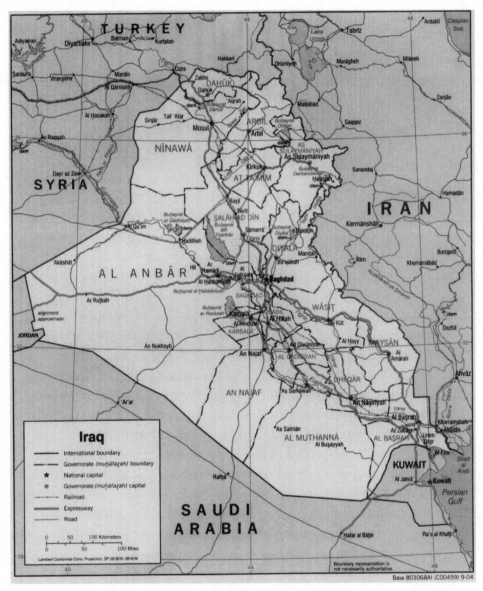

4. Map of Iraq. Produced by the U.S. Central Intelligence Agency, 2004. Scanned by the University of Texas Libraries.

Mountains, at the end of a rich and fertile plateau which is hemmed in on all sides by ranges.

What a different world this was! It was different in scenery, different in climate, and different in people and their clothes. We had exchanged the Semitic Arab for the Kurd, who is of Aryan stock. The Kurd knows he is Aryan, is proud of it, and what is more takes the opportunity to tell you so. As we stopped at villages, the people gathered about us; and when they learned that we were Americans and had a school in Baghdad, they said, "Why don't you open a school in Kurdistan? Don't you know that we are your brothers?"

This decision to test out the land of the Kurds for a summer vacation in Iraq was at first a hazard; it was a venture, for there were no inns in this part of the world, and just what accommodations we should find, when we presented to Kurdish 'aghas the letters we carried from prominent Baghdadi Kurds, we did not know. This uncertainty as to what we should find at the other end did not make for happy anticipation and confident peace of mind. But if we wanted to see the land and get away from Baghdad for a season, these mental perturbations had to be sidetracked. Reading and hearing about Sulaimania and Halapcha and Shaqlawa, our objectives, had so aroused my interest that I was armored against almost any predicament; and fortunately, as so often happens, met none.

Sulaimania I had heard frequently mentioned in connection with the Kurdish aspirations for independence, with which the name of Sheikh Mahmud was associated. This sheikh had led three Kurdish revolts, the second occurring at the time of our arrival in Iraq. Halapcha was even more vividly in my mind, because of Major Soane's book *Through Kurdistan in Disguise.* He told of a Kurdish woman in Halapcha under whose rule in a remote corner of the world a village rose to a town and a barren hillside became fertile.

That we survived these many drives in the East with reckless chauffeurs who turned hairpin corners at full speed and raced down steep hills, I lay alone to providential protection. We survived this one and reached Sulaimania without any incident. Calming ourselves, we inquired for one of the 'aghas to whom one of the letters was addressed. The 'agha was tall but flimsily built. He received us cordially and handed us over to a dapper little servant whose constant attention never gave us any chance for privacy. As necessity required, one or the other of us stood guard at the door, the key having vanished long ago. That his impetuous rushes to enter should at times be balked caused the little man's eyes to open in pained surprise. Why be so fussy, he must have thought, why keep me out? Rising early from our beds, which were placed on a high veranda without a railing and rather close to the edge, we observed a Kurdish beg using an orchard near us for his retiring-room. He likely thought that there was not much more seclusion to our dressing room, since the whole front was in windows on which were no hangings.

The 'agha's house was large, with real possibilities of which no advantage was taken. With the women of these higher families living in separate quarters and exercising no supervision over the house; with lazy servants; with an inscrutable indifference to dust, disorder, and decay, anything approaching a Western home is out of the question. As no one ever seems to be the least disturbed by the conditions surrounding him, why should I?

We let it be known, soon after our arrival, that we should enjoy attending the 'agha's *diwankhana,* a gathering of friends and visitors which in out-of-the-way places becomes an institution and a pleasant event of the day. We were informed that the 'agha received his guests twice a day: in the morning at ten and in the afternoon at three. We said we would come punctually at ten. Someone advised us to come at nine. We then said that we would wait until we were called.

That same day, we were offered for our comfort the new guest rooms in the not quite completed new *serai,* which was ceremonially opened while we were guests there. This courtesy to stay in the serai was extended to us by a Britisher, who was at that time the administrative officer of this area. We had not notified him of our coming to Sulaimania, when at that time such a notification was required—purposely, no doubt, because we feared that permission might not be granted. Kurdistan had given a great deal of trouble, and the people were still restless. Lacking in patience and given to explosive reactions which long residence in the East often aggravates, he exploded when we called with our letters. Looking at me, he said, "If anything should have happened to you, my wife, whom I had great difficulty in bringing here, would be sent back to England at once." Knowing that he had provocation, we quietly received the onset, which was followed first by calm and then by kindness.

The arrangement to stay in the serai was a happy one all round. Here we were given a pleasant suite of rooms and were next to the first to occupy them. The big enclosed garden in front of the building gave us a place to hold our diwankhanas, and here we learned to know not a few of the interesting and important Kurds. This garden in the evening was frequented by the 'aghas, the begs, and the effendis. The plebeians sat outside the garden along the fence, or in the coffeehouses across the street.

The costumes of the Kurds, of both men and women, surpass in picturesqueness those of any other people in this part of the world. Both the jackets and the trousers of the men are embroidered. They also wear a broad girdle made of yards of cloth, twisted and interlocked in front. The length of the girdle is determined by a man's estimate of his own importance, the length being sometimes twenty yards or more. In it he carries his dagger, his money, his matches, and his cigarettes. He reaches in it on one side and pulls out one thing, and on the other side, another thing. But the crowning glory of a Kurd's dress is the headgear, which is a turban made of tasseled silk squares wound about his head so that the tassels hang down around the edge. To sit in this well-kept garden was in itself a pleasure, but the nodding heads and swinging tassels gave an animated gaiety to an otherwise rather sedate affair.

The name on everybody's lips at the time was that of Sheikh Mahmud, whose genealogical chart hung in an office of the old serai. He was held in esteem as both a religious and a political leader. He was a descendant of a dervish sect who, having usurped the rule, became the ruler of southern Kurdistan. Three times the Kurds rallied around him in trying to set up an independent state, but each attempt was futile. Whenever he was captured or surrendered, he was kept for a time in exile, either in the south of Iraq or in Baghdad. The time we were in Sulaimania, he had fled for safety across the border into Iran.

The grandfather of Sheikh Mahmud won glory by building a big mosque in the town. Twice a week, in the evening, this mosque was aglow with lights; drums were beaten and men shouted. When we asked the reason for this commotion, the answer was, "It is the *zikr*," the Sufi idea of introducing the emotional into their religion; with the aid of drums and dance, they work themselves into a religious frenzy. The zikr is somewhat on the order of the meetings of the whirling dervishes in Istanbul. Sufism is a form of mysticism and has many things in common with the mystics of other faiths.

Sheikh Mahmud had two wives, each with an establishment of her own. He had summoned a wife to join him in Iran, but each one was insisting that the other go. This caused a deadlock wherein neither budged, and neither seemed to be disturbed about the absence of her lord or about her subordination. Wife Number One, called Aishah, the name of Prophet Muhammad's favorite wife, was the sheikh's cousin. On her I called first.

When the salutations were ended, and I was seated aside of the blind sister of the sheikh, the usual question was asked: "How many children have you?" When I answered "None," there was at first consternation that tongue-tied the whole group of women, who before had appeared so talkative. After they had revived from this shock, fervent prayers were offered that Allah be gracious and grant some. When this subject was brought to some kind of a conclusion, a woman asked, "When you walk with your husband, who walks first?" To my answer that we walk side by side and that women are always given first place, they replied, "Here when the husband enters, the wife must rise and wait on him, and if she refuses she is sometimes beaten."

Wife Number Two was Bahijah; her house adjoined the mosque. The three women who greeted me were, to my surprise, unadorned. I had expected the wife, at least, to be loaded with the customary gold: gold coins covering the headdress, gold chains draped around the neck and chest, gold bracelets heavy on the arms, and gold rings heavy on the fingers. Bahijah explained that it was summer and hot and that she had relieved herself of the excessive weight. There was not the animation here that had enlivened the visit in the house of Aishah's mother. But Bahijah was worth a visit in herself. I judged her as a woman of a strong personality with the qualities of leadership, and had she been placed in another environment, the strength of body and mind and spirit she evinced would have enabled her to exert a powerful influence. She sent me a basket of delicious grapes, white and green and red, firm-fleshed and sweet, enough to last for the remainder of our stay in Sulaimania.

Halapcha, which is only a few hours drive from Sulaimania, was our next goal; and as we had been invited to come there by a boarder in our school and were being expected, we were at ease and could enjoy the piping hot tea that we drank at teahouses along the way from the small slender-waisted glasses.

The student's mother was the daughter of Adela Khanum, the woman Major Soane so highly lauded. That she had inherited some of the capable qualities of her mother, her well-kept house attested. Adela Khanum, a Persian Kurdish lady, had been married to a Jaf Pasha of Halapcha. He got more than he had bargained for. Adela Khanum, whose name is best translated as "Lady Justice," had no intention of being confined to the *anderun* or harem. When her husband was away, she acted as a competent, if not superior, administrator. "She instituted a court of justice of which she was president and so consolidated her power, that the Pasha when he was at Halapcha, spent his time smoking the narghile and carrying out local improvements, while his wife ruled."

I conceived a great admiration for Adela Khanum; I liked her indomitable spirit that plowed through the obstacles of tradition and custom and that proved in a man's world a woman's ability. I saw the town she had made and the palatial houses she had built, connecting two with a bridge. These three houses, though no longer new, are imposing and impressive and are seen from afar. Her daughter was retiring and modest and was not her mother's type. But there was a Kurdish woman who began to follow in the footsteps of "Lady Justice." A few years after our visit to southern Kurdistan, we were told that Aishah, the first wife of Sheikh Mahmud, had assumed the place of authority in her husband's absence, by right of being Wife Number One, and that she presided over her own diwankhana with great ability. "Aishah," they said, "rules in Sulaimania as Adela Khanum had ruled in Halapcha."

We were invited to dine with the administrative officer of the district, who was a grandson of Adela Khanum. My fear as to how the dinner would come off as to conversation was dispelled when I learned that one of the guests, the son of the naqib of Basrah, had a degree from Oxford.

At the table, topics of conversation fairly tumbled over each other in their eagerness to be discussed, and the informality of the dinner enhanced the sociability. And since everything was on the table from the first course to the last, it mattered not whether we began at the end or the beginning, and as Kurdish dishes were strange to us, we were apt to begin with dishes intended to be eaten last. And as everybody reached for what he wanted, there was no need to waste time in polite requests, which would have interrupted the flow of the conversation. Being the only woman at the table, I emulated Adela Khanum, and presided.

The next day we rode to the Auroman Mountains, a rugged range, along the crest of which runs the boundary between Iraq and Iran. The ride was longer than I had anticipated and with more hills than my eyes had placed in the landscape. As I had asked for a horse that walked, and rode one that had to be pulled, the distance seemed doubly long. I counted twenty-five hills on the return. At the base of the mountain was a natural park with streams and lofty trees and flowers blooming everywhere. Indeed, it was worth seeing, but what a drag I was on the party! My spirits, however, were upheld on the return, as I pulled up and down those twenty-five hills, by the thought that upon our arrival at the house we would be at once refreshed by the ever-ready tea served by the *chaichi,* who in good houses has no other duty than to prepare and serve, at a moment's notice, the tea so constantly sipped.

We returned to Sulaimania in time to attend the formal opening of the new serai. The ceremony reduced itself to sixty invited guests, who listened to a few speeches, heard a mullah pray, and drank politely—that is to say, only a part of the glass of good sherbert—applauded, and departed. The serai is one of the best in Iraq, and in it are those guest rooms which were so kindly put at our disposal when we "vacationed" happily in Sulaimania, and which sheltered us from the strong "black wind" which sometimes in the night suddenly raged through the mountain passes. Grateful for this restful and uncommon vacation with the Kurds, our brothers in race as we were often reminded, we moved homeward.

We liked the Kurds. They have native ability. Not a few of the important officials in the central government and the governors of the solidly Arab districts are Kurds. In the laboratory of the Iraq Petroleum Company, at

Kirkuk, we had seen a Kurd who in a month's time had learned to grind stones containing fossils for the microscope thinner and more accurately than a trained geologist. They also have literary gifts and dramatic ability as was shown by the Kurdish coolies when they performed on the wharf in Baghdad. They are essentially a hill people, tribal in organization, Muslim in religion, most of them Sunni. The Kurds are mentioned for the first time by Xenophon, who called them the Karduchi. He found them living in the same mountains in which they are living today. They are supposed by most scholars to be the descendants of the ancient Medes. Their great hero was Saladin, who united the tribes and led the Muslim forces against the Crusaders.

The Kurds of Iraq live next to large bodies of other Kurds in Iran and Turkey. After World War I, the Kurds of these three countries had hopes of becoming united in an autonomous state. They brought their appeal for a Kurdish state before the Peace Conference in Paris and also sought to gain world opinion for their cause, and to this end they even had an office in New York City. Sheikh Mahmud, known as the uncrowned "King of the Kurds," resisted the British mandatory government,[1] and when the mandate had ceased, he defied the Iraq government as well. The repeated revolts were undertaken to secure the frustrated independence by force.

Another summer when we were fortunate to own our own car, we loaded it with air mattresses, with a simple kitchen outfit—very simple indeed—with some provisions, and started again northward by way of Kirkuk. On our way we had to cross the Lesser Zab, a tributary of the Tigris. Because a new bridge was in the process of construction, a temporary ferry was operating. One look at that makeshift ferry was enough to daunt the bravest. There was a steep embankment to descend to reach the gangway, made of two planks, which were separated the width of the automobile wheels. How could anyone descend so as to exactly hit those two planks? How could anyone stop the car on the old, small scow before

---

1. Sheikh Mahmud Barzinji revolted against the British in 1923 and declared a Kurdish kingdom in the north. British forces occupied Sulaimania in 1924.

it ran off at the other end? On the opposite side of the river it was necessary to back off down similar planks, and then climb an almost precipitous hill. To save our nerves we entrusted the car to one of those daredevil chauffeurs whose numerous amulets seemed to be unusually effective.

Crossing before the ferry took the car, we avoided the strain of suspense by walking on ahead; and when the car was handed over to us without a mishap, we climbed in and started for Arbil. After a short time, we saw at a distance a large mound rising abruptly from the plain: it was the citadel of Arbil, the ancient Arbela where one of the world's decisive battles is said to have been fought. We hailed it more because of our thirst than because of its historic fame. Before taking time even to marvel at the height and size of this artificial mound, we drank *mustow,* sometimes called Kurdish beer, which is nothing else but *laban* (yogurt) thinned with water. It was cooled by snow from the mountains, and we drank it by the bowls in a barbershop! It was not altogether a clean drink, but we had assigned our knowledge of microbes and sanitation to the rest house of the Iraq Petroleum Company in Kirkuk, our last touch with the amenities of the West, and hoped for the best.

The Arbil that is built on the ancient citadel is, as one would expect, the interesting part of the city. The walls of the houses built compactly along the steep edge form the circular wall of the citadel. Going up the three ascents in front, we called on a Kurd whose office was in the gateway building and above the gate itself, where, as in biblical times, was the place of justice. From the citadel we looked out over the plain, north, east, south, west, in the hope that our eyes would fall somewhere upon the spot where the forces of Alexander the Great defeated the Asiatic hordes under Darius, the Persian king, only to discover later that the battle was actually fought forty miles further north.

This vacation was to be spent again among the Kurds, but this time in Shaqlawa, which is north of Sulaimania. Shaqlawa is a green mountain wadi, filled with trees and gardens and abundant water, and lying between bare, ruddy hills. We had seen it once before, on a brief visit when we carried letters of introduction to the amir of the district whose guests we were. Sheikhs in Iraq rule over their tribes as feudal lords, but not in exactly feudal fashion. Yet the amir of Shaqlawa came the nearest to it. He was of lordly size and his environs were the settings for such a ruler. He was not home when we arrived, but when he later came, we had a scene more eye-taking than Scott even described in his novels.

Down a mountain road swung a company with all the bravado of a medieval lord and his retainers. The advanced guard strode in pride, shining not in armor but in color, and having guns over their shoulders instead of hanging swords. After them came the amir, a powerfully built man astride a big horse, well accoutered, and behind him on steeds his Kurdish knights in full regalia. The company flashed through the tree-bordered walk, which ends at the amir's open-air *diwankhana*. There the amir and his knights gallantly threw themselves from their horses, which "squires" promptly led away. The people came hurrying from unknown places to welcome them, eager to hear a recounting of their exploits. Here, in Shaqlawa among the Kurds, was the pomp and pride of medieval days. We saw nothing else in Iraq like it, and with the death of the amir passed the last vestiges of an ancient day.

The amir chatted with us on the clay seats, on which were thrown the beaten wool rugs in bright designs. These seats were arranged around a large rectangular pool fed by a clear rushing mountain stream. Wide-spreading walnut trees grew on all sides, and a high leafy roof covered the pool. While we conversed in this open-air diwankhana, we ate the fine Kurdish fruits, which had been cooled, not in a Frigidaire but on a ledge of concrete running around the edge of the pool and about a foot below the surface of the water.

Our second trip to this valley was very different, for we intended to remain for a month and live independently. We drove through the simply awful street of the wretched town to find the man with whom we had negotiated to rent a garden. A garden in Shaqlawa is what we would call a yard, the kind we wanted, with nothing in it but grass and trees. Ours sloped gently to a bank, below which was a small stream. We hastily blew up our air mattresses, for night was coming on, and laid them on tent cloth on the ground; insisted and persisted in having eight poles driven into the earth for the mosquito nets, as the valley was malarial; lunched sparsely; tried to bathe in the darkness behind the nets; and weary and exhausted tumbled into the beds with the sky for a roof.

Sometimes there were trying days in this garden retreat. The great difficulty was to get something done. Our landlord had agreed to erect a leafy booth from the boughs of the scrub oak the day after our arrival, but fell into the usual habit of the East by saying, "Tomorrow" when the time came. Nevertheless, my vehemence overcame his inertia, and the next day the booth proceeded with general satisfaction. The deaf and dumb workman, rather a gay fellow considering his vicissitudes—his wife had deserted him, and his son had died of a serpent's bite—sang lustily as he put up the house in a day. "House" is scarcely the word to be used. It was almost roofless, windowless; the floor was the earth, and the door never closed; but it did screen us.

It was agreed, too, that Gurjius would make for us a small clay stove, but the day he was approached, he said, "It's the 'Id; I can't work." "What feast?" I asked him with exasperation. He said, "Transfiguration." Annoyed by the everlasting postponement, I said, "Feast or no feast, we must eat." Gurjius looked beseechingly at a priest who happened handily to be around at this critical moment. The priests of Shaqlawa are darkly ignorant and far from being clean. This, however, does not disturb their minds in the least, for they are confidently certain that only the priests are to get to heaven, the rest on their recommendation. If Gurjius could feel that he would be absolved from any guilt incurred by working on a feast day, he was willing to make the little clay stove. The priest must have assured him that the recommendation would not be weakened by so simple a task; the little stove was set up.

One night we were wakened by hearing running water close to our beds; our garden was being watered. In distress we shouted for Gurjius, who, coming with a lantern, helped us to divert the courses of many rills away from our beds. The garden aside of ours was likewise being watered. In Shaqlawa, the Kurds are in the majority, and the Christian minority has often had a hard time to secure their irrigation water rights. The poor woman who owned the garden next to the one we occupied had tried in vain to have it watered. To help her in her difficulties, we sent word to the officials that our garden as well as our neighbor's would be cooler if the water were turned on. Thereupon, a full current was turned into the channel above us by night that nearly flooded and drowned us in our sleep. We certainly got our share, and more than we had asked for.

The town of Shaqlawa is disheartening, to say the least, and the lot of its people miserable and pathetic. In the summer everybody lives in the open and breathes the good fresh air, but in winter the entire family must live in a single bare room. I saw some of these rooms; they were unbelievably wretched. The walls were smoke-begrimed, and the rafters were a shiny black from the smoke of the fires, which had no chimney outlet. Everything, too, was in wild disorder and nothing was clean. I asked myself, "How can human beings exist under conditions such as these?" I shrank from the thought. In these one-roomed houses families are huddled together, and in winter there must be intense suffering. That there should be uncleanliness in a place where water is so abundant appears on the surface incredible, until one realizes that every drop of water must be carried from the springs or channels, and that by the women who do all the other work besides.[2]

These poor women walk about speaking in low, plaintive voices, listlessly and without hope. Their lives are burdensome: constant childbearing, inexpressively miserable homes, domineering husbands who are often cruel. They grow old before their time. Of course they soon grow old. Life offers them not a ghost of a chance. Whenever I saw them, whether they were sitting or walking, silent or talking, they always had dangling from their hands a spindle and their fingers were always rolling the wool.

Gurjius had a little daughter named Bari, sweet and loveable. She brought us our water, often our vegetables from her father's vegetable garden next to our grassy yard. When we first arrived, it seemed to me that wherever I looked, I saw the eyes of peering women watching my every

---

2. Due to American protection both during the Saddam era and after his downfall in 2003, Iraqi Kurdistan has enjoyed a good measure of both security and prosperity. The following headline on the Internet speaks of a Kurdish dream come true: "Kurdish Mountains Alive with Weddings in Iraqi Kurdistan." The article notes that there are "plans to attract Arab and foreign investors to establish tourism facilities in Dukan, Sarsank, Shaqlawa, Sulaf, Bekhal, and Gali Ali Bek."

move. It got on my nerves, but Bari's presence was always soothing. My only regret in leaving Shaqlawa was that Bari was left behind to the fate she could not escape.

Both the amir and his womenfolk sent invitations to dine. At the amir's dinner I was again the only woman and was given precedence in ascending the steps of his new house. At the table the amir sat at one end and I at the other. There was a teacher in the group from the Muslim School of Theology in Baghdad, whose pride was offended. It was degrading to have a woman given the place of priority, and before he left he wrote for me to read in Arabic the word meaning "masculine," and well below the word "feminine." This was to rebuke my boldness, and a reminder that in this land man is first.

The amir had two wives, but only one house for both. Wife Number Two had lorded over Wife Number One for many years, the former a big powerful woman, the latter shrunken with the years of submission and neglect. Apparently a day of reckoning was at hand. The amir was looking around for a younger wife, and Wife Number Two was in terror. She asked me to intercede with the amir. "Why this loss of favor when I have born him sons?" she said. Often, and without reason, the hard lot of women is made harder because of their own heartlessness to one another. Why does the new wife ill-treat the older wife, knowing as she must that the same fate may be hers one day? And why does the mother-in-law, having the memory of the sufferings she once endured when she entered the home of her husband and came under the domination of his mother, now inflict the same suffering upon her daughter-in-law? As regards the amir's intended third wife, the upshot of the matter was that the amir eased the situation himself by dying before she was to arrive.

We lingered a month in Shaqlawa with its copious springs and luxurious growth, living day and night out-of-doors. Out in the open, under the tall and spreading walnut trees, we ate and slept; and reclining on new deck chairs which we had brought with us, we took intense delight in reading some of the books we never had time to read in Baghdad with our busy life. We found pleasure and amusement in simple things: in the birds, the squirrels, the turtle that came up from the stream every evening, manifestly to play with us. We enjoyed the long twilights, watched the sky turn silver and then into rich sunset colors, and waited for the evening star to come up over the mountain and hang there as a beacon light.

The last evening in the garden had come. Sounds from other gardens—a bit of song, a peal of laughter, the twang of a mandolin, the murmur of happy voices—reached us. The tall trees laced a rectangular frame above us for the sky. All was beautiful and serene, but this beauty meant little to the inhabitants of the place. The music and the laughter were not from them, but from those who, like us, were summering in this mountain valley.

A heavy weight began to hang on my spirits. The misery of the lives of these underprivileged people blinded them to the beauty of their valley, and the lack of harmony in their human relationships filled them with bitterness. There was hatred and revenge, cruelty and gnawing fear, all of which turned this oasis so beautiful and luxuriously fertile into a valley of joylessness.

Early the next morning, the automobile went careening drunkenly again through the wretched street of the town, but restored itself to soberness on the highway. With the steadying of the car, we composed ourselves; we resigned ourselves for the long, tedious, and hot journey homeward over the monotonous level plain.

13

EXPLORING SCENIC IRAQ

From Arbil to the Iranian frontier five mountain ranges must be crossed. When we had reached the top of the first range, we could discern lying before us, as far as the eye could reach, range after range of mountains, each rising higher and higher in the distance. Some of the peaks toward the distant north were 14,000 feet high. The view across these ranges resembled very much a scene I recalled when, years ago, I stood on the first ridge of the South Lebanon Mountains and looked across the country of the Druses. There I saw ridge behind ridge, each rising above the other in a grand ascent. These ridges with the setting of the sun were gloriously sunset-flushed. It was not God's rose of dawn but His rose of sunset that, seeing on the mountains of Lebanon, I shall never forget.

Our first objective was the Rawanduz Gorge. It took four years to build this road from Shaqlawa to the Iranian border, with sometimes as many as a thousand men working on it. To build it was an engineering feat, for the road passed through mountains where road building had never before been attempted by any of the civilizations, ancient or modern, the reason being the technical difficulties and the intractable character of the inhabitants. In these mountain fastnesses lived a people who loved their freedom and isolation and who were fearful and jealous of any intrusion.

To reach this gorge which someone has called, exaggerated no doubt, the finest in Asia, we had to traverse the celebrated Spilik pass. Only over this pass where there is a drop considerably below the height of the mountain could merchant traffic find a way. Here is where the robbers of a famous brigand band had their dens. These brigands called their lawless profession of robbing a trade of kindness and mercy. They declared that by lessening the amount of merchandise carried by horses or donkeys or camels, their burden was eased because the amount was reduced, a queer kind of a society for the prevention of cruelty to animals.

From this robber stronghold we began to wind down to the famous gorge. The gorge matched its most lavish praise. Great cliffs towered and beetled above us, rising to a height of many hundred feet. The foaming stream rushed noisily around the great boulders that obstructed its way. Torrents even poured out of the precipitous mountainside. A rushing stream dropped in a great waterfall to join the main stream. Deeply cut gullies and a complex system of gorges met the main canyon. We crossed and recrossed the river on strong bridges, which were built to harmonize with the scenery. Stopping repeatedly along the way, we stepped down to the churning stream to dip our hands in the icy water. We ate our lunch under an overhanging cliff where the road had been "half tunneled through."

When the engineers first surveyed the road, they had to crawl around this corner on their hands and knees with a sharp fall of eighty feet to the river. Drops of water were falling from the overhanging cliff through which the road was cut. Maidenhair ferns and mosses decorated the ceiling of the road, and at one place a delicate vine had grown out of a hole and hung suspended under the cliff. The road continually winds and is often just wide enough for an automobile. I wondered what on earth would happen if, turning a curve, we would suddenly meet a car coming the other way. We were told that earlier in the summer an American touring this gorge had almost had the alternative either to be smashed by a truck or to dash over the precipice. We met trucks too, but fortunately where the road was wide enough for passing. Having traversed this gorge, we could say of both nature and man's work here, "How mightily God and man have wrought."

We emerged on an open plain, across which we had to pass to get to the Beserini Gorge. But before reaching it, we came to the much-talked-of town of Rawanduz. The town is perched on a hill. Trying to drive up the steep incline, but finding it rather dangerous to make the sharp turns on the zigzag road, we wisely halted at a place where it was possible to turn around. Then, walking to the summit of the hill, we found that the town was built upon a narrow ledge of rock between two mighty chasms. Here in Rawanduz we stood in a "place of grim deeds and blood-feuds."

A tragic incident of a blood-feud took place in this region a few years before our visit. There was a feud between Ismail Beg and Nuri, another Kurdish chief. Dead men were to be avenged on both sides, and Nuri felt in honor bound to take the life of Ismail Beg, who was the governor of Rawanduz. Now this young man was rather remarkable. Among other accomplishments he was a great linguist. He bought and read not a few of the good books in the large English bookshop in Baghdad. Once my husband saw a large order of English books on many subjects which was being prepared to be sent to him. Knowing that he was likely to be killed at any time, he never went anywhere without a bodyguard, and would stay up in the night lest evil befall him. Yet, in spite of every precaution and safeguard, he one day received the fatal shot from his avengers.

Blood-feuds have existed in this land for a long, long time, and still persist. "An eye for an eye and a tooth for a tooth" is still a tribal law. "A man is bound to vindicate the honor of his tribe, no matter what power and powers may say to the contrary." Blood-feuds and the tribal law are entrenched in this feudal social life, and one of the hardest problems with which the central government is confronted is this unwritten code observed by the Kurds and the Bedouin tribes.

Coming back to the paved highway, we arrived at the Beserini Gorge. Though less grand than the other gorge, it is beautiful in a quiet way. It is more open, though at many places great cliffs overhang the stream, which had made the gorge impassable for caravans before the road was built. Here the river is not a mountain torrent; it flows smoothly and gently. Emerging from it at the farther end, we rested awhile in a *chaikhana* (teahouse) before we reluctantly turned back. We were near the Iranian border and only a few hours from Urmia. The temptation to risk border formalities was great; but, recalling that a Britisher and his party had been detained thirty hours in prison for crossing without passports, we looked longingly eastward; voiced our regrets; and returned.

Between the two gorges we had seen a signpost marked "Diyana." Many of the Assyrians were living here who had helped to build and protect this highway. Having decided to try this settlement for the night, we were taken to the home of an Englishman who was oddly called a consul, though there certainly was no consular business in this out-of-the-way place. He received us cordially in this solitary valley. The dinner that evening was served in the open in semidarkness, because the lanterns attracted a multitude of insects. This was very convenient for us, for in the dimness the wads of chicken that would not chew up, and very few chewed up, could unobservedly be disposed of. After the meal we laid out our air mattresses on the ground in front of the house. Going to bed early, we watched the shooting stars, heard no sounds except the footbeats of the guard. Then, falling asleep, we slept the sleep of the just.

Leaving quietly in the early morning before anybody was stirring, we drove back through the Rawanduz Gorge, stopping again here and there to survey its wondrous beauty. We now had a great deal more faith in the scenic wonders we were to see farther north. Then, emerging from the gorge with a last longing look, we retraced our drive to Arbil, and from there went on to Mosul, the second largest city in Iraq.

This was by no means my first visit to Mosul. I had visited this city a few times before, and always in the spring when the country round about was covered with flowers. In some of the low places where soil and rain happily conspired, the poppies and the red anemones crowded closely and, like the daffodils of Wordsworth, they were "tossing their heads in sprightly dance." These flowers that bespangled the land here and there reminded me of the fields in Galilee in spring, when the flowers grew in such profusion that they fairly elbowed one another for room.

Directly opposite Mosul, on the east side of the Tigris, once stood the ancient city of Nineveh, the mighty capital of the warlike Assyrians. Like Babylon, it was built on two mounds, but unlike it, the mounds show no evidences of an ancient city. Despite the excavations which have been made, there are no ruins in sight; and unless informed, no one would know that mighty palaces once stood here, and no one would have any intimations that here had been discovered the Royal Library founded by Sargon and made famous by his great-grandson, Ashurbanipal, a library that has given such literary treasures as the epic of Gilgamash with its stories of creation and the flood. The visitor to Nineveh needs to rely much more on his inner resources than the visitor to Babylon.

The governor of the Mosul district, with whom we had spent a delightful morning, telephoned to Zakho that we were heading that way. We had expected to enter the town unheralded. Not so; our brief stay of two days was so well planned before we arrived that we lacked nothing that hospitable entertainment could provide. Entirely unknown to us, the administrative officer of Zakho telephoned ahead to Faish Khabur that guests were to be expected. The Christian sheikh there, who with his tribe occupies land along the Iraq-Syrian border, with kindly thoughtfulness had sent a servant ahead to direct us to his house if and when we pulled up the last hill. Now of all the vile roads we had traversed in our wanderings only the road into Sulaf matched this one. The last hill seemed to rise almost perpendicular, and how we managed to reach the top without toppling over cannot be explained in any natural way. The sheikh told us that he had built the road himself!

There are very few Christian sheikhs in this land of tribal sheikhs. In fact, we were told once that Sheikh Aziz was the only Christian one in the land. He was indeed distinctive not only because of his religion but also because of his looks. He was altogether different from the dark-eyed, dark-haired Arab sheikhs. I thought my father had returned to earth; he had the same blue eyes, the same light hair, the same build, and much the same features.

Faish Khabur is the name of the sheikh's village, which lies close to the Tigris, near the junction of the Tigris and the Khabur. At this point Turkey, Syria, and Iraq meet. The French were then mandating Syria, and on a hill across the Tigris, a French fort was to be seen. As the sheikh's house was built on a prominent knoll, the French apparently found some diversion in watching "the goings on" in this house presided over by a sheikh who enjoyed keeping the French guessing.

In the evening, when the large acetylene lamp was lighted on the terrace, our host made the remark, "Now the French are turning their glasses on us, for this light is the signal that guests have come." I suppose the French were then trying to figure out the race or nationality of the new guests being entertained here. Since this house in Iraq was near the border of both Turkey and Syria, and since Iraq was still a mandate under the British, these two strange persons on the veranda which the French could see through their field-glasses might be either Iraqis or Syrians or Turks or British—but not Americans.

Sheikh Aziz permitted no other religious group in his territory except the Yazidis, or "devil-worshipers" as they are erroneously called. These, however, are employed as servants, and are not serfs or retainers as the others are. The Yazidis are not really devil worshippers, but devil propitiators. Their philosophy, indeed, is not bad: God is good and needs not to be feared, but Shaitan (Satan) is endowed with full power for evil in the world and can do unlimited mischief; therefore, he must be placated. The Yazidis live north and west of Mosul and number about 30,000.

One of the rulers of the Yazidis we learned to know very well. Coming to Baghdad, he occasionally called on us. I greatly admired the fine workmanship on his long dagger. In the Orient, admiring something is often taken as a hint that you really want it. But for some reason or other I never received the coveted sword or one like it. Once we had invited him to dinner in the evening, but he neither came nor sent word. The next morning he appeared as we arose, saying, "I decided to come for breakfast rather than dinner."

The Sunday we spent with the sheikh at Faish Khabur, he gathered his people on the lawn of his house in order that my husband might talk to them. Then he called on me to say a few words, and I pled for kindly treatment of the women. The sheikh laughingly told me afterward that the men said, "Should she come again and talk the way she did, we would lose all control over our wives."

We returned on the alternate road which the sheikh had mentioned, and which fortunately had been improved forty days before for the governor of the district, who had visited these parts. At any rate it was a more level road even though at times you did not see where it was. We were now driving in an uninhabited land, a region where we met no human being and saw no signs of life until we drove up to the door of the brother of Sheikh Aziz.

The people of this village were out in the gardens and fields when we arrived, but hearing the automobile, they all came flocking to the beg's house. Without any invitation or assigning of places, the men came immediately into the house and seated themselves on the clay benches along the wall. Apparently the women knew their place, too, which was standing in the doorway.

I have never forgotten the beg's wife, just as I had never forgotten Surma Khanum of the high commissioner's garden party. I thought I had never seen a face of such sweetness and strength. What molded this face? Few opportunities had ever come her way: she probably had little schooling, if any, and this village where she was happily living was isolated and cut off from the currents of modern life. With quiet dignity she moved about so simply in her efforts to please, with a face that was a benediction.

I said that the village was apart from the currents of life, and so it was; but we were treated to "American watermelons," ripe and sweet and delicious. In this remote and unfrequented corner of northwestern Iraq, American watermelon seeds had found their way and were bearing fruit. We were unquestionably the first Americans that had come to this remote and solitary place in Iraq, but wonderful to relate, the "American watermelon" got there before we did.

That we might not lose our way, the beg sent a guide with us. He was such a happy-faced fellow, who entertained us with local stories. Passing some boulders, he told us this story. Once upon a time when there were strained relations between Muslims and Christians, two men came along here from opposite directions. Neither could tell at a distance the religion of the other traveler. Fearing the other was an enemy, each took refuge behind a big rock with a no-man's-land between. Peeping behind the rock with his gun loaded, each was ready to shoot if necessary. This position, however, could not be held indefinitely. Finally, to test whether the other was friend or foe, one shouted, *"Halleluyah"* (Praise ye the Lord), whereupon the other loudly answered, *"Amin"* (So be it). Immediately both threw down their guns, ran toward each other, and embraced, crying out, *"Al-hamdu lillah"* (Thanks be to God).

Turning then to the northeast over a delightfully metaled road, we crossed mountain ranges timbered with pine and oak. Storm clouds hung low, and the sun threw cloud shadows on the mountains and in the valleys. It was altogether like American scenery. All along the way were villages hanging on the mountainsides, whose white houses contrasted with the red soil and the deep green trees. Some of these villages were inhabited by Kurds; others by Assyrians. The latter were being molested by the Kurds, and in their distress came to the road, halted the car, and pleaded for help. Apart from these unhappy interruptions, we were peacefully driving over these grand old mountains, getting ever to higher and higher elevations, when all of a sudden the good road ended, and fright took the place of calm. An execrable road! Then, after nervous exhaustion we suddenly reached wondrous beauty.

Here was real Swiss scenery: lofty mountains, jumbled ranges, upland meadows, cascading streams, all on a grand scale. Some years before we had traveled in the Tyrol Alps; later we saw the Swiss Alps. The scenery we found in Switzerland was much the same as that of the Tyrol, only much more magnificent and glorious. So it was around Sulaf and Amadiyah. Everything here was on a larger scale than in the Rawanduz Gorge that we had first visited on this trip.

After having lived for years under the burning sky of southern Iraq, on a dry and thirsty plain, devoid of running brooks and mountain ranges, I became almost intoxicated with the grandeur of this scenery. My younger days were spent in one of the most fertile valleys in eastern Pennsylvania, with the Blue Mountains on the one side and the South Mountains on the other. I also had spent seven years on Puget Sound in the State of Washington where mighty mountains reared themselves. The serrated Olympics were in view when I turned to the west, and the Cascades with snow-capped Mount Rainier or Tacoma, when I turned to the east; and between these magnificent ranges were great forests; rushing streams, crystal clear; and lakes and waterways. Then to live in a level country, with no mountains in view, no babbling brooks to listen to, no green lawns as I had been accustomed to, and few shade trees except the everlasting palm tree which is a poor excuse for giving shade—was starvation to my soul. Little wonder that I became ecstatic in this mountainous region. Yet my nostalgia for mountains did not overtop my deeper subconscious longing to be linked with the past.

Very reluctantly we left this wealth of beauty, cool climate, and invigorating air. Returning, we stopped at Duhuk, a rather large and important town. Driving into a shed built to receive cars, we failed to see a little goatskin, filled with ghee, lying where it should not have been; and alas, a wheel burst it. Out of it ran the liquid sheep's fat that was to be taken to the market. A vessel was hastily brought and most of it was saved. Observing that we were Westerners, the person to whom this liquid belonged demanded a greedy compensation for the loss. To avoid a noisy haggling and to make a just payment, we said that we would take the case to the *mudir* (mayor).

As it was Friday, the Muslim Sabbath, we had to call the mudir at his house. When this official saw my husband at the door, he exclaimed, "My father! Welcome, welcome!" and almost embraced him. Up there in Duhuk, to our utter surprise, one of our former students was the mudir. On the walls of his room were pictures of the school and his class, and what a warm and royal welcome we received! As the accuser beheld the warmth of our reception, his hope of enriching himself faded. We told our story, and the administrator said to my husband, "What do you think is a just amount to pay?" My husband named the sum and the case was settled.

Finding the plain exceptionally hot after we had come down from the mountains, we decided to travel from Mosul to Baghdad by night, and so informed an official friend of ours. He said, "Better take a policeman with you," and kindly provided one. This was wise and turned out to be providential. In a lonely place in the night where the road was rough and where we had to move slowly and cautiously, a Bedouin suddenly stepped in front of the car with a gun and halted us. Immediately the policeman stuck his gun out of the automobile and pointed it at the man, who quickly melted into the darkness of the night, and we quietly drove on.

These journeys to the north changed our whole conception of Iraq. Iraq, we found, was more blessed than we had judged her to be. Besides a very rich, alluvial plain, the richest in the Middle East, and two mighty rivers, sometimes referred to as two Niles, the country possesses rugged, majestic mountains, running streams, fruitful valleys, and an invigorating climate. We had found a treasure-trove in these mountains. Nature has provided here in Iraq, in the land of the Kurds, the climate, the water, the trees, and the scenery for those pilgrims who seek the shrine of nature where the dome of the temple is the sky and doorway open to all seekers.

14

THE BEDOUIN TRIBES

One cannot live in Iraq without being conscious all the time of the tribes. Almost the whole population outside the cities is subject to the tribal system. Someone who has lived in the country the major part of his life, and who knew the tribal ramifications, has stated that seven-eighths of the country is still tribal. Not a few who live in the cities still belong to a tribe, either as tribesmen or tribal leaders. Once in a while one hears a city-bred Arab boastingly say that he has a certain number of men belonging to him who will do his bidding. "Tribal," of course, is more comprehensive than "Bedouin."

The tribes have always interested me, especially the Bedouin tribes, with whom a certain glamour is associated. I had not only read much about them, but while in Baghdad I constantly came in contact with them. I saw the Bedouin in the bazaars, on the street, in the government offices, and in Parliament. In our school, too, we had the children of many of the tribal leaders. These sheikhs called on us not only on business pertaining to their sons, but they came also to our public functions and occasionally were invited to tea when they were in the city. Their sons who were with us were usually more of a problem than other boys, for the life confined to walls, and to the ringing of bells and the attending of classes was the very opposite to the free and open life of the desert to which they were accustomed.

Every stage in tribal development can be found in Iraq. There are the Bedouin tribes who are pure nomads, tending camels, sheep, goats, and horses; the cultivator tribes near the rivers and in the uplands; and the semisettled, seminomadic tribes—a blend of Cain and Abel—half-agriculturist, half-herdsmen. The tribal leaders, whether Bedouin sheikhs or big landlords, do not always live anymore with the tribesmen, or *fallahin*. Not a few have two establishments, one with the tribes and the other in the city. A paramount sheikh like that of the Shammar lives most of the time in a tent with the tribes, but has also a house at Shergat, at Mosul, and at Baghdad.

Looking forward to visiting a Bedouin sheikh in his tents, we were given that privilege a year or two after our arrival in Baghdad. It was arranged by a Syrian doctor of Kadhimain whom we had learned to know well and who was a personal friend of the sheikh. The plan was that a small party should spend the day with the tribe as guests of the sheikh, the doctor himself going along to conduct the party.

The tribe we visited was the Bani Tamim, now practically a settled tribe, not far from Kadhimain, near Agar Quf, a ziggurat or temple mound, which in its ruined state still stands over two hundred feet above the level of the plain and where excavations were recently made revealing a Kassite city. The sheikh and his tribesmen are Shiah Muslims. They live summer and winter out in the open plain in black tents, though the sheikh has now also a house in the city.

Driving over a desert waste, we suddenly and unexpectedly came upon these black tents surrounded by flocks of sheep and goats, and by growing fields of grain in a well-irrigated area. In this unlikely spot we found charming courtesy awaiting us. We were saluted with the dignity of the true Arab and welcomed with the hospitality native to the tent. Sheikh Hassan Suheil with his three brothers received us in his large, airy guest tent, which was in readiness for the expected guests.[1]

Along one side of the tent mattresses were laid, which were covered with rugs, taking the place of chairs. On these we sat leaning against the stiffly stuffed cushions which we could adjust at will; I cannot say that we were very comfortable; no Westerner ever is, sitting for hours on the floor. I was readjusting my cushions and my position all the time. To the sides

1. I had one of the two Suhail boys as a student at the American School for Boys, where they lived as boarders. Their family had the Buick agency in Iraq, its shiny cars exhibited in an elegant showroom on the main street of Baghdad, Shari' al-Rashid.

and to the front of us along the edge of the tent sat the leading men. Sheikh Hassan seated himself in the middle of the tent facing us as we conversed with him.

The salutations occupied some time, since they are always repeated: the assurance that you are welcome, the inquiries as to your health, the latter always receiving the same answer, whether sick or well, "*al-hamdu lillah*" (Thanks be to Allah).

In the guest tent of the tribe with its earth floor was a small shallow depression where a charcoal fire burned low. In its embers stood the coffeepots that are always in readiness for the visitor. Should we have come unannounced, the coffee would have been ready to be served just the same as it was for us to whom the courtesy was at once extended. The drinking of coffee is an act of ceremony and a symbol of hospitality and should be carefully observed. The servant pours in a small *finjan* for you a tiny bit of bitter Arab coffee. You take a sip, turn your cup, and sip again, repeating the process a few times. The servant will come around at least three times, and it is etiquette to take the third.

After the usual salutations had come to an end and the coffee was served, the conversation, after a few general remarks, took the form of questions and answers.

"Your tribe," began my husband, "is one of the few attempting to settle, not so?"

"Yes," said Sheikh Hassan, "for our land is well irrigated and is therefore productive, supplying the needs of my tribe."

"The government is pleased that you have set an example, I judge." continued my husband.

"Very much pleased," said the sheikh, "for it is ever so much easier for the government to deal with us if we remain permanently in one place than if we roam about."

"Are the tribes eager to settle?" asked another member of the party.

"There are many problems arising in the matter of settlement," responded the sheikh, looking concerned. "Which system shall we follow? Shall the sheikh own the land and the *fellahin* work it as a serf, or shall the land be divided and each member of the tribe become an independent farmer? In this present system there is a mutual advantage; it provides social and economic security and protection to both the sheikh and the tribesmen. An independent farmer would need, at least, a small capital to start, and a lot of initiative and energy to succeed. He would be thrown entirely upon his own resources. Really, it's a problem."

"How large is your tribe?" asked the doctor, knowing full well the size, but injecting this to accentuate the difficulty of the solution by the largeness of numbers.

"It consists of one thousand able-bodied men, which means that with women, children, and aged, there are about ten thousand souls," was the answer.

"If the land should be divided, what would happen to the sheikhs?" asked one of the ladies.

"Our authority and position would go," said the sheikh, "and like some other sheikhs now, we would most likely migrate to the city and find a government job."

Now the tables were turned and the sheikh became the questioner. As he took his turn, he surprised all by turning to world affairs. This visit took place before the days of the radio, and nowhere did we see a newspaper or a magazine in his possession; and yet, he conversed most intelligently on world affairs and the topics of today. He knew President Woodrow Wilson's Fourteen Points better than many a college student; he knew what was going on in the League of Nations at Geneva; what the Great Powers of Europe were thinking and doing. These men have a zest for international news and take every opportunity to widen their knowledge. Once in an isolated village between Damascus and Palmyra, where we were entertained, the host kept awake one member of the party all night asking all sorts of questions to become better informed.

The sheikh then invited us to dine, and after he arose, we followed him to that part of the tent where the meal was served in true Bedouin fashion. Three husky men carried in a huge vessel of nickel-plated copper on which was the food, rice cooked with raisins in which were pieces of chicken and mutton in large chunks. We sat cross-legged on the rugs around the common dish; and because the Bedouin believes that Allah made our fingers that we might eat with them, we pushed back our sleeves and dived into the food. We rolled and squeezed the rice with our fingers into balls, and put them into our mouths; we took chunks of meat and ate as our remote ancestors did; we drank the thinned laban out of a common bowl.

After we had eaten, a tall Nubian slave, whom the sheikh had brought from Mecca, came around to each one with a basin, an ewer, soap, and a towel, in order that we might clean our greasy hands and faces. We left the mound of food not much lower than it had been and watched to see what would happen next. As guests we were the first to partake, eating with the sheikh and his brothers. Then came the men who had been sitting in the tent, and afterward the children. If anything remained, the servants likely consumed it.

After the meal, we rested in a tubelike room made of matting until the doctor started to drive around to look after those of the tribe who were ailing. Accompanying him, my husband and I saw a side of tribal life that took away whatever romance I had attached to it. When it was noised abroad that the doctor was coming, the sick were brought to him, and he tried to heal them. Bilharzia was causing much suffering, and trachoma, of course, was common; there were also cases of malaria and tuberculosis. These are germ diseases, which in the early stages can be cured, but the doctor's visit was only a chance visit. The tribes have no attending physician, and the people suffer without help.

The life of the tribe certainly holds out no attraction when viewed at close range; disease, poverty, harsh conditions, a poor tent, no family life, and no social life except what the men create among themselves. These are the things that make living hard and for the time depressed me. But when the camels and the horses were brought out to ride, and there were races and sports and contests and the dancing of the *debki,* my spirits rose again as I saw real fun and heard genuine laughter.

Where were the women? Muslim custom would not allow them to join in the games and sports, not even to be present to watch them. The sheikh's wives lived in a long mud house surrounded by a mud wall where each wife occupied her own room. There was nothing romantic about this either as I and the other women of the party saw it. What did these women do all day? All these women were just ordinary Bedouin women, living one wonders how! Since our visit, the sheikh has built a fine house along the Tigris in Kadhimain, and to it he has brought an educated wife from

Damascus who was formerly a teacher. She speaks good English; with her I had delightful visits.

We came back to the big tent again and lounged on the cushions while drinking tea or coffee and listening to worthwhile talk, which appeared to be the right thing to do in order that we might link the last impressions with the first that had been so favorable. The time for departure having come, we said, "Fi 'aman Illah" (May you be "In Allah's protection") to our host, who always appeared neat and attractive in his Arab dress, and who has a pleasing smile and a most dignified bearing. From that day on, he and his brothers became loyal friends.

Ever since this visit, the problem of the Bedouin life pursued me, and as the years went on, I became aware that this problem is really one of a larger one: that of Iraq's landless multitudes, whether settled farmers, Bedouins, or seminomads. "The problem of landlordism is one of the most unsettled forces in Iraq," and unless there is some sort of land reform in the near future, no one can predict what may happen. The problem is not as simple as one might think. Just to change a nomadic Bedouin tribe into a settled or sedentary agricultural community does not do the trick. To change the status of a sheikh into that of a landlord, and the tribesman into a fellah, keeping the latter still a serf and landless under the mercy of a powerful and often absentee landlord, does not solve the problem. The fellah still continues to live in abject poverty and is unable "to rise above the subhuman conditions of living." To exchange the tent for the mud hut is no solution as long as the other conditions remain the same. Often it makes for a worse condition.

When the Bedouin becomes the cultivator under the tribal conditions, he usually degenerates physically and morally. This can be observed in this tribe I visited. They have now exchanged the tent for the hut. The swaying stride that proclaimed the man of the tent is exchanged for the dragging and slovenly gait of the cultivator. When the dirt accumulates in a tent, the tent can be changed to another place, whereas the man of the hut becomes infested with germs that lower his vitality. Then, too, the change from the nomadic to the sedentary is registered in moral deterioration. We speak of the agricultural life as a step higher than the nomadic, but in the case of the tribesmen it has been a step downward in character.

Someone has said that when the dweller in tents of hair becomes a riverine cultivator a certain moral and mental decadence follows; he is no longer an aristocrat but often a boorish churl. The Bedouin has a code by which men live, and in the desert this code is maintained; but in a settled state and under a different environment, it becomes obsolete.

The land problem in its ramifications is possibly something like this. It is obvious that neither the tribesman nor the fellah will have any incentive to improve his lot unless he becomes or has the hope of becoming an independent farmer and is dissociated from the semifeudal system. In this role he should be helped financially to secure livestock, machinery, and water rights, the help coming from the government or from some foreign source. At the same time he should be guided in modern ways of farming. Then, too, a revolutionary change must be wrought within him that will revive his inner life, remake him and revitalize him so that he can shake off the accumulated lethargy of the centuries.

But how can the landless get land? That again is a serious problem. Will those who have received large shares from the state domains be willing to share, giving up part of their holdings? And if this is not done, will Iraq be able to put all the available thirty million acres under the plow by elaborate schemes of irrigation?

One Easter vacation we accepted the invitation to visit the Shammar tribe near Mosul, the invitation having been extended to us by the sheikh's eldest son, who was then a student in our school. The Shammar tribe is the largest in Iraq and numbers 300,000 souls. A part of the tribe is also in Syria and a part holds a principality in northern Arabia, but the main body occupies land south and west of Mosul and is constantly moving as it is a nomadic tribe. The paramount sheikh at the time of our visit was Sheikh Ajil al-Yawir, an ideal Arab host. The way he managed men and the affairs of his tribe, as well as his personal appearance, satisfied the most idealistic notions of what a sheikh should be.[2]

2. During the current war, Ghazi al-Yawir, of this powerful Sunni tribe, became the first interim Iraqi president in 2005; prior to that he held the monthly rotating presidency of the U.S.-appointed Iraqi Governing Council.

A great surprise on this trip came to us at noon at Hatra, when the repast was spread out on a rug. We were served chicken, a lamb stuffed with rice and raisins, bread, eggs, oranges, and to cap all this, cans of mixed fruit. Where on earth was that lunch stowed in the car packed with stout men and guns? Canned fruit never tasted better than in this ruined Parthian fortress, and the mixed party showed its good spirits in a mixed way. The Bedouins went at the business of eating without any ado, as if famished. In comparison our eating here was as dainty as at Najaf. Sufuq tore the head of the lamb apart and offered us tongue or brain. They sang lustily, and we, sharing their gay spirits, felt as free in forgotten Hatra, in the heart of the desert, as the nomads.

Leaving Hatra, we drove about two and a half hours more until we reached the main camp of the Shammar tribe where the paramount sheikh at the time had his headquarters. A special tent, carpeted with rugs, was assigned us, and on the floor was a spotlessly clean bed. Many of the up-to-date sheikhs who frequently come to Baghdad and stay at the first-class hotels, where they dine with officials, now entertain in their tents more along modern lines. Tables and chairs, however, are still tabooed, since this is just so much extra impedimenta when the tribe is on the move. With this sheikh we did not eat with our fingers, neither out of the common dish.

After eating with the sheikh, we were led to the tent where he entertains small groups. Here we spent the evening in profitable conversation. The desert life and desert ways educate men in remarkable ways. It teaches them to observe carefully and to reason from cause to effect. The great prophets and founders of religion received part of their education in the desert. This was particularly true of Moses, Elijah, Amos, John the Baptist, Jesus, Paul, and Muhammad. As we left the sheikh's tent for our own, we stopped in the moonlight to feel the vast spaces of the desert and its sublime silence—the silence of earth and sky which speaks to sensitive souls "in deafening tones of God."

The next morning we were introduced to an interesting institution in the tribal life. We were invited to attend the sheikh's *majlis* (council) in the main tent, which is so huge and heavy that it takes six strong camels to carry it and which is held down by strong cables. This long black tent focuses the sheikh's activities. In one part of it, the sheikh, as head of a confederation of tribes, meets with a hundred or more men who come from near and far to attend this assembly. Under the other end of the tent, the work is done to maintain the proverbial tribal hospitality, while the center shelters his harem, consisting of two wives, a matrimonial restraint rarely found among the sheikhs.

I counted that day 140 men as we sat beside Sheikh Ajil on a mattress at the honor end of the majlis. To the sheikh's right were the senior sheikhs, and close to him was little Muhammad, a favorite son. Near him, too, but slightly behind, was a man who did a great deal of whispering in the sheikh's ear. "What was that whisperer saying?" I asked later. My informant told me that he brought all kinds of information about the tribes to Sheikh Ajil and about cases between tribesmen that needed attention.

One learns a bit here and a bit there. I was told that the men preferred to bring their troubles to the sheikh rather than to the government, that sometimes he acts as a judge; at other times he appoints a council which listens to both sides and then renders a decision. Through these assemblies the sheikh keeps informed as to the condition of the tribe in every part of his realm, enabling him to formulate a wise policy.

In contrast to the quietness with which the work of the majlis was carried on was the way the work in the other end of the tent was carried on. This was alive with activity and chatter. Here the women held their own meetings, presided over by the sheikh's first wife, who directed the business of the day. This wife did not seem Arab in either appearance or bearing. Sufuq, who was not her son, spoke of her in terms of respect and admiration, saying how capable she was, and how thoughtful and kind.

Her daily business was to see to it that food was prepared for the assembly and the family, "a hard and constant work," the wife said. Girls were grinding *burghul,* wheat after it had been boiled and dried, between two millstones; others were swinging back and forth the goatskins that churned the butter; rice was being cooked, and the meat was ready for the fire. Some were weaving, some were nursing their babies, and there were tasks for all. There was no time to sit cross-legged by the hour drinking the ever-ready coffee or tea.

In the middle of the tent three small rooms were fenced off by bamboo canes tightly woven together, each one being occupied by one person: the first wife who carried the heavy responsibilities lived in one; in the other lived the young second wife sitting on a mattress holding a baby; and in the third we met a daughter about fourteen years old heavily burdened with clothes and ornaments.

I returned to the men's assembly where business had just come to an end. The sheikh invited us to walk outside with him to see something of the daily life carried on in the open. The lambs in the spring are kept apart from their mothers except for a short time twice a day. We happened to come along as the sheep were being brought back, and the straining lambs were left free to run and meet them. Such a scampering and such a bleating! "Bah, bah," quavered the little lambs, and "Bah, bah, bah," answered the mothers. We wondered how the sheep could be distinguished one from the other in that big flock; but unerringly each lamb found its overjoyed mother, and together all came back in a cloud of dust.

The sheikh had opened a school at his headquarters. It was the first tribal school in Iraq for boys and limited in the number attending. It was a pioneering work and an exemplar. The school was attended by the sons of the sheikh and by a few other tribal boys. It was held in a tent, and the children sat on the floor with their papers and books. For the first time in their own environment children of the tents were attempting to learn the three Rs. It was a "peripatetic school," moving with the tribe.

One day I said to Sufuq, "You are being educated; will you be happy again to return to the tents and the desert?" The answer was, "Yes, because in the desert we are free." I know that Sufuq was never happier than the day he received his certificate and could go and live as a free man in the tents. I gathered, too, from the conversation that it is the birthright and prerogative of the ruling family to command, which satisfies a natural propensity and is worth sacrificing the city for.

In the afternoon of this day we returned to Shergat, and as a storm was brewing, it was necessary to make time. Sheikh Ajil accompanied us, leading the way with his car. We dared not ask him to slacken his speed, for the clouds threatened rain, which would turn the solid earth into a morass in which we would flounder. We clipped along, said little, tried to think less, and held our breath many times as we hoped for the best. We drove for three hours under a lowering sky before we reached the road.

Then, just as we were about to enter the house the storm broke out in fury. The winds of heaven were let loose, it lightninged and thundered, but not a drop of rain fell. And though the dust befogged the day, yet through this well-built house very little sifted.

We were glad to sit again in the comfortable chairs, and as we talked Sheikh Ajil slid easily off his chair to the floor where he seemed happier and more at home. The relative who managed the Shergat house, without any remarks, followed suit; and Sufuq, unnoticed on our part, landed on the floor too. On one side of the room everyone was down on the floor, sitting cross-legged, pleased as boys when they have found what they want; we, on the other side of the room, were equally happy in stretching out our limbs from cushioned chairs.

There were so many things about the tribe we wanted to know that we turned the conversation in that direction: further information concerning the unwritten tribal code, blood-feuds, and the execution of a girl because of unchastity. I wanted to know how a sheikh finances his little state within a state. I knew that his tribesmen create for him revenue, and that there are other sources of income, but I also knew that the outlay is great. I put to Sufuq a question much on my mind, "Your father is head sheikh, and has brothers, and all have sons. What work is there for all these sheikh-al people?" He said, "In the old days a sheikh's family was not so large because in raids and feuds many lost their lives; but now since raiding, in which the Bedouin gloried, has ended, the growing families of the sheikh do present an ever-increasing problem."

The next morning we prepared to leave early. We thanked Sheikh Ajil for his hospitality, Sufuq for his thoughtfulness, and others for their helpfulness in making our visit to the tribe a rare experience. As we said farewell and looked again at this sheikh of sheikhs, we realized his far-reaching influence and the breadth of his interests, which were wide enough to include two trips to London and versatile enough to keep himself informed concerning national and international affairs.

He was a fine specimen of physical manhood, very handsome and unusually tall and well proportioned. He looked the picture of perfect health. No sheikh in all Iraq, and possibly not in the whole Arab world, was like him in appearance. Sometimes as he stood and talked with us, his two little sons slipped in and out of his long, camel-hair 'aba as chicks slip in and out from under the mother hen. Then, a few years later, came the shock of his untimely death, "from heart failure" as the newspapers reported. Little, too, did we dream when we said goodbye to Sufuq, who was then only a student, that in a few years he would be called upon to take his father's place and assume his responsibility as paramount sheikh.

15

THE UPROOTED ASSYRIANS

Strange to have a train conductor in ecclesiastical robes," I said to my husband in the train from Basrah to Baghdad on our arrival in Iraq in 1924. He was a friendly, bearded man, this priestly conductor, or guard as the British would say. The black robe he wore had a rusty look, and the purple trimmings had faded some; otherwise, it was strictly churchly. He was of middle age, and very energetic as he took up the tickets and saw to it at every station that the train would not move until everything was attended to.

This conductor, we discovered later, was an Assyrian priest of the Nestorian Church, who, having fallen upon evil times, was earning a livelihood for himself and his family as best he could. Because he knew English, the British, who then owned the railways of Iraq, were glad to employ him as a conductor. He belonged to a refugee people who had no means of supporting their priest. This was our first contact with the Assyrians, of whom we had no knowledge before we came to Iraq. This priest, who was really of higher rank than just an ordinary priest, we learned to know very well later on when he brought his sons to our school.

These Assyrians were an uprooted people; they had fled for safety toward the end of the First World War from the lands in which they had dwelt for centuries, in southeastern Turkey and northwestern Iran. They had been a Christian folk since the first and second centuries. Like the Armenians, they remained faithful to their religion after the Arab conquest; Christians and Jews were not forced to convert to Islam. They remained a Christian island in the ocean of Islam.

The Assyrians form a group set off distinctly from all the other Christian minorities of the region. The origin of these present-day Assyrians is unknown (Joseph 2000, 1–32). They are a strange remnant of a race whose

169

history is veiled in mystery. They themselves claim to be the lineal descendants of the ancient Assyrians, that proud, warlike, and conquering race whose mighty kings created a vast empire and built for themselves great palaces in Ashur, Nineveh, and Khorsabad.

In the narrow valleys among the snow-crested peaks of the Hakkiari grew up Lady Surma, whom the people called Surma Khanum. How was it possible for Lady Surma to grow among unlettered and untutored mountaineers into the educated and cultured lady I found her to be?[1] She was never married, being regarded sacred by the Church, and set apart for the special duty of caring for the Patriarch, who was also a celibate and a member of her immediate family. She owed her training to the English, whose first knowledge of the Assyrians is accounted for in a story which contains fact interwoven with legend.

The existence of this Christian remnant was hardly known in England before 1837, and it was not until 1876 that a mission was sent to the field by the archbishop of Canterbury to investigate. Later on the archbishop's Mission of Inquiry that was sent to these people made its report. It wrote that the people were "abysmally ignorant, and that even the bishops could hardly read or write. They appeared to be better judges of a rifle than a doctrine." In consequence of this report, a mission was then established in 1886 in the mountains, and in time there came to Qudshanis a Reverend Browne, who for more than thirty years lived in the household of the Mar Shimun and was the tutor of Lady Surma. This explains how it happened that she so perfectly fitted into the garden party of the British high commissioner in Baghdad (Coakley 1992, 197–98).

How the Wheel of Fortune creaked and groaned as it bore downward this people of an ancient church, a church which had once been great and influential, and in which there was such missionary zeal that its outposts were in Persia, India, and China![2] Early in the twentieth century they were

---

1. For the first impressionable contact of Ida Staudt with Lady Surma, see chapter 4.

2. Because the New Testament was originally written in Greek, the language of learning for centuries prior to the Arab conquests of the seventh century, the hierarchy of the Aramaic-speaking Christian churches of Mesopotamia and Persia had to learn Greek. During the golden age of Islam, with Abbasid Baghdad as its capital, some of the

caught in the whirlpool of World War I. Casting their lot with the Christian nations, they brought down upon themselves the fury of their Muslim neighbors and were gradually sucked down to oblivion as a national unit.

Who would have dreamed before 1914 that anything tragic could ever happen to disturb the established order of these Christians or to draw them into the maelstrom of a world war? Away from the world's highways, in the strongholds of the mountains, far removed from city centers, Qudshanis spelt the last word in security. World War I then started; the Assyrians were wedged in between the Russians and the Turks, each trying to win them to its side. The Turks promised the Mar Shimun, their patriarch, arms, schools, and salaries to be paid to their religious and tribal leaders; the Russians promised arms and other material assistance. The patriarch's decision to favor Russia brought down on his people the wrath of the Turks, who retaliated by mercilessly ravaging the country.

The Russians were having trouble of their own at the time; their promised help never came. Forsaken by Russia in their day of dire need, the mountaineers were soon fleeing from their stone houses in the valleys to their highland summer pastures. Forty thousand of them struggled over the mountains, crossed the border into Persia, and joined their fellow Assyrians on the Urmia plain in Iran. This was a trek only mountaineers could accomplish; the feat amazed both Russians and Turks.

In Urmia, the Russians had a strong force; under the aegis of this nation, whom the people so implicitly trusted, the Christians for once could domineer over their Muslim neighbors, which, in true Oriental fashion, they did as arrogantly and inconsiderately as the Muslims had previously lorded it over them. Consequently, wrath was stored up against them for the days that were to come.

---

outstanding men of learning there were these Aramaic-speaking Christians, most of them "Nestorians"; it was they who introduced Muslim Arabs to the mysteries of Greek learning, translating into Arabic its scientific, philosophical, and medical treatises, already translated into Syriac, a dialect of Aramaic. These Arabic translations, which survived the original Greek, were translated later into Latin in Muslim Spain by, for the most part, Jewish scholars there (Hourani 1991, 75–79; Appiah 2008, 59–62).

Who could foresee a revolution gathering force? Suddenly the bulwarks of the Tsarist government began to crumble. Bolshevism sprang up, and by 1918 Russian aid and support had ended. The Assyrians were now under the heel of a vengeful and infuriated group. To add to their calamities was the sad news that the capable and energetic Mar Shimun Benjamin had been treacherously killed by a Kurd, called by the people Simco. Having accepted an invitation with other Assyrians to a conference to discuss the present situation and to make plans for the future, the Mar Shimun and his party were shot down by their hosts.

The Turks, taking advantage of this baneful situation, attacked in this moment of weakness. The mass rose as one man, and in a wild tumult fled headlong south to join the British. What a flight that was! What tales were related to me of children lost in the crowd, of the aged abandoned to their fate, of persons dying on the way, and of the efforts hurriedly made to scoop out a shallow grave. There was hardly a family that had not lost someone on the way. Sometimes the whole family perished. This line of retreat, marked by an endless trail of dead men, women, and children who had dropped in their tracks while on the march, remained indelibly impressed upon the minds of the survivors. Worn out and weary and against the will of many, the refugees continued their trek till they came within thirty miles of Baghdad. There a huge camp was erected for them at Baquba, where they were cared for and remained for a few years, after which they were settled in various parts of Iraq.

All this help and friendship which had been given to the Assyrians by the British must have been in the mind of Lady Surma that day when she was honored by having the high commissioner's private launch put at her disposal. The British had been good friends, and Lady Surma knew that her people owed them much; in this friendship she must have felt was the sure hope of her people. But now, all at once, the British whom they held as friends seemed to have deserted them.[3]

---

3. There was a downside to this British help: When it became clear in the 1920s that the future of these refugees would have to be assimilation within the frontiers of Iraq, the British, instead of pursuing a policy that held out hope for such an assimilation, persuaded

Trouble was bound to arise, and it did when the Assyrians themselves began to cast around for some solution of their problem after the British mandate had ceased. The Assyrians feared a massacre, and the Iraqis felt the Assyrians were a dangerous element in the land. Massacres did actually take place in some of the Christian villages in the north, especially at Simel (Summayil). After these troubles, the Mar Shimun was deported, followed by Lady Surma with her family. They were taken by airplane to the island of Cyprus. I met the Mar Shimun in the States, where he worked among his people who have migrated there.

The Wheel of Fortune will never lift the old Nestorian Christians up again to a national unity, a people among peoples. That chapter is closed. When Iraq secured her independence, she agreed to safeguard her minorities, and the government was willing to have the landless, jobless Assyrians settle in the land in homogeneous units, but not to allow them, and rightly so, administrative autonomy. This was a thorny problem.

Assyrian hopes for a permanent home somewhere on the earth came to an end after about twenty years of searching and waiting. The search ended where it had begun. Iraq, the land of their sojourn, became their permanent home. The old grievances are forgotten and the Assyrians are no longer treated as refugees. Their conditions have been improved; and many through their intelligence, ability, and enterprise have become prosperous and are now (1950) living a contented life.

---

a large body of the Assyrian mountaineers to enroll as mercenary troops for the suppression of local revolts. Winston Churchill, then secretary of state for the colonies, stated it bluntly: "I have been endeavoring to form out of the [Assyrian] refugees who have so long enjoyed our reluctant hospitality," a fighting force by enlisting their able-bodied men into the Iraq "Levies." Until 1921 the Levies were manned by Arabs, Kurds, and Turkomans; eventually the mercenaries were wholly Assyrians, used to safeguard the resented British air bases in independent Iraq. The French in Syria and Lebanon exploited the Armenian refugees there, following the same unconscionable policy: using them against the countries that had provided them refuge.

16

IRAQ'S GREAT STATESMAN

Three armies in the First World War were on the march to break up the Turkish Ottoman Empire. These three campaigns were spectacular and of staggering consequences. General Allenby marched his army from Egypt into Palestine; Prince Faisal and Colonel Lawrence headed toward Damascus, holding the restless tribesmen in their army together by gold and Faisal's persuasions; General Maude pushed his army along the Tigris to Baghdad and held out high hopes for this ancient land.

When General Maude entered Baghdad, he issued a proclamation that revived life in the valley of dead bones. He pronounced kindling words: "It is the hope of the British government that the aspirations of your philosophers and writers shall be realized, and that once again the people of Baghdad shall flourish, enjoying their wealth and substance under institutions which are in consonance with their sacred laws and their racial ideas." When the people heard this message of promise, it was as if a breath had entered into them coming from the four winds. Old Mesopotamia was reborn, and its people began to live anew.

In addition to General Maude's proclamation, to which there was a full-time reaction, which even the British had not anticipated, there were other declarations made by the Allies that aroused the hope for independence. In an Anglo-French pronouncement something was said about the establishment of a national government in Iraq. Then, too, President Wilson's ideas of the self-determination of nations had seeped in and were known and discussed in surprisingly out-of-the-way places.

What this newborn land needed in its infant days when it began to walk toward this intimated freedom was the guidance of a great personality who would so acceptably lead the people that the diversified groups could be united in loyalty both to himself and to the country. It was a fortunate suggestion on the part of the British that Prince Faisal would meet the requirements, and a fortunate decision of the Iraqis to accept the British suggestion and acclaim him as their first king.

I saw King Faisal for the first time at the garden party of the British high commissioner, as he stood in the dignity of his Arab garb, surrounded by high-ranking officials. Some weeks later I met him personally. It was when my husband and I called at the palace on a feast day when he was receiving. This day he was dressed in his military uniform, decorated with braids and medals. "My, but he is handsome!" I said when I wrote down my impressions.

I found myself to be the only woman to extend to him the feast greetings. He generously attributed my blunder to my being a *franji* (a Frank, a Westerner) and acknowledged my good intentions in his kindly way. He shook hands with us, and asked us to sit down with him; and being greatly pleased with the compliment, we talked with him a short time. He said he was delighted to know that we had come all the way from America to open a school and assist in the educational work in his realm, and we in turn told him of some of our plans.

At the palace where we met the king, we were first led into the receiving room, where we were served sweets and a sherbert. Here we met a few of the important people of Iraq, especially those who were connected with the palace and associated with the king. From that day on these officials were our friends and were always helpful to us during our long stay in Iraq.

Faisal had a background. He was from the revered Hashimite family of Mecca, of the tribe of Quraysh, considered the noblest of the Arabs. The house of the Bani Hashim was the very family of the Prophet, and also the family from which the Abbassid caliphs, who founded Baghdad, had descended. For Faisal to be king of Iraq would link him with the former rulers of the golden age of Islam who had made Baghdad their capital. There was something highly significant in this proffered kingship and strongly appealing to the Arab imagination. He was born May 20, 1883, the third son of Husayn, the sharif of Mecca. His mother, who died soon after his birth, was to him a precious memory. He and his two brothers received their education in Istanbul at the "invitation" of Sultan Abdul Hamid II.

When the British proffered to the people of Iraq Prince Faisal to be their king, it apparently was not done out of singleness of heart; it was rather an act of appeasement and a design to cover broken promises. But whatever the cause, it was a wise and politic move.

The Iraqis had thoroughly believed that immediately after the armistice of World War I, "the process of nationalizing the administration" would proceed. Things, however, moved slowly; in the interim of waiting for developments, people employed their time in talk. In the coffeehouses, on the street, in the tents, and wherever Arabs congregated, the one topic of discussion was "What form will the new government take?" As to the government to be formed, the crucial question was, "Who can command our allegiance?"

When in 1920 the decision of the San Remo Conference was made known, the people of Iraq shockingly discovered that instead of independence their country was to be a mandate, a fancy name for a colony, of Great Britain. The news of the decision placing Palestine, Syria, and Iraq under mandatory rule came as a bombshell. The Arabs loathed the word *mandate,* and from the day of its announcement until the mandate ended, the people of Iraq never ceased to storm and struggle against it. They were suspicious of the word, not knowing exactly what the term implied. One day a member of Parliament called at our house with an English book under his arm about mandates. My husband asked, "Why are you reading this book?" His reply was, "I want to find out what mandate really means."

What Iraq really wanted was a treaty of alliance between two free people and not to be under a mandatory power. When this was not forthcoming, an insurrection broke out in 1920 despite the proclamation that Mesopotamia was "to be constituted an independent nation under the guarantee of the League of Nations and subject to the mandate of Great Britain." Subsequent to that uprising, it took four different treaties, negotiated at four different times, before Iraq finally gained her independence in 1932. Jafar Pasha al-Askeri, who was many times a minister, once said, "Independence is not given; it is taken."

After the revolt was put down, Sir Percy Cox, who was then high commissioner, persuaded the British government that a national Iraq government might succeed. He determined upon a Council of State consisting of eight men as a start. With this council begins the story of Arab rule. The rise of Arab power and the wresting of power from Great Britain between the period of occupation and the final granting of independence is another great story of the land. It was this Council of State which accepted the proposal of the *naqib* of Baghdad, the venerable and highly esteemed Sayyid Abdul Rahman al-Gailani, who presided over the council, to declare Amir Faisal king of Iraq.

Until 1921, Prince Faisal had moved here and there seeking the fulfillment of the promises the Allies had made—to London, where he was welcomed but disillusioned; to Paris, where he pleaded before the Peace Conference for unity and independence for the Arab-speaking people of Asia. Then returning from Europe to Damascus, the center of the Arab nationalist movement, Faisal was reticent. How could he tell the people the unvarnished truth!

Regardless, however, of contrary plans and adverse decisions, the Arabs boldly forged ahead. A national assembly was formed, which met in Damascus, and a resolution was adopted demanding the recognition of the independence of Syria including Palestine, with Prince Faisal as king. This kingdom was short-lived, having been forced to succumb to French imperialism. A decisive battle was fought in the Anti-Lebanon mountains in which the Syrian army was defeated. At the time the engagement took place we were summering on Mount Lebanon, not far from where the engagement took place. The grave of the Syrian commander who fell in the battle is close to the highway between Beirut and Damascus and is a constant reminder to everyone who passes that Faisal was once king of Syria.

It was then, after Faisal was compelled to flee from Damascus, that the British government proposed to the people of Iraq that he become their king. The British suggestion was accepted not only by the Council of State, but by an enormous majority of the suffrage.[1] Before he was crowned, the tribes gave him the oath of allegiance in a huge tent on the banks of

---

1. Long excluded from Ottoman administrative positions by Sunni Turks, the Shiahs of southern Iraq were now excluded from the major administrative offices by both the British and the Sunni establishment (Tripp 2002, 45 et seq.).

the Euphrates in the territory of the Dulaim tribe. He sat on a dais, and the tribesmen, four or five hundred of them, sat below him. Outside were drawn up the horsemen and the camel riders of the tribes. Inside the tent, Faisal began to talk "in the great tongue of the desert, sonorous, magnificent—no language like it. He spoke as a tribal chief to his feudatories." When he had finished, the sheikhs laid their hands in Faisal's and swore allegiance.

Then came the ceremony of crowning, which was also thrilling but more formal. It took place in the courtyard of the Baghdad serai, which had been built fifty years before by the Turkish *vali* Midhat Pasha. The proclamation of Sir Percy Cox was read, and the people saluted Faisal with "Long Live the King!" Since Iraq as yet had no national anthem of its own, the British anthem was played; the guns fired a salute, and Faisal was king.

With his crowning there was ushered in a period of high hopes and real accomplishments; but best of all the air was charged with a certain elixir that had a transmuting power. Under its potency life surged. From the narrow streets and congested quarters people moved out into the open spaces; the various communities were united in a bond of mutual confidence and common endeavor; children and young people pushed into the schools that were opened; shops outside the bazaars were established; business picked up; new enterprises were started. A new era was ushered in.

The country over which Faisal began to rule is not a large and populous region when compared with many other countries. It is about the size of New York, New Jersey, Pennsylvania, and Ohio. The estimated population is less than five million, less than the population of a few of the largest cities of the world. Nevertheless, Iraq is important in other ways, and that is why its ruler should also be important. The importance of Iraq lies in its geographical position, in its strategic location, in its fertile soil and valuable oil fields, and in that it has had a glorious history in the past.

There was about Faisal an innate kingliness; it never had to be assumed, for it was inborn. Then, too, "he combined a practical mastery of affairs with shrewdness and patience." By wise statesmanship he adjusted the relations between Iraq and Great Britain as the country was passing toward self-government. In his attempt to make Iraq modern, he preserved the best in Arab culture and linked it with the best of Western civilization. He was endowed with both the Arab and the international mind. There was with Faisal, as with the great caliph Harun al-Rashid, an understanding and a just estimate of the other than the Arab population dwelling in his realm; and this attitude induced a love for His Majesty and a loyalty to the throne on the part of the minorities.

On the great Muslim feast days, the king received, usually early in the morning, but men only. Our household was astir on those days to aid my husband in getting off; and upon his return, we hung on his words as he related all that he had seen and all that had taken place at the palace. A cosmopolitan gathering, such as one rarely sees, came out to honor the king and wish him "*Idkum mubarak.*" In this gathering were prominent Arabs, Turks, Iranians, nawabs, rabbis, patriarchs, and bishops of the Eastern churches, ministers of state, members of Parliament, Europeans, Americans, ambassadors and other foreign diplomats, Bedouin sheikhs, Kurdish chiefs, mullahs, army officers, educators, lawyers, doctors— indeed, as notable an assemblage as could be found anywhere.

We remained in Baghdad the summer of 1933. The previous year we had been in America on a furlough, and during our absence Iraq had attained her statehood. This independence changed the atmosphere, a change we keenly felt upon our return. A rampant nationalism was ham- pering the fine and more delicate growth that promised so rich a harvest. Iraq had entered the second period of her history, and there were ominous forebodings. Yet, as long as the king was at the helm of the ship of state, it was felt that nothing ill could happen.

This was the summer when some Assyrians had taken matters into their own hands to find a national home for themselves. King Faisal would have clearly understood the situation had he been in Iraq, but he had gone to Switzerland for health reasons. When he was informed of the Assyrian unrest, he returned but came too late to prevent trouble and unfortunate incidents. His heart was burdened, and he was tired in body and mind. After a few weeks' stay, he went back to Switzerland to continue the recu- perative treatment. I did not know at the time that he had become so feeble that he had to be carried to the plane.

It was true that the king had died, for the drums began to beat—the Baghdad drums that brought laughter and tears. They were beating heavily with a rolling sound that made the heart sink. All day the drums filled the air as processions moved up and down Rashid Street; all night they beat, beating into our teeming brains "The king is dead!" Kings die, it is true; all that lives must die, but this death seemed particular and different.

Crowds milled up and down Rashid Street, repeating antiphonally, "O, father of Ghazi, you have left us when we needed you most," "our souls are desolate, and our hearts are numb!" We, too, were heavy of heart, wondering how this new nation, which was so gallantly and bravely steered to statehood by him the previous year, could, in these still infant days, walk without his aid. The future appeared imperiled, and in reality it was, as history has shown.

Something died with Faisal besides kingship, something the land needed greatly and which no one else could supply. His was a gracious, understanding, and broadly tolerant nature. He was the kingly protector of all his five million people, unusually diverse in religion, race, and language. How securely everybody lived when he was on the throne. His whole life career had a kingly tinge. Had he not tilted for the independence of the Arabs? Had he not struggled with imperial powers for the fulfillment of promises avowedly given, but faithlessly kept? Had he not maintained his poise under the overpowering situations and responsibilities with a knightly bearing?

An airplane brought the king's body to Baghdad. On a rooftop which commanded a view of Maude Bridge over which the cortege had to pass, I with others stood watching. It was a long wait. Nine airplanes which had gone out to meet the king's body circled above us in perfect formation. The Boy Scouts below were keeping the kaleidoscopic Rashid Street crowd from obstructing the way for the funeral.

Most of the inhabitants of Baghdad, young and old, rich and poor, had abandoned their homes to observe the funeral of their beloved king. Many from all Iraq had come for the same purpose. For four or five miles the street was jammed with hundreds of thousands of people. The flat roofs and balconies of the houses along the route were black with women. The street, too, was one mass of humanity, with a narrow opening kept in the middle for the cortege to pass through. From the street human beings overflowed into the alleys and the lanes like the tributaries of a river. Like clusters of grapes on a wall, persons even were hanging along the front of buildings. There was not a foothold that was not occupied.

There was no music, no outcry, no audible wailing, no sound save the soft tread of the mourners. The men on the street and the women on the roofs and balconies were mute. Not a sound escaped from a single person while the gun carriage, draped heavily in black, drawn by six horses that were also covered with black and guarded by soldiers, bore the king to his last resting place. It was one of the most moving occasions I ever witnessed.

The invited mourners, among whom was my husband, were asked to assemble in the palace grounds and to follow from there the body to the grave. There was a long wait, and twice came the report that the casket was approaching, whereupon the master of ceremonies formed the mourners in the order in which they were to walk according to their rank and importance. When it was discovered that these reports were not true, the orderly lines were broken up each time, and everyone sought shelter under a tree for the sun was hot.

Suddenly and unexpectedly, however, the gun carriage arrived, and since the invited mourners were to follow immediately after the distinguished guests and the immediate family, there was no time to bring together again the men in the prescribed order. My husband and the king's treasurer certainly were not to walk together near the head, but they were pushed there and pushed together by the dense throng which lined the street or followed the body. Because of the pressure of the throng no change was later possible.

At the grave, the mullahs, in Arab dress with spotless white bands wound about their tarbushes, grouped themselves around the casket and repeated the prayers for the dead. After the body was lowered into the grave, the guns fired the salute, the buglers sounded "The Last Post," and all was over. One of the noblest of the Arabs, he who had led Iraq to her promised independence passed on. The first chapter of Iraq's history was closed.

17

AND SO THEY PASSED

The death of King Faisal was a great loss to the country. Indeed, it was a calamity for he could not be replaced. Then there were other very influential people who passed away after our arrival in Baghdad. The number is really appalling. Death seems to have singled out Iraq as his special field and kept the door of the other world constantly swinging open to receive them, these men and women who figured so prominently in this newly born nation. These deaths removed experienced leaders sorely needed in piloting the course of the new state, in a land where statesmanship had not been encouraged for hundreds of years. The loss of these conspicuous leaders robbed Iraq of indispensably useful men.

Three big houses stood on the bank of the Tigris adjoining the grounds of King Faisal's official palace. The first and largest house was occupied by the queen. It was a house of some pretensions, but unfortunately the foundation was gradually being undermined by the swift current of the river; one day after the queen had found another residence, the large building collapsed with a mighty crash. The second house was occupied by the king's grandmother, the most distinctive of all the characters I met in Baghdad, in a class quite by herself, and by the three princesses. In the third house lived the king's treasurer.

The first two houses were joined by a short bridge, which I eagerly crossed one day with Madame Safat Pasha, the wife of the king's treasurer, to make an unscheduled call. The appointment was with the queen, but as we had time, it occurred to my friend that we might fill in the interval by calling on the grandmother. This was a happy thought; for of all the calls I paid in Baghdad, none left such an indelible impression as this brief visit with a very old lady, who, though living in retirement, cherished memories that kept her aglow.

We found her sitting on the floor on a mattress covered with crimson velvet, leaning against crimson velvet cushions. She lifted her eyes as we entered. And such eyes! They were big and alive, as though life had been, every day of it, full of interest. Time was to her a precious legacy, guarded in order to revel in great memories and present glories. Were not her three grandsons *muluk*s (kings)? Time could neither dim her vital pride in these three grandsons who were her care after her daughter's death, nor could time, she was sure, tarnish their glory. So dearly had she loved these kings while they were still little boys living in Istanbul that, when they left the house to visit friends or go to the bazaar, she waited at the latticed window for their return. This lady's age was ninety-four. She was frail of body, but age had not touched her mind.

From our chairs we looked down on the quaint old lady on the crimson, velvet-covered mattress. She drew one of the princesses who had come into the room to her, kissed her, and held her by her side as she talked. She said, "The world closed on me when my daughter died." Her daughter was her only child and was the mother of the three kings: King Ali, who, for a short time, was the ruler of the Hijaz; Amir Abdullah, now (1950) king of Jordan, whose guests we once were when he lived in tents on the hills above Amman; and King Faisal, the youngest and most famed, the king of Iraq. The walls of her room were adorned with their pictures, but in her mind many more were treasured. Her daughter had died two months after the birth of Faisal, at the age of twenty-seven, "and all Mecca went into mourning, for so was she loved."

Her eyes laughed as she told of her daughter's rival for the proud position of the wife of the sharif of Mecca, keeper of the Ka'ba; of Husayn's choice, which was victory for her daughter and defeat for the rival; and of her rejoicing in the triumph. "Husayn chose *Sitt* (Miss) Abdia, the most beautiful woman in Mecca, my daughter, as his bride," she said with the accumulated pride of years of telling. We, looking down on the big-eyed little lady, judged that the mother had been no less beautiful. We told her so, and there was no dissent. Among her choice memories were those of admiration and rapid advancement because of her beauty. There was no dissatisfaction with the guidance of her life, save that her daughter had died so young, but happily, died the wife of the sharif of Mecca; in that there was solace.

This grandmother of kings was a Cherkess, the tribe of the Caucasus, famed for the beauty of their women. She had been adopted by a high Muslim family in Istanbul, and later became one of the four wives of Amir Abdullah Pasha, the uncle of Sharif Hussain. So great was Hussain's love for this daughter of the Cherkess that no other woman was received into his harem while she lived. He married again after her death but only once. King Ali has only one wife, who is the mother both of the present queen-mother of Iraq and of the regent; King Faisal I also had only one wife. It had not been customary for Muslim rulers and sultans to lead so curbed a domestic life.

The time had come to call on the queen. Reluctantly we salaamed and bade farewell to the grandmother of the kings. Recrossing the bridge, we entered the house of the queen and were conducted into her presence. She sat on a couch in the place of honor. There was nothing regal about this first meeting; it was all very simple, very cordial, and very informal. The queen's face in repose was not beautiful but it was a sensitive face that lighted up when she smiled; and as the conversation was rather animated, the face was alight most of the time. With the grandmother we drank Turkish coffee, and tea with the queen. Warmed by the pleasure our visit had obviously given, we said good-bye both times with considerable fervor. This auspicious beginning with the queen when we met in simple friendliness continued through the years. The grandmother I never saw again; she passed away soon after my visit.

For a time I called quite regularly on the queen. Every month, at least, I would call when she received in the big red house on the Tigris, to which she later moved. She wore European clothes, due perhaps, to the English governess who took in hand the education of the princesses and supervised these receptions. I was always happy to call on the queen. Apparently we had much in common, felt mutually drawn to each other, and never seemed conscious of the things in which we differed. She was brought up under a certain culture and religion which was altogether different from mine, and yet we found in common likings and common interests a common bond. Never strong and robust, the queen grew more and more frail after the death of the king. She rests beside her husband in the beautiful mausoleum erected in honor of Iraq's first king.

In the East, death is surrounded with such impenetrable gloom. I called on the princesses after their mother's death and tried to relieve the oppressiveness of their surroundings. The room in which they were seated was small and meagerly furnished. The girls were in deepest black, and the Muslim ladies in attendance in unrelieved black, seemingly ready on short notice to wail and weep as is the custom. After my entrance, weeping, for a time at least, was suspended. We became almost cheerful as we talked. We talked dress, think of it, and I carried away the simple garment worn by Muslim ladies which belonged to the elder daughter of King Faisal. This garment which she pressed upon me is a treasure I greatly prize.

When I turn to the Land of Memory and recall the persons who had helped to make Baghdad a city of enchantment for me, figures seem to awaken as in Maeterlinck's *The Blue Bird*. Among those that greet me is the queen, whose face never failed to light up as I approached her.

One morning, Baghdad was startled by the news that Miss Gertrude Bell had passed away in her sleep in the early morning hours—startled because her death was altogether unexpected. She was in her usual health the day before, and according to her custom, had sailed up the river in her launch in the afternoon for her usual swim. No one dreamt that it was for the last time.

Miss Bell, as has already been pointed out, was a unique, vital, influential woman. She chose to spend her adult life with the Arab peoples. At the time of her death she was Oriental secretary to the British high commissioner. She had been a fearless traveler, and actuated by her interests in archaeology had gone into unfrequented and dangerous parts of the Middle East, traveling among the desert tribes by camel. On these trips she took with her everything needed for her work and comfort, and, to keep up her customary British ways, evening dresses and cutlery and napery went along. Her father was Sir Hugh Bell, for whom she had the deepest admiration and affection.

She was a welcome guest of many Arab sheikhs, who delighted in her sincere friendship. In their tents as well as later in her office in Baghdad, she immensely enjoyed their "desert gossip," as she called it, with which they entertained her. Few sheikhs came to Baghdad who did not visit her first before being recommended by her for an interview with Sir Percy Cox or Sir Henry Dobbs. "She acted as a strainer," Sir Percy said, "through whom the individual filtered through to me."

During World War I, when the British were fomenting new plans, it was thought by those in Cairo that Miss Bell's knowledge of northern Arabia would be of value in the planning. Thereupon she was called to Cairo. Britain's authority and influence in the Persian Gulf and in India was being threatened by the building of the Berlin-Baghdad Railway. The construction of this line was steadily advancing. It was a growing menace that had to be offset. Accordingly, two almost identical plans were worked out, independent of each other: one by the Arabs, the other by the British. The Arabs wished to free themselves from the Turks, and to this end wanted British aid. The British, on the other hand, perceived that if the Arab provinces of the Ottoman Empire would form themselves into an autonomous state or states friendly to Great Britain, they would become, as it were, an "Anglo-Arab dam to stem the Turco-German tide."

After General Maude's victorious entry into Baghdad, Miss Bell was called to this city by the British high commissioner. Here she began to play her important role in helping to recreate a reborn land. Wholeheartedly she devoted herself to this cause; or as she expressed it, "To make Baghdad a great center of Arab civilization, a prosperity; that will be my job partly." She was an indefatigable worker, worked with ardor, put out piles of papers, and followed the shaping of Iraq with zestful interest. The information she had gathered on the Arabs was useful in solving many problems. Perplexities and uncertainties were clarified by her knowledge of sheikhs and tribes, their locations and their tribal animosities. She was sometimes even called "The Uncrowned Queen of the Desert" or "The Real Ruler of Iraq."

Someone wrote of her irresistible vitality that overflowed into the museum project that her antiquarian bent naturally made her desire to establish. Into this museum she put her spare hours, and her last letter was almost entirely about it—a museum which under her skilled direction has become a repository of marvelous objects unearthed by excavators. A brass plaque at the museum ascribes to her the creation of it in 1923.[1]

I saw her buried with the honors of a military funeral, and it seemed fitting that she should be buried in this way. Her pioneering work, her courage and fearlessness, and her valuable service to the British Empire and the Arab world made her deserving of such an honor. She lies in a British cemetery, a homelike burial place, green and restful and walled in from the encroaching city.

As I stood beside her grave, my thoughts wandered to General Maude, who lies in a cemetery at the other end of the city. Maude's death strikes a tragic note. For he, like Alexander the Great, who died in Babylon, and like the Emperor Julian, who died in Samarra, "had conquered the ungrateful soil of Mesopotamia only to become its victim." Nevertheless, he had brought the gift of a great hope to Iraq—a hope that the land might be free and independent. Although Miss Bell did not live to see that cherished hope of independence become a reality, still she did see the framework of an independent state fully reared, in the setting of which she had been a prime mover.[2]

Miss Bell's death was the first break in the procession of persons who had figured in the founding of the new state. After her death the Norns busied themselves in cutting off the life-threads of many of the makers of Iraq. One can only speculate on the kind of a nation Iraq might have developed into had some of the large-minded men at the helm, who had to relinquish their hold, been granted a longer time to steer.

1. The Museum of Antiquities was looted after the lawlessness that followed the American occupation of Baghdad in 2003. When parts of the museum were opened six years later, thousands of the works stolen from its collection, "some of civilization's earliest objects, remain lost." *New York Times*, Feb. 24, 2009.

2. Gertrude Bell was very conscious of Iraq's sectarian divisions: "The Sunni nationalists wanted an Arab kingdom, the Shi'ites wanted an Islamic religious state, the Kurds in the north sought an independent Kurdish entity." In her opinion, it was beyond consideration to turn over control of the country to the local population: "To give them total power would have been like handing over the reins to a riderless horse" (Wallach 2005, 215–16).

The mantle of the naqib, who was the first prime minister in King Faisal's cabinet, fell upon the shoulders of Abdul Muhsin Beg al-Sa'dun. This cabinet continued for only a year. Prime ministers in Iraq resign and again come back to office, resign and are recalled. It was so with Abdul Muhsin Beg. The struggle over treaties went on, and it seemed as if a new one was always drawn up to be ratified. Because of British opposition to government demands, the ministry would fall, and the ministers would be reshuffled with a few new ones added to change the complexion. Then, a former premier would try again. In an interview with an English lady, King Faisal once said, "I believe in England. I think she means to help. But the promised treaty which is to take the place of the mandate is always postponed. The delay has already cost one prime minister his life." King Faisal, of course, referred to Abdul Muhsin Beg al-Sa'dun.

Chopin's "Funeral March," poignant with sorrow and heavy with tragedy, was played on the streets of Baghdad by a military band as the body of al-Sa'dun was carried to the Gailani mosque for burial. It was the first time, and to my knowledge the only time, that this funeral march was ever played on the streets of Baghdad. Perhaps because it was strangely exotic, perhaps because there was such a pathos in the tragedy, the music was weirdly moving.

When he was prime minister the second time, al-Sa'dun invited my husband and me to be present at the opening of Parliament. As only a very limited number of guests apart from the diplomatic corps could be accommodated, we considered this a great honor. He sat facing the deputies, and I recall with what keen interest I followed his speech, though I understood little. After Parliament had adjourned, he sent word to us to come to his room in the building. Here, while drinking Turkish coffee, we had the opportunity to thank him for his thoughtfulness in inviting us to this parliamentary session. He answered with the courtesy of good breeding and education. We left carrying away an impression of dignity, quiet reserve, and a certain gentleness that placed Abdul Muhsin Beg high in our esteem.

These were trying days for men in high office: they were between Scylla and Charybdis. An ever-pressing constituency was demanding that more and more power be yielded by the mandatory control and that the day of Iraq's independence be hastened. When these demands were not granted, the officials were taunted with words that cut deep.

Abdul Muhsin Beg was a capable prime minister, but he could not accomplish the impossible. One day after a heated debate in Parliament, in which he had been accused of a betrayal of national interests, he dropped in at the Iraq Club, where he was again accused of treachery. He returned to his home in a nervous state. At the evening meal he repeatedly professed his love for his family, after which he withdrew to write a letter to his son, who was studying in England. Soon a shot was heard, fired by his own hand. Muhsin Beg was dead.

He was carried to the tomb in solemn state. Mounted police rode slowly; the military band voiced the sorrow felt by all; behind the bier came the throng of men, a very great throng, on foot; and, according to the custom, all were impressively silent. Up through the palm-girted road the funeral procession moved into the congested city to his last resting place in the mosque.

The next day we went to the house of mourning. Men sat with men in one room; women with women in another. The Eastern way of showing your sympathy is to be silent and drink bitter coffee. This is more impressive than words. Around the large room were seated the friends who had come to share in the grief. There was no wailing. I sat between the mother, so still in her great sorrow, and the daughter who in low tones told me the sad story.

A statue of Abdul Muhsin Beg stands at an intersection of two busy streets in Baghdad. Whenever I passed it, I seemed to hear Chopin's "Funeral March" that alone broke the stillness of the great procession silently winding its way to the grave. I recalled, too, other tragedies that happened because of a reluctance to give statehood on the part of the British and an overzealous desire to secure it on the part of the Arabs.

Next, the life-thread of King Ali, brother of King Faisal, was cut off. Their father, Hussain, six months after the Revolt in the Desert, was proclaimed "King of the Arab Countries," which title, however, was reduced by the Allies to "King of the Hijaz." His downfall later was due to his failure to keep in friendly relations with his powerful neighbor Ibn Saud, paramount sheikh of the Najd. They quarreled over a boundary, and the

Wahhabis easily overcame the Hijazis. Hussain was compelled to abdicate in favor of his son Ali, who was then forced to withdraw to Jeddah, and Mecca was occupied by Ibn Saud. Unable to cope with so strong an adversary, Ali surrendered and came to Baghdad, where he lived, quietly but with dignity, till his death in February 1935. He was fifty-six years of age.

What a burial day for one so gentle and likeable! A high wind swirled the dust all day long and raised whitecaps on the Tigris. The funeral plan of bringing the body up the river on a boat from the southern extreme of the city to Adhamiyah, a northern suburb, had to be changed. Here in an open space those who were invited to attend the funeral were asked to assemble for the purpose of following the body from there to the grave. In the meantime, the storm increased in intensity: the wind howled, clouds of dust turned day almost into night, and the palm trees tossed in fury. Because of the changed plans there was delay, and those who waited and waited in the open began to look like the bleak landscape about them. The Britishers nervously busied themselves in brushing the dust from their top hats.

At last the body arrived, and the procession, after being formed, moved forward in quiet order to the grave, which was about half a mile away. Directly behind the casket, which rested on a gun carriage, came the chief mourners: Amir Abdul Ilah, the son, who was now the regent; King Ghazi, the nephew, who was then king; and Amir Abdullah, the brother of the deceased. In the slow march the army officers found their bright decorations growing dimmer as the dust particles clung to braids of gold and the insignia of office, and all appeared to be returning to the dust of which they were made. The service, like that of King Faisal's, was brief. And long after the crowd had hastened away, a mullah sat near the tomb praying for the soul of the departed.

Suddenly one day, the quiet of the school was interrupted by parents and servants entering the court, and excitedly and anxiously asking for their boys, whom they hastily took home with them. It was the morning of October 29, 1936. Bombs had suddenly fallen from a clear sky near the government building, and one of these had dug a hole in the court and shattered the windows of the offices of the prime minister and the Ministry of the Interior. It was Bekr Sidqi's coup d'état. It took only five hours and the crisis was over. The coup was so carefully planned that neither the government nor the public knew anything about it till the moment it was sprung upon them. Important British officials were recalled because of their unawareness of this move on the part of the Iraq army.

It took only five hours, but how fateful those five hours were! The cabinet was forced to resign. Yasin Pasha al-Hashimi, who had been prime minister for nineteen months, fled to Syria; so did Rashid Ali al-Gailani, the minister of the Interior, who later returned and became a Nazi agent as well as premier; Nuri Pasha al-Said, the minister of Foreign Affairs, was taken by a British airplane to Egypt; but Jafar Pasha al-Askeri, the minister of Defense, remained and heroically met his death. Hearing that the army was only a two-hour march from Baghdad, he insisted against earnest protests to go and meet it, believing that a loyal following of his in the army would divide allegiance and stop the march. Bekr Sidqi foresaw just such a contingency and had prepared for it by depending upon four of his trusted followers. Jafar Pasha was shot and buried at once where he fell.

For several days rumors were current of his death, but three days elapsed before they were confirmed. To many it was a grievous loss. Both Nuri Pasha and Jafar Pasha were close friends and were related by each having married the sister of the other. Both had served in the beginning of World War I in the Turkish army. When Jafar Pasha heard of the Arab awakening, he volunteered for service with the sharif. He was given command of the Arab military operations, and by his untiring efforts, he greatly improved Faisal's army.

Jafar Pasha had such a big heart, which fitted well into his big body, and his hearty voice and jovial disposition created an atmosphere of genial warmth and friendliness wherever he appeared. Just shortly before his death he brought personally to our school his two nephews to be boarders. My last conversation with him was on the trivial subject of sheets. I thought that the sheets were missing among the listed articles, but Jafar Pasha laughingly assured me that they were included. I found he was right, the sheets having been buried deep in a trunk.

When we came to Baghdad, he was prime minister, and he honored us with his presence at our first commencement. He also had been the first among the higher officials to call, and in any function of importance in our home, we could always depend upon Jafar Pasha's encouragement.

Next to King Faisal in our esteem and affection was this devoted leader. For a number of years he represented Iraq at the Court of St. James, where he was extremely popular. He used his spare time in London to study law and was admitted to the bar.

When the nation regained its normalcy after the Bekr Sidqi eruption, Jafar Pasha's body was lifted from his desert grave and brought to the beautiful mausoleum of King Faisal, whose trusted adviser he had been for many years. On the other hand, retribution came to Bekr Sidqi, whose heart was as hard as the rocks of his Kurdish mountains.

Next to Nuri Pasha al-Said, Yasin Pasha al-Hashimi was probably the most capable among the small group of Iraqi statesmen. He was usually the leader of the opposition in Parliament. He had a most pleasing voice, which together with his strong physique and natural poise made him a magnetic speaker. After his flight to Syria, he lived in Beirut for only a short time before his death. He is buried near the tomb of Saladin in Damascus and suffers by proximity to a hero with whom no one would compare him. Unfortunately, he had lost the confidence of the people of Iraq while he was premier because he was assuming too much power, and it was feared he was aiming at dictatorship.[3]

Whenever interesting travelers came to Baghdad, it was our pleasure to invite officials and people of worth to meet them. Then the samovar steamed, the living room took on a festive air as guests gathered, and conversation became animated. Yasin Pasha not infrequently was a guest at these special teas. One summer morning in July, I went to his office early, to avoid the heat of the day, to request his intercession in behalf of some of our boys who wanted to continue their studies abroad but were having trouble with their passports because of one of the many new regulations always popping up. When I left he walked with me to the door of the building and shook hands cordially. That good-bye was the last.

---

3. After Bekr Sidqi's assassination in 1936, the history of Iraq for the next few years is largely a record of army intervention in politics and of invitation by politicians for the army to intervene. This series of coups d'état almost paralyzed the government, paving the way for the pro-Nazi revolt of 1941, the subject of chapter 20 (Khadduri 1951).

Still another procession, another body for the beautiful mausoleum of King Faisal: his only son, the young Ghazi. A drive; a crash into an electric standard; death! The chronicle is brief; the ending final. Life's fitful fever—it was that for Ghazi—was over.

It was only four years before this tragedy that a reception was held for Ghazi's new queen, Aliyah, the daughter of King Ali, soon after their marriage. Only sixty invitations were issued for this formal affair. The royal ladies did not appear until all the guests had assembled. At the end of the room was a tiered dais, canopied with deep red velvet, on which chairs had been placed for the new queen, the queen mother, and the princesses. Over these chairs had been thrown velvet coverings embroidered in gold, while on the arms were laid yellow satin cushions. On the front drape of the canopy was a crown, the center of which was lighted by an electric bulb.

When the appearance of the royal ladies was announced, the guests who were standing in a semicircle around the room assumed an air of expectancy. The ladies came in the order of their rank, all wearing white satin dresses, the young queen's being the only one having a long train.

Whenever I had called on her mother, the daughters were never in the room, and I had thought of them as being very young girls. Queen Aliyah was young but had grown to be tall and slender, resembling her mother. This was her first public appearance as a grownup, and naturally she appeared shy, knowing full well that all eyes were on her. When each one of the royal ladies was in her place on the dais, the guests began to move. They passed in front of the ladies, curtsied to the queen, and then crossed a corridor into a room where refreshments were served.

I wondered then, as I have always wondered whenever I went to her receptions, what this girl thought of this homage. She had had some tutoring in her home, in English as well as in Arabic, though I could never induce her to speak to me in English. When a little son was born in the new Qasr al-Zuhur (Palace of Flowers), there was great rejoicing. "Guns and proclamations" announced the event. The son is now [1950] the king of Iraq, called King Faisal II. His uncle Abdul Ilah, King Ali's only son, acts as regent. The nephew and uncle are great friends and have had numberless pictures taken together.

King Ghazi died in the late evening of April 3, 1938. The whole next day crowds shuttled up and down Rashid Street, where all traffic was suspended. Student groups marched, then halted to hear someone extol Ghazi, then marched again. From different quarters of the city men formed as in the Muharram processions, beating their breasts as they walked. The tribes, among whom King Ghazi was very popular on account of his daring and reckless courage, came in large numbers to the city. Everywhere the drums were beating, and the drumbeats mingled with the wailing of the women. Strange indeed, that the death of this young king should occasion a reversion to the primitive at his funeral, something which was not displayed at any other royal burial.

And so they passed. At the mausoleum three mullahs read the Qur'an and offer prayers daily for the dead. A blind mullah prays daily for King Faisal I; another reads and repeats the prayers for King Ali, who also is buried there; the third reads and prays for the soul of King Ghazi. A good Muslim at any grave repeats the first sura of the Qur'an, known as the *fatiha*. At the mausoleum the mullah may repeat it for you. These prayers and readings please the angels who intercede for the soul of the dead. The mullah begins, "In the name of God, the Compassionate, the Merciful, King of the Day of Judgment. Thee do we worship, and to Thee do we cry for help."

18

THE MAGIC HORSE
AND THE MAGIC CARPET

Routes! Routes of migration, routes of armies, routes of travel, routes of trade; land routes, sea routes, and air routes girdling the earth like Ariel! Nowhere else in the world had I ever become so conscious of routes as in Iraq. Whether I was thinking of the ancient highways of the land or observing the opening of new ways of communication, my mind always stretched beyond the confines of Iraq. These new routes, the "new-old routes," passed across the land to countries near and far. Whether I willed it or not, living in Baghdad obliged me to become world-conscious, a devotee to geographies, atlases, and globes.

It was the reading of George Adam Smith's *Historical Geography of the Holy Land* that gave me my first sweep of the understanding of this part of the world. The book opened to me new and vast vistas. The author showed that Palestine and Syria in ancient times were a land bridge between two continents—Asia and Africa; between two civilizations—Western Asia and Egypt; and a bridge lying between two river basins of immense fertility. Then, my long residence in Baghdad made me realize that Mesopotamia, too, was an important land bridge; that from its earliest days it was a bridge between the East and the West, between Iran, India, and China on the one hand and the Mediterranean world on the other. Over these routes came and passed not only travelers and armies, but also streams of ideas and goods of trade.

Through the centuries, most of these trails and routes and highways disappeared. They were obliterated through centuries of change and turmoil. Yet, in our travels we must often have crossed and recrossed these forgotten routes, and sometimes, unknowingly, followed in their unmarked tracks. Some of these roads, I discovered, had lustrous and poetic names—names that were both appropriate and beautiful. Not only the names but also the routes as well haunted my mind and fired my imagination. These trunk roads swung across the Mesopotamian plain from the Persian Gulf to the Great Sea; from the plateau of Iran to the Aegean; from the various Islamic centers to the holy cities along the littoral of the Red Sea; and from the China Sea clear across the continent to the Mediterranean and Egypt. Thus, from the early Babylonian days through the five hundred years of Baghdad's position as the capital of an empire, world routes were crossing this ancient land. Mesopotamia was then as now on the crossroads of the world.

There were two ancient highways that particularly stirred my imagination: the celebrated Royal Road and the Golden Road to Samarkand. The Royal Road was a magnificent road in every way. It traversed almost the whole length of the land for a thousand years. Starting from Susa, the Persian capital, it swung through the valley of the Tigris and Euphrates, and then zigzagged through the mountain passes of the Anatolian plateau until it reached Sardis and Ephesus. The road was primarily built as a great postal road for the king's messengers.

Whenever I read about this road or had my mind dwell upon it, I imagined I was at one of the relay stations or post houses observing the world pass by. I watched with eager eyes the coming of the royal messengers and the caravans weaving in and out through the plain; and as they came and went, I dreamed of lands they came from and the goals they sought. From the great palace of the king at Susa couriers carrying royal mandates hastened on horseback, knowing that on the way at the relay stations, fresh mounts would be instantly ready to avoid any delay in forwarding the king's orders.

At these relay stations, I would also get the stirring news of the world—of battles, fresh revolts, imperial policies, disaster, scandal, crime, assassination. While the courier's mount was being changed and new food and fresh water were placed in his saddlebag, I could get a few scraps of news before he spurred his fresh horse to get to the next station. But for the more complete and detailed news, I had to rely upon the merchants of the caravans and other travelers who came along leisurely and unhurriedly. I might be fortunate also to see some of the great armies on the march, for over this highway marched the great armies of Darius, Xerxes, Alexander the Great, and the Roman, Parthian, and Sasanian generals with their armies. Maybe some travelers coming from the West had astounding and almost incredible news of a great artistic and intellectual center in Europe which they called Athenai.

But of all the roads of long ago, the Khorassan Road, or as it is more commonly called, the Golden Road to Samarkand, touched something within me that fails to find words. Perhaps I was hypnotized by the poetic name, which, if you pronounce it slowly and properly, goes trippingly on the tongue in poetic cadence with a measured order of successive short and long syllables: The-Gol-den-Road-to-Sam-ar-kand. Once I read that a certain orator or actor could speak the word "Mesopotamia" in such a way that it produced sadness to the point of tears, and then again, he could pronounce the word in such a way that it brought spontaneous smiles and laughter. You cannot do that with the poetic name "The Golden Road to Samarkand"; there is only one way of saying it and that is the musical, poetic way.

Not only the name but the road itself stirred my imagination. It led into vast and strange distances, into ancient lands with its frigid, monotonous, semiarid tablelands. At Samarkand the road continued as the Great North Road, which, in reality, was the great silk route that penetrated into the Far East. No road so leads the mind into space—out into vast distances of desert and grasslands and high mountains and into cities peopled with men of strange faiths, strange costumes, strange manners, strange rulers living in reckless splendor—as the Golden Road to Samarkand. When Baghdad was founded, the road started from the Khorasan gate of the Round City. Merchants traveled that long, long distance from China to Tyre and Sidon to have their silk dyed the royal purple, that precious dye once made from Murex shells, or to sell their silk together with ivory and jade to the merchants of western Asia.

Up and down, hither and yon, on the highway to Samarkand passed the splendor of the Tartar court and the Mongol hordes. Back and forth went ambassadors with their trains, merchants with their wares, and artisans who were sent here and there, according to the whim of sovereigns, for the purpose of embellishing their cities. On the road could be met weary captives, lamas from Tibet, Nestorian priests and missionaries, pilgrims visiting shrines, Chinese mandarins, Buddhist bonzes, Manchurian lords; and always the line of laden camels or donkeys with their ringing, tinkling bells, carrying their burdens east and west.

There were two other roads in this area that were once famous; both are often mentioned or alluded to in history and in the Bible. Both of them connected the valley of the Tigris with the Mediterranean. They were two entirely different routes: the one swung around the Fertile Crescent; the other moved more directly across the Syrian Desert. The one is known as the Syrian Road and the other as the Great Desert Way.

The Syrian Road was probably for a long time the only route to the Great Sea. It was much longer, about twice as long as the more direct way, but was preferred because it passed through a region where there were inhabitants, grasslands, and cultivated fields. Besides, there was no lack of water, especially where the caravans are long and where armies are on the march.

In the early days of the Abbassids, the road emerged from the Syrian gate of Mansur's Round City, Baghdad. Let us suppose a merchant had come all the way from China with silks to be dyed in Tyre or Sidon or merchandise to be sold in Syria and Egypt. He would enter the city through the Khorassan gate and leave from the Syrian gate. Or if goods were brought from the Persian Gulf, caravans would enter the Basrah gate and also emerge from the Syrian gate.

Over this route trekked Abraham when he went forth from Ur of the Chaldees and became a sojourner in the land of promise. The journey is clearly mapped out in the biblical account, following the familiar route around the Fertile Crescent. Through the millenniums innumerable caravans passed along here, as well as the armies of the Babylonians, the Assyrians, the Chaldeans, the Persians, and the Greeks, not to mention those of the Christian era. Today a railway traverses this entire arc-shaped area.

But it is the Great Desert Way, the direct route between Baghdad and Damascus by way of the Rutba Wells, that I know best. I do not need to depict it in imagination; I know it better than many other things. Thirteen times I traveled this monotonous and wearisome way and always in the blazing heat of summer except once. Each time my thoughts turned to the multitudes who had crossed it on camels or on foot in the exhausting and pitiless heat of summer or in the bitter and piercing cold of winter. The Great Desert Way evidently did not always follow the same trail. For a time it went around by way of Palmyra or Tadmur, still a wonder city in its ruins, in the days of Zenobia when the merchant princes of Palmyra had charge of the caravans that traveled between the Persian Gulf and the Mediterranean Sea.

It was this Great Desert Way that Isaiah presumably had in mind when he spoke to the released captives after the emancipation proclamation of Cyrus the Great. The Jewish exiles were now free to go back to Jerusalem from Babylon, but between them and the sacred hill of Zion was this arid desert with no food and no water, a barren waste with ravenous beasts. When the exiles came to Babylon, they were led and escorted by an army; now they had to make their way back solely by their own efforts. They were dejected, weak-kneed, and afraid to undertake this long and risky journey of six hundred miles and to endure the hardships and dangers they would necessarily have to encounter.

There is another desert road, which was once much used by the adherents of the Muslim faith, and which was reopened since we came to Iraq. It is the Great Pilgrim Road to Mecca and Medina. When the Round City was in existence, the caravans left from the Kufah Gate for the long, hard journey to the holy city of Mecca.

Both Harun al-Rashid and especially his wife, Zubaida, did much to alleviate the suffering of these "way-worn multitudes traveling in the great terrible wilderness" by digging wells and building rest houses along the road, placing them at such intervals that meals could be eaten in comfort and rest enjoyed in safety. Later these wells and cisterns on the Hajj Road caved in and were filled with sand, while the rest houses disappeared. But in Mecca and the nearby plain of Arafat, Zubaida's determined effort to quench the thirst of the weary pilgrims has, through all these centuries, kept her memory alive, as the pilgrims drinking at her fountains gratefully say, "God bless Zubaida" (Tschanz 2004, 2–11).

One of the tragic stories of history is the sudden disappearance of these famous roads that either started in the valley of the Tigris and the

Euphrates or passed through it. These highways which were once so useful, and which had caused Mesopotamia to be on the crossroads of the world, suddenly disappeared when the country was invaded and Baghdad sacked by Hulagu in 1258 AD. The country was devastated, and its great highways were destroyed. In fact, they as well as the canals were deliberately demolished by the Mongol hordes. Trade, travel, and communication with the outside world practically came to a standstill, and so it remained for centuries. Seldom did people travel, even within the country itself. The post houses which had been a boon to travelers in former times had disappeared, and the rapid postal service that had been in operation in the days of the kings, the khans, and the caliphs had come to naught.[1]

Suddenly, not by degrees, a change took place as though an Aladdin's lamp had been rubbed. Magic began to work, and to the astonishment of the world back to this land came once more the magic horse and the magic carpet, the means of easy and quick travel devised in the *Arabian Nights* tales. World communications as in the olden days was revived, and that in a world grown very much larger. Once more highways traversed the "old-new kingdoms." To these were added the railways and the airways. All these means of communication now link Iraq with a much bigger world than the ancients and the Abbassids ever dreamed of. Mesopotamia is once more a junction on the world routes. The story of how this came about is another Scheherazade tale.

The first of the old routes to be opened was the Great Desert Way. It occurred to two New Zealanders, the Nairn brothers, that it might be possible to connect Baghdad and Damascus by a regular automobile service for passengers and mail. This was an epoch-making idea and became a concrete venture in April 1923. The Nairn brothers summoned the magic horse to carry people over the trackless desert in an unbelievably short

---

1. The Crusading wars waged against the Muslim East during the two hundred years preceding the Mongol invasion also took their toll. Then came the Age of Explorations, from the fifteenth century on, when Western countries circumnavigated the globe along routes that bypassed the heartlands of the Islamic world. They returned to it in the eighteenth century and with full force when the Suez Canal was opened in the mid-nineteenth century, and when oil was discovered early in the twentieth.

time. In opening a regular service, they shortened the time to reach the Mediterranean from almost a month to twenty-four hours, now actually reduced to fourteen and half hours by special service.

The first time we crossed this desert, seven passenger automobiles were used, the open kind, and the minimum number of cars required for a convoy was three so as to be mutually helpful. Native companies soon began to compete with Nairn at lower rates, capturing the "lower bracket populace." The start from Baghdad in those first days of service was hectic. The baggage had to be strapped on the sides of the car, necessitating the climbing in and out the best one could. Provisions were stacked inside, and a watchful eye had to be kept on one's place lest there be no room for the feet and no room for an occasional change of position.

There were passports to be examined, the porters to be paid, all shouting at the same time for more *bakhsheesh;* and then when the car tuned up and it did seem that everything was in readiness for the journey, a number of other stops were made for trivial things which had been put off for the usual "tomorrow." I recall seeing a friend in another car whizzing past us on one of these starts in order to clear the bridge before it was opened for river traffic, something which we failed to do. The next morning at dawn, when all the cars had assembled at one place in the desert so that the drivers might have a little rest, I could not believe my eyes when I saw in the neighboring car this same friend whose advantageous start I thought had landed him in Damascus. There he was no farther than the "dilatory we." "Oh," I said to him, "I thought you were in London!"

We always crossed in midsummer for our brief vacation when the desert fairly sizzled, and returned in August when the withering heat almost annulled the gain of Lebanon's refreshing air. How hot it was and how long the day! I had strange sensations, a desire to knock that flaming sun out of the sky or force it down under the earth when it began to move toward the horizon. I was willing to resort to anything to rid the earth of this tormenter.

But when the sun had disappeared and the western sky was shot through with crimson streaks and the coolness of evening had come on, I more or less repented of my rash intentions. The desert in the twilight has, no matter what the day may have been, a beauty and fascination of its own. But this cool and delightful twilight was only for a few hours. Then it began to get really cold, and woe to those who had not provided themselves with wraps or blankets in these open cars. No matter how hot the day may have been, the night in the desert can become uncomfortably cold. As the driving went on all night, and I could get only a few winks of sleep over a bumpy road, and in a car where I had to sit stiff all the time, the cold was keenly felt.

Except for the brief periods of early spring and late fall, a person in this part of the world is always sun-conscious. The sun assumes an importance out of all proportion to life's general program. The year is largely spent in loving the sun and hating it; in seeking the sun and escaping from it; in basking in it and hiding from it; in speaking of its blessedness and rising in wrath at its cursedness; in suffering for lack of it and suffering because of it.

Added to these discomforts were the dust and the dirt. I looked gray like the desert, and thick layers of grime stuck to my sweaty skin. All I could think of now was a bathtub in a Damascus hotel where I could wash this deposit of desert dirt into the city sewer. I grew weary, too, of constantly bolstering myself lest a sudden stretch of rough road should send me rocketing through the roof of the car. Indeed, I once was jolted through the roof and thought my face was disfigured for life until I felt it with my hands and found to my infinite relief that it was still all there, but it took an American osteopath to put my head back to where it belonged.

Some years after the desert route was opened, busses took the place of automobiles. Later Nairn put on semi-trailer caravan coaches, described as desert trains. In these roomy, air-conditioned coaches one travels deluxe in almost Pullman comfort, and the desert at all seasons can really be enjoyed: the long ranges of the eye, the green birds, the shimmering mirage, the illusory dark forest that seems to close in at night, the wondrous star-sown sky, the weighty stillness.

But to travel in these deluxe coaches is more or less conventional, and differs little from travel in America, another example of the standardization of the world. If you want amusing incidents and local color, you will find these in the native busses. The passengers carry their own food, usually in large baskets, enough for a week. In summer each basket is surmounted by a large "American watermelon." As the baskets are too big for the racks, they encumber the aisle. In the front part of the bus is a faucet which taps ice water as long as it lasts. Children begin early to fall over the baskets, from which roll the melons, in order to reach the faucet, carrying a drink to each member of the family and never failing to slop water on those who happen to occupy the inner seats. The faucet is steadily engaged until the real thirst begins in the afternoon, when, to the dismay of all, the supply is exhausted.

In the many times I crossed the desert, I never lost interest in three places along the way. The one was Ramadi, along the Euphrates, where we directly turned west, leaving all greenness behind. Here some time had to be consumed in custom and passport formalities. Looking down from a balcony into a court, where in the earlier days the automobiles were parked, I was endlessly amused by the "doings" of all kinds of people. Men under suspicion for some reason sweated and buttonholed officials, gesticulating wildly. On one of the trips into Iraq some men who were suspected of being diamond smugglers had their suitcases emptied unceremoniously on the ground, and the contents clawed through and scattered. These men had specialized in winter underwear, the last thing to be thought of on that day when the thermometer in the shade had registered 112 degrees. In dripping sweat they patiently gathered, lifted, folded, and meekly replaced their belongings in their suitcases.

Equidistant from Baghdad and Damascus are the Rutbah Wells, where the Iraq government had built a fort in which is a police post, radio station, post office, rest house, and other offices. Here the automobiles always stop. Late in the evening or in the night, I eagerly scanned the horizon for the red light raised high above the walled enclosure, a beacon light that heartens the traveler. Out in this vast desert, more than 250 miles from either end of the road, surrounded by desolation, are these oil wells. Here travelers can clean up a bit, eat a good meal, drink tea, lounge in Morris chairs, hear the victrola records, listen to the radio, and read the recent newspapers and magazines.

We always said that it was worth crossing the desert just to be in Damascus, with its fifty thousand acres of gardens, its background of ruddy mountains, its gushing fountains, and the tree-bordered Barada

River flowing through the city. Damascus to the desert traveler is now, as it always has been, paradise. Should you ask me to which city in my travels I should like to return, I think I should answer, "Damascus." I don't exactly know why.

Seventeen years after the Nairn brothers had opened the desert route, a railroad was opened or rather completed, which, if it had not taken place in wartime, would have made exciting international news. This was the Berlin to Baghdad Railway. No railroad has owed so much to its name; none has attracted more attention; none has given more scope to the imagination; none ever exhausted more power and resources of diplomacy; none provoked greater struggle for control; and none had been a greater menace to the world than this Berlin to Baghdad Railway.

In the local English newspaper in Baghdad, there appeared on the second page, on July 18, 1940, the following headline:

The Baghdad Railway
First Train Leaves for the Bosphorus

A railroad that plagued the chancelleries of Europe for years was eventually completed and started to operate with no more fanfare than an article in the newspaper with that simple headline, not even on the front page! As General Allenby had walked into Jerusalem very simply, and as General Maude had entered Baghdad quietly, so this famous railway that makes possible the running of trains from Baghdad to Istanbul, and from there to the capitals of Europe, opened without even a simple ceremony.[2] The intention was to have a little ceremony at Mosul, but even this was waived because of the war.

2. Research done after Ida Staudt wrote her memoir shows that General Allenby's entry into Jerusalem had caused a major stir. To Allenby himself is attributed the boast as he entered Jerusalem: "Today ended the Crusades." Even if this attribution were anecdotal, the capture of Jerusalem in 1917 was given a "crusading color." The *Times of London* commented, "The deliverance of Jerusalem is a most memorable event in the history of Christendom." Britain's Foreign Office wondered why King Hussein, the sharif of Mecca, had not sent his congratulations for the British liberation of Jerusalem (Tibawi 1967, 84–85).

I watched the train pull out from the Baghdad station that was to run without a change to Istanbul. It may have meant less to others, but it meant much to me. Some years before, I sat for a few minutes in a coach of this historic railway at Mersina in Turkey just before the train started, and for no other reason than to have the satisfaction of having been on it. I rode more than once on the German-built stretch of seventy-five miles between Baghdad and Samarra. I had traveled on the road that had been completed from Aleppo to Istanbul; I was thrilled when I saw the train start on its virgin run. When the engine puffed to pull after it the string of cars, my heart began to beat just a little faster. When anyone on my visits to America asked me whether I knew anything of the magic carpet, I replied, "Yes, I have traveled on it, and that shortly after coming to Baghdad."

One day John Randolph, the American consul, came to the house and said that Larry Rue, of the *Chicago Tribune,* had engaged a twelve-passenger Imperial Airways plane, the only kind then available, to fly to Khanaqin the following day. Seven seats were put at the disposal of the consul and we occupied two. Larry Rue was flying to Kabul to get a firsthand story for his paper about Amanullah, king of Afghanistan, who had abdicated because of a revolt against his attempt to Westernize his subjects.[3]

Larry Rue certainly had made no special effort to impress the Afghans by his appearance. He wore the baggiest trousers and the flattest derby I had ever seen, and his ample pockets bulged with the oranges with which I had filled them. The plane took him only to the Iranian border, where another plane was waiting to fly him to Kabul; we returned as we had come. If riding on the magic carpet was like riding on this plane, then it was easy going. I wondered whether he whose imagination created this

---

3. Emir Amanullah founded the Afghan monarchy in 1926. He encouraged a number of reforms, such as coeducational schools, and allowed women to remove their veil, moves that offended the conservatives and tribal leaders. After his abdication, Afghanistan remained a monarchy; its last king, Muhammad Zahir Shah, ruled for forty years (1933–73). The country then became a republic; its tribal divisions, its invasion by Soviet Russia in 1979, and a ruined economy eventually led to the ultraconservative Taliban takeover. The Taliban were helped by Bin Laden and his followers, and both were aided and incited by the United States in their successful war against the Soviets.

swift way of travel ever dreamed of how it would feel up in the air, no sensation of movement and so great a sense of freedom from bounds in the unbounded space.

Anyone living in Baghdad between the two world wars could not help becoming air-minded and, through it, world-minded. Many international air routes passed through Iraq. By virtue of her geographical position, Iraq soon became an air-junction for services to many nations. It is recorded that the month before World War II broke out more than 250 planes were handled at the airports of Iraq.

This necessitated the building of up-to-date airports with facilities for landing, unloading, and refueling. The first airport was established in Baghdad, modeled after Croydon in London. Maurice Hindus, who had certainly seen many airports, was so impressed with the comfort and luxury of this one that he spoke of it in his latest book as one of the finest in the world. What would he say of the more elaborate and luxurious one in Basrah, which is designed for both seaplanes and airplanes, and which has an air-conditioned hotel as a part of it?

Because Iraq stands astride the airways of the world, the air routes of the world cross it as naturally as the world highways had crossed Mesopotamia in the days gone by. But with the outbreak of World War II, civil aviation practically ceased; the remarkably rapid growth of air communication was checked. It had been prophesied that the day would come when Baghdad, and to a lesser extent Basrah, would be among the busiest airports in the world. The airplane, like the railroad and the motor vehicle, have been vital factors in the development of the country, and these have hurled and plunged Iraq from obscurity, remoteness, and isolation into the existing world confusion.

19

THE STORY OF OIL

Three letters of the alphabet spell the little word *oil,* which, like the little word *atom,* is charged with tremendous power, both for good and for evil. Oil has shaped and shapes national and international policies. It causes plans and intrigues to move as does that dark and thick and oily flow. It brings about international complications and is politically explosive. That is one side of oil. That it is the lifeblood of industry and a vital force in civilization is the other side. In no small way does it contribute to a nation's prosperity and a nation's influence in the world.

The rich oil fields of Iraq are a blessing both to Iraq and to the world; but there is also the other side, a very shady side. Iraq would certainly confirm the statement that her oil fields have not been an unmixed blessing. Oil and strategy may not be synonymous, but, as it has been observed, they are inseparable, at least so far as Iraq and the Middle East are concerned. Oil and strategic location equal power, and this expresses the importance of Iraq in international affairs. It was this background of oil that invariably determined the nature of the treaties in which Iraq was involved. From the Paris Peace Conference that followed World War I to the later treaties pertaining to Iraq, we detect the smell of oil.

It is Iraq's oil that has made her one of the vital areas from any point of view, not only in the Middle East but in the world as well. The story of oil in Iraq is often stranger than fiction and equally engrossing. The tale is an epic in a major key.

My first contacts with oil, and men connected with oil, were not shadowed by any thoughts of darkling scheming either by nations or by men, or by the "ups and downs" of international oil politics. On the contrary, we met those delightful and interesting people who were sent to Iraq to prospect for oil, to develop the oil industry, and to manage the oil business. These people had come from different countries. The first to arrive on the field were business executives, who were all British; then came the geologists, who were an international group; and lastly came the drillers and welders, who were Americans.

Having fallen into the English custom of four o'clock tea, we met most of these men around the tea tray, where in their relaxed state and under the stimulus of tea, we learned so much about oil that I fell in heartily with Reginald Hine's encomium of tea. He said, "There is black magic in tea . . . I shall have much to say of this blessed beverage which has neither the arrogance of wine, nor the self-consciousness of coffee, nor the simpering innocence of cocoa. If tea can make the most taciturn Quaker talk, what will it do to an ordinary conversable human being? Blessed be tea whose gracious influence can so wondrously enliven the intellect and stimulate the flow of soul. For my part I am constantly declaring that the day does not begin till tea time. Sydney Smith gave public thanks to Almighty God that he had not been born into the world 'before the age of tea!'"

This comment on tea would have been incomprehensible to us had not the British inducted us into this afternoon ritual so yielding in returns. Besides, not a little of my information in regard to the production and distribution of oil I learned by reading the essays on oil which some of our students yearly wrote in a prize competition. For a number of years a group of students were annually sent to the oil fields, where as guests of the Iraq Petroleum Company, they saw and had explained to them matters pertaining to oil. But the most satisfactory introduction into the mystery of the knowledge of oil came to us when we were the guests of the manager of the company in the oil fields. We spent two days on the field not only enjoying his hospitality but also seeing things with our own eyes as we were driven around in his car and officially guided. We visited the stores and laboratories and saw the actual drilling.

For a number of years our host had been our neighbor in Baghdad. Only a thin wall, lower than the roof, separated the court of the Baghdad offices of the company from the court of our building. I frequently could tell what was going on on the manager's side, and he certainly knew more of what was going on on our side. Occasionally we were teased about one of the hymns sung at the morning assembly of the school, "Work, for the Night Is Coming." Meeting me, the manager would jokingly say, "It is very important for us that you sing that hymn more regularly; it peps us up; not hearing it this morning, we slumped. Too bad!" So in order to stimulate the oil industry as well as to encourage the boys in their efforts to get an education, the school often sang "Work, for the Night Is Coming."

Thus, gradually we became thoroughly oil-conscious. We learned that it is an established fact that the center of gravity of world oil had shifted to the area of the Persian Gulf. The greatest and richest reserve area of oil in the world lies in a triangle where one angle is in the Russian Caucasus, another in southern Iran, and the third in Saudi Arabia. In the middle of this triangle is oil-soaked Iraq. It is indeed oil-soaked, for beneath its surface are not only pools of oil, but a continuous sea of oil, or more accurately, a limestone reservoir rock whose pores are filled with it. Here, then, within this triangle are the world's richest oil deposits, and here, too, on the Shatt al-Arab near the Persian Gulf, is the second largest refining center in the world.

While others were digging in the ground for oil, I dug into books to discover who it was that drew attention to the fact that there were valuable oil deposits in Mesopotamia. In my digging I came across a pamphlet that was written during World War I by an Englishman who was a missionary in the land, entitled *Mesopotamia: The Key to the Future.* The pamphlet was for British consumption, but the information it contained became world knowledge.

The pamphlet describes how the author, on coming down the Tigris from Mosul, beheld a stream of oil gushing out of the bank of the river. This to him was evidence that large deposits of oil were beneath Iraq's soil. The pamphlet was a forceful presentation of the geographical position and the natural resources of the land. The author advocated that this oil should be exploited. Thereupon Great Britain lost no time to dig herself in, despite protests from abroad and from Iraq herself. This establishment of Britain's control over the oil fields in Mesopotamia was looked upon by the imperialistic leaders of Great Britain as one of the greatest achievements of the First World War.

Britain soon found that she could not gobble up all the oil herself. Hungry oil nations were at her heels, demanding a share in the bonanza.

France was the first to press her claims. She forced herself into the picture so strongly that the San Remo agreement provided for French participation. Speedily the British government promised to place at the disposal of the French government a 25 percent share in the company, this being the confiscated German interest.

America, too, came into the picture. The exclusive nature of the agreement aroused strong American objections. A vigorous note was sent by the State Department, followed by another, warning that the San Remo agreement would result in a grave infringement of the mandate principle. In reply, America got a real stab, one she possibly deserved for not having entered the League of Nations. The British answered that since the United States was not a member of the League, she should not interfere in mandate questions.

In spite of this snub, America did not cease her insistence upon her open-door policy. The result was that Sir John Cadman, who was the technical adviser of the Anglo-Persian Oil Company, was obliged to make two trips to America to arrange for some agreement that would satisfy American insistence to be included in this company. In consequence of these visits, the Anglo-Persian Oil Company handed over to Standard Oil and other American interests one-half of her 50 percent holdings in the Turkish Petroleum Company.

The Turkish Petroleum Company, which later took the name of the Iraq Petroleum Company, became an international combination of British, American, Dutch, and French oil companies, each holding a 25 percent interest; or to be more exact, a 23.75 percent share, since a 5 percent holding was retained by the oil magnate Calouste Gulbenkian.[1] The Iraq government granted to the company a seventy-five year concession to exploit the oil resources in the Mosul and Baghdad area.

1. According to a 1912 British document at the India Office (London), Gulbenkian, an Armenian, was a financial agent of the Turkish government in London. He and Sassoon Haskel were reported as two of the most conspicuous promoters of an Iraqi Concessions Syndicate formed "to obtain as large a control over irrigation, railways, and navigation in Mesopotamia, as circumstances admit" (Great Britain 1912).

From the geologists I learned that when the concession was given to the Iraq Petroleum Company to exploit the oil, it was stipulated that the company could select within a certain time a number of square blocks or areas from which the oil might be taken, the idea being that there would be, as at most places where oil is extracted, pools of oil here and there. But it was soon discovered that there were no scattered pools but a continuous area of oil. There were not only riches here but "unsearchable riches."

This necessitated the making of certain revisions in the stipulations of the former concession. The Iraq government, learning that it was in possession of "unsearchable riches," naturally demanded a higher royalty. The "conversations" between the company and the government were long and tedious, and at the last meeting the representatives of both sides sat up in the Royal Palace until the early hours of the morning. The agreement that was finally reached provided that the company's concessions were to be confined to the entire area between the Tigris and the Iranian border; that a pipeline carrying not less than three million tons a year should be built to the Mediterranean; and that the company should pay to the Iraq government an annual sum of 400,000 pounds in gold.

After the Iraq Petroleum Company was organized and had received its concession, the history of the production of oil passed through certain stages. First came the work of the surface geologists. Their purpose was to locate the probable oil beds and to determine where wells should be drilled. These were memorable days for us. Their visits we prized in many ways. Their work obliged them to live Bedouin fashion in a tent. But when they came to Baghdad and were present at a dinner party, I had the impression that they had never known anything else than dinner-dress occasions. On the field they had to carry with them supplies of canned goods; once when the head geologist left for America, he presented to us his surplus stock, which we received as manna from heaven, a veritable windfall.

It was an American geologist, a professor of a state university, who located the first well that yielded oil. He related his experience to us while drinking tea. He examined a terrain that to him looked promising, having a rather unusual rock formation. He said, "Drill here." There was sometimes international jealousy, and in this instance a geologist of another nationality spoke up: "If you drill here you won't find a spoonful of oil." The American said, "Drill here." They drilled. All of a sudden, after a certain depth was reached, a powerful column of oil shot into the air. It was the great Baba Gurgur well, possibly the largest of the wells drilled in the Kirkuk area.

The Baba Gurgur "gusher" spouted out fifty thousand tons of oil before it could be capped. Three lives were lost, and Baghdad was alarmed for a river of oil began to flow toward the Tigris. Should this oil have reached the river, it would have contaminated Baghdad's only water supply and would have brought untold suffering. For a number of days the Baba Gurgur spouted its oil heavenward like a geyser and defied man and beast to come near it. Yet this well, which wasted so much precious oil and brought so much terror to the hearts of men, still had left in it, after it was under control, enough oil to pay for the pipeline, which cost ten million pounds and which "monopolized the energies of thousands of men."

After the oil reservoir was located through the Baba Gurgur well, a number of American drillers, mostly from California, arrived, and comfortable houses were especially erected for them. I was so impressed by the way these Americans lived. It was when my husband and I were the guests of the manager of the company that one morning we shared a breakfast with some of the drillers. That breakfast crowned the sightseeing. How were they able to bring together such delicacies? Cans and cartons were opened, hot cakes were flapped on our plates, syrup and honey flowed freely; and during the meal, at least, we wished we were in the employ of the oil company.

The initiative and ingenuity they displayed, in diverting some of the oil to heat their unheated houses during the winter, so contrasted with the inertia of the millions who for millenniums have suffered the cold without anyone concocting a method of relief, that they seemed creatures from another very much more advanced planet.

The management and business side of this international company was British, while the technical men were Americans; being thrown closely together, Americans and Britishers had opportunity to do a great deal of talking. I was told that the American Revolution was fought over again many times on the Kirkuk oil fields. The bookshop in Baghdad did a thriving business importing and selling histories to verify assertions made on both sides.

Near the Baba Gurgur well, we saw the Everlasting Fires, already mentioned by Marco Polo in the thirteenth century. The fire is perpetual, and for ages it has been burning unceasingly. In vain have men tried to extinguish the flames. This fiery furnace is in a little hollow on the arid foothills from which natural gas escapes to the surface, emitting a blue, lambent flame. There is nothing miraculous about it, though it is a singular curiosity in nature. Many have come from far and wide, as we did, to see this strange phenomenon. Some say that this is the "burning fiery furnace" of the Book of Daniel, in which Shadrack, Meshach, and Abednego walked unscathed because the Lord was with them. Some, too, have thought that the fire-worship which spread over Persia may have originated in this place, or, what is more probable, that it furnished the perpetual fire for a Zoroastrian temple here in ancient times.

We walked to a primitive refinery which refined the oil that seeped out of the earth nearby; a refinery which had been monopolized by the same family for generations. The seepage collects in a well about twenty feet deep and is reached by descending the most villainous steps that ever snared men to perdition. Watching men go up and down, I expected any minute one would slip and be drowned in the pool of oil; but the awful thing never happened while I was looking on, and never did happen, we were told. This primitive method of securing and refining oil stands over against the highly mechanized oil industry around it. Nothing so visualizes the differences in Iraq between the past and the present and contrasts the old and the new, as this source of oil with its crude refinery and very limited production, on the one hand, and the modern installations to meet world demands, on the other.

Passing the oil fields one time, I noticed that a huge plant had been erected. As it had silver pipes and high cylindrical tanks and other receptacles for oil, glittering in the sun, I took it for granted that it was a refinery. I was mistaken; it was a stabilization plant. This plant does not separate the crude oil into its constituent parts like lamp oil, gasoline, lubricants, and various by-products. It eliminates the hydrogen sulfide and other noxious substances and delivers the "sweet" crude oil to the pipelines, through which it is then easily pumped. Because of this uniformity, the value of the crude oil is increased: it is made suitable for the diesel engine and is also more readily refined.

As the oil business steadily moved forward, the laying of the pipeline across the desert to the Mediterranean was the next step to be undertaken. While the construction of this important outlet for the crude oil was under consideration, friction arose between England and France on the question of the terminus of the line. Shall it be Tripoli in Lebanon or Haifa in Palestine?

The cheaper, shorter, and easier route would be from Kirkuk to Tripoli, and the company most likely would have chosen this had not international politics entered into the problem. France was the mandatory power for Lebanon and Syria and urged the port of Tripoli as an important factor in her defense. England and Iraq favored the less desirable route to Haifa. There was an impasse—neither side budged. The work of producing the oil was held up; the interest on the capital invested continued; and the royalties to the Iraqi government had to be paid whether oil was sold or not.

Eventually, Sir John Cadman, then chairman of the Iraq Petroleum Company, found a way out of the dilemma. Two pipelines were proposed, the one to reach the Mediterranean at Tripoli and the other at Haifa, both to carry an equal amount of oil. With this arrangement agreeable to both parties, the laying of the pipeline began, at a cost practically double in labor and materials. The total length of both lines was to be 1,150 miles.

Nonetheless, it has turned out to be a statesmanlike decision, for history has already shown the wisdom of it. When the pro-German Vichy French in Syria opposed the British during World War II, the flow of oil was cut off from Tripoli, where it could have been advantageously used by the Axis powers; the oil was allowed to flow to Haifa where the Allies could make use of it. Again, more recently, the oil was not allowed to move through the pipeline to Haifa because of the Palestinian situation, whereas it was allowed to flow freely and unhampered to Tripoli.

The difficulties of building the pipelines and the enormities of the task became very real and concrete to me, for most of the area over which the oil is carried I had occasionally traversed. I could fully apprehend the utter daring of the project. Railway facilities were almost null; there were hardly

any roads; most of the country was desert, without water, without culti-
vating, and without habitation save wandering tribes. Everything had to
be conveyed by trucks, from machinery and supplies to water and food,
for the six thousand men employed on the pipeline construction. Besides,
four rivers had to be crossed.

The formal opening of this pipeline, which started the flow of oil from
Kirkuk to the Mediterranean, was a significant event in the history of Iraq;
it was fraught with consequences which none attending the ceremony
foresaw or faintly surmised. The ceremony took place on January 14, 1935.
In itself it was simple: in the engine room of the pump house, after brief
talks were given by distinguished guests, King Ghazi opened the valve
of a container charged with air; within a second or two after it had been
opened, it started the great engines to which the pumps were coupled and
the oil began to flow, to flow westward in two invisible channels carrying
5,500 tons to Haifa and the same quantity to Tripoli. This flow had to be
visualized by the guests for not a drop of oil was seen by anyone in the
pump room.

At the opening ceremony of the pipeline, King Ghazi said, "I pray that
this unique project may bring peace and prosperity to all concerned, that
it may be of lasting benefit to mankind and that, with the help of God, it
will unite people in the spirit of brotherhood and security and be a real
agent in the creation of peace among the nations of the world." Alas! The
Iraq oil did not usher in this millennium of brotherhood and peace, and
oil never will as long as men's hearts are still brutishly selfish and nations
selfishly greedy.

Oil was a commodity so coveted that nations were willing to stake
much, even honor, if that word is still current, to possess it. Iraq was sitting, as it were, on a volcano. She was soon to have trouble. In the late
1930s Germany would begin nazifying Iraq in her desperate effort to get
control of the rich oil fields, which she would desperately need in times of
war. (For more on Nazi Germany's involvement in the affairs of Iraq, see
the next chapter.)

The pipeline which carried the first oil to the Mediterranean was only
a twelve-inch affair. The American welders jokingly called it "macaroni."
Because it was not adequate for the large oil deposits in the center of the oil

triangle, a sixteen-inch pipeline was later built, terminating also in Haifa and Tripoli. I wonder what name the American welders have given to this. I should not be surprised if they would call it "the tunnel." And what more shall I say? For the time would fail me if I told of the Mosul Oil Company and the Basrah Oil Company that have concessions to exploit the oil west of the Tigris.

My last touch with the Iraq Petroleum Company was upon my last return from America to Baghdad, in 1943. This was toward the latter part of World War II, when as a guest of the company, I traveled from Haifa to Baghdad. Not having had time in America to secure a French visa to travel through Syria, I tried to secure one at Haifa; but when I was told that I had to wait for days, possibly two weeks, before a simple transit visa would be authorized, I decided to outwit the French—and indeed I did.

While staying at the German hospice in Haifa, where, ironically, nearly all the guests were Britishers, I learned from one of them that the Iraq Petroleum Company had a weekly bus to the oil fields. I hastily inquired at the office only to be told that the bus had left that morning. Fortunately, something better was offered. The next morning I was sitting in a Buick car belonging to the company, headed for Baghdad via Transjordan. I bypassed Syria; I bypassed the French! I had rubbed again an Aladdin's lamp, and my wish was fulfilled. Never had I crossed the desert in greater comfort and ease than in the car of the Iraq Petroleum Company, and what is more, at no other time gratuitously.

The car moved along the pipeline, stopping at the pumping stations. At these stations, we—an employee of the company, his wife, and I—rested, had our meals, and stopped for the night. The fine metaled road, the telephone line, and the pipeline kept nearly parallel. The automobile road through Transjordan was excellent, and with my eyes closed I could have told when we had crossed into Iraq by the feel of the road and the jolts over the Irish bridges.

In this deluxe traveling, we scorned night driving. We always stopped at a pumping station, where we had good meals and enjoyed the spacious, steam-heated bedrooms with private baths. We appeared at dinner, not in evening clothes but spruced up, ready for congenial companionship either in a private home before a bright fireplace or in a social room of the guest house. Here we had books, magazines, comfortable chairs, and all the amenities of life in these desert pumping stations.

What a contrast between the way I had traveled across the desert the first time and this last time! What unbelievable changes had taken place! When later my big, unwieldy trunk, which had to be carried across the desert in a truck, was delivered at our door in Baghdad, my gratitude to the Iraq Petroleum Company was brought to the point of speechlessness.

I wish I liked the British policy as well as I liked the Britishers at the pumping stations—so hospitable, so friendly, so generous. In a give-and-take spirit, we showed up to each other our nations' faults in the evening in front of the fireplaces. How kind and helpful they were along the way, and how superlatively kind to have allowed me a seat in a car of the company. I vowed to spend my vacations with them, selecting the winter as the time, for then I could revel in the warmth of oil-heated houses, a thing I prayed for through every January and February while living in Baghdad. It was a comfort we were deprived of even though we were living on a "sea of oil."

The story of oil in Iraq—from the first intimations that oil in large quantities was here, through the search for it, to the measures to control it and the flow of it to the tankers in the harbors of Haifa and Tripoli—is an epic story that should be classified under the heroic. It is an achievement that should be included in the tales of a modern *Arabian Nights.*

20

A Nazi-Inspired Revolt, 1941

Crossing Faisal Bridge one morning, an automobile stopped at my side, and a friendly voice invited me to share the car. It was the wife of Herr Doctor Grobba, the German minister to Iraq. Incidentally while conversing, she made some reference to her husband, and this gave her an occasion to say, "My husband is the most popular man in Baghdad." I did not disagree with her, and no one else would have questioned her statement. He overtopped and outshone every other diplomat in Iraq. He knew how to win people and how to stay in the spotlight. He belonged to that group of men occupying key positions all over the world who by their suavity and friendly patronage ingratiated themselves into the very core of the life of the people.

Herr Grobba was the outstanding agent in Goebbel's espionage network in the Middle East. Through his untiring efforts he caused most of the minds of Iraq to become infected with Hitler's madness. For six or more years he kept the propaganda machine going day and night. His house was constantly thrown open to social functions, and he entertained lavishly. He appeared at most of the public affairs, even at our school plays; with his gold and his promises he was generous. He saw to it that his compatriots in the land became aggressive missionaries for the Nazi cause, and the literature they left with me was voluminous and attractive.

One evening in Baghdad, we saw the house in which dwelt, openly, unmolested, and in state, the grand mufti of Jerusalem, Haji Amin al-Hussaini, brilliantly lighted and full of people as if for a special occasion. It was not a special occasion but a nightly occurrence, we were told. "Who attends these conclaves?" I innocently asked. The answer was "The mufti's house has become a rendezvous for Nazi sympathizers and anti-Britishers."

218

The mufti, after his escape from Palestine and Syria, came to Baghdad, where he was allowed to live freely in a house once occupied by Jafar Pasha al-Askeri. At this time there had also come to Baghdad a large number of inflated and bigoted nationalists from Palestine and Syria, who either received subsidies from the mufti himself, who was generously aided financially, or who were employed as teachers in the schools of Iraq or given other posts in the government. Both the mufti and his satellites were received as heroes and given full freedom of movement and speech and the best of good treatment. After the unsuccessful revolt against the British, the mufti fled Palestine to Iran, where he was in hiding. General Wavell offered a reward of 25,000 pounds for his capture. I was dazed; in Baghdad he could have been seized for nothing.

Passing the coffee shops one evening at seven o'clock, I saw something unusual. Not only were the coffee shops crowded, but people were standing outside, overflowing into the street, and all were listening eagerly. I thought possibly the prime minister, or some other important official, was giving a message to the people. But when on another night there was a recurrence of this, I became curious and asked what was going on. My informant told me that the men were listening to a radio broadcast from Berlin, and that the broadcast was given by an Iraqi citizen, Yunis al-Bahri, formerly the editor of a newspaper in Mosul. While traveling in Europe, he wrote a series of inflaming articles for his paper, with the result that the paper was suppressed, and he was forbidden to return to Iraq. Hitler then picked him up to broadcast to the Arab world from Germany, which he did daily.

In his radio talks he usually spoke directly to the Iraqis, many of whom knew him personally, and he did this with vehemence and fierceness. Nothing was more pernicious to the Arab mind than his colossal and fantastic lies, his frightful invectives against the Jews, and the promise to the Arabs of an Eldorado when the Germans come. He took a special delight in meticulously and maliciously relating the terrorism in Europe and the Nazi atrocities against the Jews. So menacing were these radio utterances of his to which the coffee shop crowd listened every evening that the Iraq government, before a Nazi-inspired ministry was in power, tried to intercept them and to jam Berlin at the local station.

There were other ways by which the people were won over into the German camp. All kinds of promises were made, and these were accepted as gospel truth. Bribery was offered on a large scale and many succumbed to the glittering gold. Medals were awarded under the pretext that they were for special services to Iraq, whereas, in reality, they were for services to the German cause. Students were induced to go to Germany to receive an education, so that when they returned they would be key men for the Nazi regime. Notables were invited to visit Germany, where they were generously entertained. German "tourists" offered to teach the German language in schools and privately. In some mysterious way certain local societies became Nazi clubs.

Looking back over those years, I wonder how it was possible so thoroughly to change the thinking of the people when the British were there. Nothing went on in the land that the British Intelligence Department did not know. The British often speak of taking a "long-range view." What was the "long-range view" in regard to this German propaganda that fashioned the inexplicable British policy? At any rate, it went on full blast and with brazen openness until after the May Revolution in 1941.

This well-planned Nazification of Iraq was bound to bear fruit, and it certainly did. The stage was being set for the German occupation of the land, both in what was happening in Iraq and also in what was going on outside of it. After a year and a half of fierce fighting between the Axis powers and the Allies in World War II, the situation became threatening for Iraq. The Axis powers were pounding at the gates of Egypt in the south; in the north they were trying to get across the Caucasus; in the west severe fighting was going on on the island of Crete.

One just needed to look at a map to know what might happen any day. If Crete fell, the Axis powers would be free to move on to Iraq. To Iraq they wanted to come for a double purpose: to close the pincer movement between North Africa and Russia and to get control of the Iraq oil fields. Germany must have said something like this to the Nazi element in Iraq: "You start to fight against the British, get the country into a mess, and as soon as we have wiped the British from Crete, we shall come to your assistance." Alas for Hitler's timetable! It took longer to dislodge the British forces in Crete than was calculated, and the promised aid of the Axis powers never came.

Inside Iraq a storm was brewing; its first mutterings were heard toward the end of January in 1941 when a few members of the cabinet who were pro-British resigned. Among them was Nuri al-Said, the minister of Foreign Affairs. Shortly after his resignation, I saw Nuri Pasha at a dinner party and made light of his ample leisure, asking him to use his time in some service for the school, to which he gave laughing assent.

A rather exciting announcement made at the time was that Sir Kinahan Cornwallis, who for fourteen years had been connected with the Ministry of the Interior, was returning to Baghdad to be the British ambassador. He knew almost everything about Iraq and its people that is of value to a man in public life. He was versed in the "ins and outs" of Mesopotamia, and personally knew its key men, their temper and character. He was intimately acquainted with the tribal sheikhs, many of whom he had himself appointed. Sir Kinahan was a man held in fear in the land, and the Nazi element did not want him. Some even openly declared that they hoped something would happen to him before he reached Baghdad. But it didn't; he arrived. Revealing also was the news item that he was met at the airport by some friends, and not the customary news item that he had been met by the prime minister, ministers of state, and other high officials.

More alarming was that the Iraqi army was under the command of four generals, known as the "Golden Square," who were notoriously pro-Nazi. The army, through a coup d'état, put Rashid Ali al-Gailani back again into the office of prime minister after he had been out of office for a few months and placed the ultimate power and sovereignty of the government in the army, with the four generals in the saddle.

The appointment of a premier by the army needed a whitewash of constitutionality. On the morning of April 10, 1941, I woke up to find walls placarded with posters calling for a meeting of Parliament at twelve o'clock for the purpose of electing a regent. The atmosphere became tense; many shops and business houses closed their doors for the day, and students in the schools welcomed the occasion for another holiday. What happened was succinctly stated in the "Stop Press" of the English newspaper of that day:

Iraq Parliament—New Regent Elected

They voted for the dismissal of Amir Abdul Ilah from the regency, and elected H. H. Sharif Sharaf as regent until King Faisal II attained majority. The vote was unanimous. Sharif Sharaf must have rubbed his eyes at this sudden, unexpected, and unforeseen hoist—the Wheel of Fortune having taken him on a hasty spurt upward. It is true that he was related to the royal family, but he had lived simply and humbly; and be it said to his credit, he refused to exchange his house for a palace. Perhaps, back in his mind was the thought that the honor would not be lasting enough to be worth the bother of moving. The king's majority, it is true, was a long way off, but Sharif Sharaf was seventy years old and times were uncertain.

What was going on behind the scenes in the days that followed not many knew, but there were indicators that pointed to stormy weather. Life inside our walls moved on according to the regular school routine, and the daily duties were scrupulously performed. Nothing really upsetting to this routine occurred until April 29, when the British Embassy ordered the British subjects in the school to come to the Residency for safety. Not many British subjects were enrolled, but the two in the graduating class we were loath to give up. That same day a letter came from the American Legation stating that "owing to sudden developments in the political situation in Iraq there was grave danger of disorder." The letter stated further that the American women and children who wished to leave Baghdad would be evacuated by the British that afternoon along with the British women and children. One hundred and fifty women and children gathered at the airport and were conveyed by motor busses to Habbaniyah, the British air base, the plan being to fly them to Basrah the next day. Alas for human plans! That night the Iraq army moved en masse to Habbaniyah. In the morning their howitzers and other guns made it difficult, well nigh impossible, for the British planes to leave the ground in the cantonment.

The day following the evacuation of women and children, the remaining American and British subjects were asked to come either to the American Legation or to the British Embassy, whichever place being the nearer to their home. The five hundred British residents and the few Americans who had sought refuge and protection expected to be confined for only a few days. Actually, they were imprisoned a whole month, and during this time both the American Legation and the British Embassy were in danger. Both were surrounded by armed guards, preventing anyone from coming in or going out. The American Legation was once definitely threatened to be bombed since it had given refuge to Britishers.

Happily, our lives did not partake of these dangers, remaining as we did in our own dwelling. Since America was not involved in this fight there was no reason, so it always seemed to me, why we who were Americans should flee and seek refuge in the Legation. We carried on our work without a day's interruption, the only school in Baghdad that was able to keep open during the month of fighting, as though no planes were zooming over our court, no fighting going on at Habbaniyah and Fallujah, and no bombing of objectives on the edge of the city.

What a month May was! Actual shooting began, on the little king's birthday, at Habbaniyah, which came within almost an inch of falling into the hands of the Iraq army. The air base was totally unprepared to resist the force that threatened it, and only British strategy and the fighting ability of the Assyrian Levies saved it. In spite of reinforcements and additional Bedouin help, the Iraq army was finally defeated and driven to the outskirts of Baghdad. The four generals of the "Golden Square," the prime minister, the ministers of state, the grand mufti, and the aged and unfortunate regent scampered across the border into Iran. An armistice was signed by those who were left behind, and fighting ceased.

No one, except those who have gone through it, can really understand how life is broken up and the social structure dislocated by war. All business slowed down or stopped, banks froze their assets, the local money was worthless on the foreign exchange, all communication with the outside world was cut, prices soared, and food became scarce. Few people at any time were seen on the streets, and there were no friendly visits. Should a Christian or Jewish woman venture to go outside her house, she discarded her hat and put on the black 'aba and veil that she might not be identified. Even the men were afraid to be seen with sun helmets.

A signaling racket went on the whole month of May, making this a fearful month of uncertainty and dread. No one knew when such a racket might be drummed up against him, and he might become the victim of a mob. Adjoining one of our buildings was a large house marked by the rapacious rabble for looting. It must have been a prearranged affair, since the crowd that I saw from our upstairs window could not have gathered so quickly in this quiet street. Someone shouted that he had seen signaling from the roof: he had sighted a man with the British flag in one hand, in the other a revolver, and in the third a wireless set, three hands, so the story was transmitted! The mob rushed to the door of the house and forced its way in. I heard the shrieks of the women, loud and piercing, as they were stripped of their jewelry and the house ransacked.

Pretending to search for the guilty person, the looters overflowed by way of the roof into one of our buildings, seized the janitor, who was alone at the time, by the throat and accused him of the act. Frightened out of his wits, poor Pera denied the accusation and produced his residence book which all non-Iraqis must carry. The loot here was not large, but seeing a book in a teacher's room with the picture of Winston Churchill, they took the book and tore it to pieces.

Other looters ran into the garden, and by climbing over the wall reached the high school building when the boarders were at dinner. They pilfered the simple things the boys had in their rooms, such as soap and combs and toothbrushes and small hand mirrors. One of the boarders, however, fared worse. Old sandals were left behind in exchange for his fine new pair of shoes.

Gradually, I grew accustomed to the droning of the bombers and the fighters flying over the city. When I learned that the explosives were dropped only on military objectives outside the city, the flights fascinated me. Our confidence in our safety was only once disturbed. Close to our house was the telegraph station which also supplied the power for the loud-mouthed local broadcast station. One day British planes circled over it half a dozen times. Our neighbors living in small, sun-baked brick houses, in fear, hurriedly sought the protection of our thick-walled dwelling. Nothing happened.

That same day, looking up into the sky, I said, "It's raining silver." Leaflets were being dropped by British planes over the city, and, touched by the sun, they glistened as they fell. A severe penalty was meted out upon those who had leaflets in their possession or who were found reading them.

The radio repeatedly announced the coming of the Germans. This assurance of German help soon to come bolstered the Nazi-inspired government and the army. The Berlin announcer would tell of hundreds of planes that were soon to arrive. To substantiate these claims, something dramatic had to be done. A rumor was widely spread that Herr Grobba, who had been ordered out of the country at the beginning of the world war, had returned with a retinue in three planes and that one of these pilots was shot down by the British. One of our helpers had actually seen a funeral procession entering the German cemetery, the kind of a funeral to attract attention. But this was a pure hoax, a spectacular pageant to keep up the morale of the people. Later, when the Germans had actually come, a German pilot who was really shot down was buried.

The London radio had prepared us for this coming of the Germans. I shall never forget the evening when some of our teachers sat with us in the serdab to listen to the British broadcast. We sat in gloom when we heard that the Vichy French in Syria had allowed the Germans to occupy the Syrian airfields. This brought the Germans within a few hours of Iraq, and they would unquestionably arrive. They arrived that very night. The flares hanging in the sky that I saw from our roof were to assist the nine planes in landing. Three of these planes were shot down and the rest returned to Syria, but not until they had done some damage to the British air base.

The widespread rumor that Herr Grobba had returned to Baghdad was a fact. He came with a political mission to dictate the terms under which the Axis powers would give assistance to the Rashid Ali government. These terms by which Iraq would have been gulped down by the Germans were fully accepted by those who had seized power illegally. The man on the street and the coffeehouse frequenters, so obsessed with the idea that the Germans were supermen, treated them accordingly. When the few Germans who had come to Baghdad during the revolution walked the streets, the people kept at a reverent distance. In the shops no payment for purchases was accepted. The hotel keeper where they lodged was not so impressed. He handed to them a bill as they were leaving, which they pushed aside, saying, "Send it to the British Embassy."

There was a blackout and a curfew every night; and when in the evening I looked out over the city from the roof, it seemed like a deserted or forgotten city in a waste and barren wilderness. No one showed his face at a door or a window, lest some fantastic accusation should be trumped up against him and he be taken to the police station and mercilessly fined. A friend of ours was once fined twenty dinars for inadvertently turning on an electric bulb. We were once guilty of the same offense but fared better.

After the revolution had come to an end, and the troublemakers had fled, and an armistice was signed, the tone of the radio changed in the twinkling of an eye. For weeks the voices had been bold, and the tones strident and loud, especially after a jihad had been proclaimed. Just a few hours before the rebel government fell, the commentator, in giving the world news, called out boldly, "Ber-r-lin, To-kyo, Stockholm, Rome, Ve-echy, Hee-tler." But after the armistice in truckling tones, "Washington, Mr. Roosevelt, London [with accent on d-o-n], New York." But the most surprising statement that came over the radio that Saturday was this. Without a quiver in his voice and without choking, the announcer spoke of the unsurpassed gallantry of the British troops on the island of Crete, paradoxically, the very thing that delayed Hitler's Middle East program and prevented him from giving the hoped-for military aid to the insurgent, Nazi-inspired government of Iraq.

Sunday morning, I woke as from a nightmare. All was quiet—no planes flying, no lorries passing, no bombing around the city, and no booming of cannons. The radio had announced that life was to return to normalcy, which I was gullible enough to believe. It seemed good to walk out of the house, for I had been out only once during the month of May. We went to a nearby Arabic church, where I greeted friends by saying, "How long it is since we last met; it seems like years." The month had changed us, and we appeared older, more careworn, somewhat remote, and certainly sadder. Obviously, this day we were not wanted in this church where we were always welcome because strangers seeing us go in and out might report that we were Britishers.

Returning to our peaceful home, we lived for a few hours in a fool's paradise. I had swallowed the word "normalcy," and thinking all was well, my husband and I drove around the city in the late afternoon of Sunday to see the evidences of a month's struggle. At the American Legation the small guard booths were empty, and the great veranda of the building, modeled after the White House, was deserted. The place had lapsed into silence within and without. But this was not the case at the British Embassy. It still had the appearance of a fortification with its sandbags and wire entanglements. Sandbags and barbed wire had certainly been needed by the British on the west side of the city, as was patent by the hostile crowd we saw hanging around outside the embassy, even on this day when the revolt was supposed to be over. That crowd gave one a disquieting feeling; neither was our nervousness allayed by driving through the Shiah Muslim street beyond the embassy, for here the people looked angry. With relief we turned on the boulevard, which appeared decidedly safer.

Recrossing the river, we drove to the Royal Palace and then started back by way of King Ghazi Street. It was after six o'clock, the time when the poor people in this quarter literally pour out of their wretched houses into the wide open spaces of the new boulevard. At this time of the day in summer, the street is always crowded, so that there seemed to be nothing unusual about this teeming multitude.

Suddenly we saw men in uniform jump upon a carriage in which a man was seated, and to our amazement, they began to beat him. A throng immediately gathered, as if the whole affair had been prearranged. The man was then thrown headlong over the back of the carriage, the crowd closed in upon him, and he was in all likelihood killed. This man in this part of the city was possibly the first victim of the planned outbreak against the Jews. Now the violence of the mob was unleashed. We were informed later that as we steered through that wildly excited crowd, a few who were noticing us shouted, "*Inglezi*" (English); but because the attention of all was riveted on the victim, we passed on unscathed.

Greatly disturbed and ignorant of the planned carnage, I kept repeating the question, "What could that man have done to have so infuriated the mob?" Behind the windowless walls of the ground court of our house, we remained for a time unaware of the terrible deeds that were being enacted. It was only after we had gone on the roof to retire that the real truth of the matter drove itself into my mind. At first, I thought the *tat, tat* of the guns sounded like fireworks, and that the people were celebrating the return of the regent, Abdul Ilah, who was expected that day; and that the shrieks that here and there pierced the air came from women mourning for the dead who had fallen in battle. No! The guns were used for another purpose, and the shrill cries were those of fright and fear—and of death pangs.[1]

Late in the afternoon, however, order was restored and lawlessness ceased. Then the city became deathly still as though a silencing calamity had struck it; stupefied with terror and grief sat the sufferers; and stunned were those who felt the shame of what was done. The dead had to be buried, and the wounded had to be taken to the hospitals. Many stores were emptied, and in some of the bazaars like the Shorja almost every shop was broken open and completely looted. Some of the houses were so completely stripped that even the water pipes and the electric fixtures were taken and tiles removed in the hope of finding treasures.

The darkness of evening came on. Martial law was declared, and an early curfew was put in force. Dumbly, I went through life's routines; dumbly, I sat with folded hands; and when night came, I sought what rest I could with burdened sighs. For a week or ten days no one cared to do any business. Those whose shops were looted and had no more goods to sell declared that they would not open up business again, though most of them did open after they had recovered from the shock. Money in the banks remained frozen for a time, and the little money we had stored away to pay the salary of the teachers for the summer, we could not draw until some weeks later, and then only in small amounts. And just as business was at a standstill, so were also all social communications. People did not call; they sat listlessly in their homes.

Almost directly after this political upheaval, an anti-Nazi government once more came into power. It courageously faced the situation and at once became active. The land had to be cleared of German agents and German hirelings. Those who had done villainous and murderous deeds had to be brought to justice; the country had to be purged of its lawless, criminal leaders; and precautionary measures had to be taken to prevent another outbreak, all of which was a gigantic task that was enough to make men

1. This mob violence, known as *farhud,* was mainly directed against Baghdad Jews on June 1, 1941, when lawlessness reigned prior to the British takeover (Kedourie 1974).

quail as they surveyed the devastation. Besides, this had to be done in the face of continued radio propaganda by the Axis powers.

The new government was strengthened by the support of the good people of the city, who deeply lamented the happenings and deplored the wrongs that were committed by those who had been so basely misguided. These good people felt the shame and the humiliation of the blot on Iraq's escutcheon. Nevertheless, dispensing justice, however thorough, could not dull the poignancy of terrible memories. Rancor and gnawing bitterness was bound to persist.

21

CHANGING AND CHANGELESS BAGHDAD

In July of 1941 we left Baghdad with nothing in our possession by way of booking except railway tickets from Baghdad to the port of Basrah. As World War II was on, we were advised to go without booking and pick up chances along the way. Happily, chances followed one after another in such perfect coordination that we have always spoken of this home-ward sailing as Our Miracle Voyage. Of the many voyages we had made between the two hemispheres, this was in a class by itself.

No sooner had we left the train at Basrah than we learned that there was a ship in port leaving the same evening for Bombay. By six o'clock, we and our baggage were aboard. It was one of the British troop ships that carried soldiers from India to Iraq; and inasmuch as these ships on their return were empty, they were privileged to carry British subjects, and by arrangement, American citizens as well.

It was a poor boat. It might have been all right should the sea have been calm. But when we got out of the Persian Gulf, we were at the mercy of the monsoon; because the ship had neither cargo nor ballast, we became the plaything of the wind and the waves. Rolling into the harbor of Bombay, our next problem was how to get out from here. We soon learned that one of these ships, called "hush-hush" to conceal its identity, was to arrive in a few days which might take us to Vancouver, British Columbia, but whether we could sail on it or not was in the hands of the British admiralty.

When the ship arrived we were informed that only men passen-gers would be allowed on it, since the sailing would be through danger-ous zones. This was indeed disappointing, and so I earnestly pled to be allowed on it. "Tell the authorities," I said, "that I'll give no one any trouble

5. Ida Donges Staudt in her later years.

if the ship should be in danger, and tell them, too, that no one needs to be concerned if I drown." Other women who were waiting to sail must have pled as urgently. That august body, the British admiralty, was moved. They reconsidered the matter, and before the day was over I received the good news that women and children were being allowed to sail on the boat and that I could go with my husband. Revived and happy, we proceeded at once to hurry along and hustled about attending to the innumerable details that make travel so burdensome. We went down to the dock wondering on what kind of a vessel we would sail from here, and saw there, ready to receive us, a great ship, the flagship of the Canadian Pacific, the *Empress of Japan!* What a stately ship it was!

We stopped at both Ceylon and Singapore. At the latter port the two thousand or more Indian troops that were being carried were disembarked; and this big liner was thereafter left with only a few passengers; we were allowed to occupy the deluxe cabins! Because of the tension at that time between Japan and the Allied powers—this was only a few months before Pearl Harbor—the boat did not venture to take the direct route from Singapore through the mandated territory of Japan in the Pacific; we went between Borneo and Java, sailed through the Torres Strait, passed the Fiji and Samoan islands, and then on to Hawaii and Vancouver. We had a smooth sea throughout the long voyage, which so far as I was concerned could have gone on forever, so satisfying and restoring were the good ship and the calm ocean.

We were forced to remain in America for nearly two years. When we returned to our work in Baghdad we each went by a different route. My husband was on a military ship coming again across the Pacific, but this time through the Southern Seas below Australia and New Zealand, being on the sea for seventy-three days; I, coming a few months later, was able to get through the Mediterranean.

While in America we received the welcome news that Iraq had declared war against the Axis powers. This was on January 17, 1943, just a little more than a year and a half after the Blind Revolt. Though the country had been more Nazified than any other Arab country, Iraq was the first Arab state to take this step. This action followed the invasion of the American troops in North Africa, an achievement that had profoundly impressed the Arab world. In his letter to President Roosevelt, the prime minister of Iraq wrote, without restraint, of how impressed he was "with the stupendous undertaking," and how amazed he was "at the daring conception, the perfection of organization and the magnificence of achievement."

Upon my return, I found Baghdad greatly changed. It was not merely a change in atmosphere such as I had found in Baghdad once before upon my return; Baghdad itself now appeared to me to be both a changing and a changeless city. It was a different city; its ways of life had changed, and it appeared strangely new. With ease I had fitted into the old Baghdad; with difficulty, I adjusted myself to the new.

The city was no longer "Oriental," neither was it Occidental. In few other countries did the old and the new so strangely intermix as here. This strange juxtaposition of the ancient and the modern was everywhere in evidence. Just as certain colors clash when they are together, so this strange medley of old and new, of East and West, of antique and modern as they appeared side by side, often jarred.

Nevertheless, it was the ancient, the changeless in the midst of the changing that still appealed to me; and this I sought out with the fresh eyes of an adventurer. I was thrilled whenever and wherever I found that which had not changed. "Ah, this is my world," I would say as I felt again "the vibrations of great times and tall deeds." At all times and in all places where the changeless was manifested, I would seek it with my whole heart, for it touched that something within me to which my inner life was akin.

Of the many events during the last years we resided in Baghdad, there are two outstanding ones I shall never forget. One of these occasions was the Silver Jubilee Celebration in appreciation of the twenty-five years of my husband's services as an educator in the Middle East. It was held under the patronage of the prime minister in King Faisal II Hall and the sunken garden contiguous to it. The Alumni Association of the school arranged the affair. This meeting was significant in more ways than one, and in its ramifications it was international, too. Even the chairman of the Educational Committee of the U.S. Senate sent a message in which there was an expression of gratitude for the useful educational work rendered to Iraq, and a touching message of friendship and goodwill toward Iraq.

The beautiful new hall, built like a theatre with a balcony and private boxes, was filled with an audience made up of Iraqi ministers, members of Parliament, high government officials, and diplomatic personnel, as well as the friends and graduates of the school. It was a very cosmopolitan gathering and in that lay partly the importance of the meeting.

At this Silver Jubilee Celebration there was the same mingling of various groups which had characterized all our school functions. It was a temporary exhibition of a one world. The graduates sat in a body filling the center of the floor of the theatre. On the stage were four alumni who had a part in the program, each representing not only a different profession but also a different creed. The same can also be said of the rest of the platform party. There was the minister of Education, who represented the Iraq government; the American minister, who represented the American government; and a local teacher, who represented the faculty.

In his address the minister of Education spoke in beautiful Arabic, expressing his appreciation and the appreciation of the government of Iraq, for the cultural and educational contribution of America to the Arab East, and the humanitarian spirit which led Americans to assist in the education of the youth of Iraq.

My husband, when he spoke, made mention of his desire to labor in this part of the world because of the ancient glories that once were here which the West inherited. He said that the values inherent in Western civilization were created in this area, and that he had come to repay his own spiritual debts as well as those of America by rendering a service to the people who now live in this part of the world. He also spoke of his longings to promote mental and spiritual growth in young people, declaring that the most precious thing in the world is the individual human mind and spirit with its capacity for growth and service.

In conclusion, he said that he had also come as an ambassador of friendship, striving to do his part in creating a reservoir of good will between Iraq and America. Nations, he continued, must find a means of living together on a friendly basis, for civilization is the result of the common work of all nations. The East needs the West, and the West needs the East. Each has much to learn from the other. And in that mutual need and mutual richness there will spring a life for mankind richer and better than anything we have known.

A full translation of this speech was then read by the president of the Alumni Association; and as he concluded, the band, having caught the heart-stirrings of the people, played a lively selection prior to the unveiling of the two busts, which stood on high pedestals, and a covered portrait of my husband on an easel between them.

Then the piano struck a chord; the school chorus stood up at this signal; the alumni arose; and forth pealed with fervor the school song. The rest of the audience of their own accord stood up; and immediately when the song had come to an end, the King's Guard Band played the national anthem. The Jubilee program, dignified and moving, was over.

The other occasion was an elaborate garden party on the twelfth anniversary of King Faisal II's birthday, a delightful affair. Similar affairs were held before to celebrate the king's birthday, but the one held on the evening of May 2, 1946, will always be remembered as having been unique—for me doubly unique. It so happened that I had attended a garden party a few days after my first arrival in Baghdad, the colorful garden party of the British high commissioner.[1] I attended an equally colorful garden party a few days before my departure from Baghdad on the occasion of the anniversary of the birthday of the young king. No wonder these two garden parties are so unforgettable: the one introducing me to romantic Baghdad, the other leaving with me an aroma upon my departure. Between these two garden parties was sandwiched my life in Baghdad.

What was special on this occasion was the singing of Umm Kalthum, the prima donna of Arab singers, universally acknowledged as the best singer of Arab music in the Arab world. Together with her orchestra, she flew from Cairo to Baghdad in order to grace this birthday celebration of Iraq's young king. A temporary stage was erected for her in the spacious palace grounds of the regent, from which she sang at intervals from ten o'clock in the evening until two in the morning. She showed poise and dignity and appeared very much at home before the public, this woman who once had been a little Bedouin maid. She moved freely and gracefully on the stage, using with considerable effect a rose-colored handkerchief which, as she well knew, contrasted with her heliotrope gown.

Here was the charm of Baghdad again. The garden with its shrubbery, its many trees and spring flowers, and the thousands of colored electric bulbs strung all over it had a most festive air. The garden was artistically

---

1. See chapter 4.

236 · LIVING IN ROMANTIC BAGHDAD

laid out and was well kept. As I sat in the midst of this beauty, I listened to Arab music at its highest level. Umm Kalthum's singing was accompanied by an orchestra of five musicians, most of whom played Arab instruments. The playing of these instruments as well as her singing intensely interested me. I cannot say that I really enjoy Arab music, but I enjoy seeing others enjoy it. My ear was never educated for the appreciation of Arab music, and I was always so busy with other things that I could not include this in my agenda for a rounded education.

As I listened to it, Arab music rests upon laws entirely different from those which govern Western music. One thing I easily detected was that its tonal range is very limited; a musical selection stays within four or five full tones. Another thing was that all musicians played in unison. There is no harmony in pure Arab music. Umm Kalthum's singing and her orchestra performed in unison though each freely embellished. Some scholars of Arab music have said that there are as many as fourteen scales or modes in Arab music, whereas in our Western music there are only two, major and minor. In addition, Arab music has thirds or quarter tones. Hence, it is not suitable to be played on a piano.

As I listened to Umm Kalthum and tried to catch what was distinct in her music, I discerned that she embellished the melody, if we can speak of a melody. These variants or ornaments seem an important factor. Then, she continued to sing on a single word or phrase for a long time. In one of her selections she was singing *"Ana aghanni"* (I am singing). After four or five minutes, I turned to a friend who was sitting next to me and asked what the prima donna was singing now. The friend replied, *"Ana aghanni."* After a little while I repeated my question, and to my surprise received the same answer as I had before. This, I understand, is characteristic also of Arab music. A singer continues interminably to sing on a phrase as she did in this case.

My mind wandered from the music frequently, but I never lost interest in the effect of that music upon the audience. A number gave vent to their feelings in approbation and frequent exclamations of "Allaaaah!" especially when Umm Kalthum held a quivering note for a long time or when she reached a climactic pause. Someone has said that in the constant repetition of the same motive within a narrow range of tone there is something that "little by little steals over the soul." No question but those habituated to Arab music were emotionally moved.

Now the time had come for me permanently to leave Iraq, where for twenty-three years we had been welcome resident guests, and where life had been so crowded, so diversified, and so full of adventurous experiences. It was fitting and natural that I should leave on a magic carpet, carrying with me the memory of a life framed between two memorable garden parties.

As the seaplane lifted itself from the surface of Habbaniyah Lake, I looked down, I trust not for the last time, upon the desert waste I had so often covered. As I thus surveyed these barren stretches, this life of mine which I had spent in the city of the caliphs unrolled itself before me as the plane sped on its way to Cairo. I recalled the checkered course of Iraq's history; I recollected the many changes that had taken place in Baghdad within this span of life.

In an effort to analyze this overall picture, I discovered that my life had fallen into four marked periods, consonant with four distinct periods in Iraq's history. My life in Baghdad had not been an even succession of years, imperceptibly running into each other; it was rather an assemblage of years sharply divided from each other by the sharp changes in Iraq's history.

The first was the period under the British mandate, which continued until 1932, when Iraq was admitted into the League of Nations and secured her nominal independence. It was a glorious period, a period of awakening, of a new birth. Iraq was reborn. She had passed after the First World War from Turkish misrule to set her face steadfastly toward the promised goal of independence. It was a time of progress, of great endeavors, and of great hopes; the men who were leading in these beginning years projected their high hopes and endeavors into the life of the people.

During this period Baghdad had for me all the charm of the *Arabian Nights* tales. I lived, as it were, in a city enchanted. Baghdad was still purely Eastern, and was as yet neither spoiled nor standardized by Western ways. Much of what has been written in this volume reflects the charm and aspirations of this period when life was rich in romance and when hope budded though never blossomed. As I look back over those years in Baghdad, that which is still most vivid in my mind is what took place during those fascinating years.

The transition from mandate to formal independence came about while we were in America, and upon our return I keenly felt that a decided change had taken place. Sensitive to a changed atmosphere and to changed conditions, my exuberant spirits were toned down, and my former buoyancy gave place to staidness.

In the third period the country moved into the German orbit. The well-planned Nazi penetration, which had begun about 1936, commenced to bear fruit a few years later. The British hold upon the land rapidly declined in the spring of 1940 and continued to diminish until eventually an insurgent, Nazi-inspired government came into power, a government that plunged the country into a revolution against the British. This period will forever remain a dark chapter in Iraq's history.

During these years Baghdad retained for me very little of the old flavor. Its quaint charm had disappeared. During this time I was often depressed. When I came to Baghdad I carried with me a wand that turned everything it touched to beauty and happiness. This wand, which was needed more and more as the years went by, dropped from my hand during the May revolution, and as it fell a ball of gloom descended upon me.

In the last period, which began toward the end of 1941, Iraq's Wheel of Fortune once more started to turn upward. The country was on the march again and made strides, in spite of the fact that retarding problems began to show their ugly faces above the horizon: the never-ending tussle with British policy, the infiltration of communism, and the tragic situation between Arabs and Jews brought on by the Palestinian question. But that which I noticed the most, especially upon my return from America, was the fact that Baghdad had rapidly changed, materially and socially.

During these years, despite these untoward circumstances, I felt that a rebound had come. But that is not what particularly affected me. It was something else. The city I had so enjoyed was no more. That which once had been so appealing was only so at certain times and in certain places. The city of *A Thousand and One Nights* was no longer purely and fascinatingly Oriental. The world including Baghdad was being standard-ized and was becoming more and more colorless.

Now that I am living in retirement in America, my heart again moves to the East, and I am often attacked by nostalgia for Baghdad. Iraq and the whole Middle East possessed and still possesses, notwithstanding its many changes, a peculiar charm and appeal that I have found nowhere else. This is an experience, too, which I share with others. When we left Lebanon where we previously had resided, I had the same feeling. The dirt and the heat and the insects and the discomforts are not of lasting memory, neither are abnormal political obsessions, nor the changed con-ditions, but the changeless unchanged that still persist.

There is something in this part of the world, as I had said at the begin-ning of my life's story, to which I was akin and into which I fitted without any effort on my part. I moved about everywhere, whether in Lebanon or in Iraq, as if I had been born and bred there. Upon my arrival in Baghdad I had said that I knew I would like it. That was not a momentary feeling but a deep conviction. My reaction to Lebanon was the same, though there its breathtaking beauty first enthralled me.

I never felt a stranger in the land, and my feelings toward the people became warm and affectionate as I learned to know them. In Beirut I had given my services to the American School for Girls, where I had my first experience in teaching Middle Easterners and my close contact with them. Every school day I used to walk from the university campus to the school compound; and if today I want to evoke an ecstatic emotion, I walk in memory the familiar way to the school in the spring when the wisteria hung over the walls and the almond blossomed, while before my eyes in all seasons stretched opalescent Lebanon. And then when I walked into the large assembly room of the school, the friendly glances of the girls made light the day's work.

In Baghdad I missed scenery, but its substitute was a closer and more intimate contact with the people, especially with eager, ambitious young people who crowded about us through the length of the years. They had had limited opportunities; life had not satiated them; and simple pleasures more than met their desires. In their eagerness to learn they drew out from me the best I had to give, and this best I gave to the boys in our school and the girls in my club.

The ever-changing Baghdad was, after all, only a trivial undertone in my life there. What enthralled me was the changeless Baghdad. In it I happily lived and moved and had my being. Here my inner life was satisfied; here my youthful dream was realized. The Baghdad which ever was so dear to my heart is still dear to me today. My husband and I often say to each other, "When we go to Baghdad"—and saying that, our eyes shine.

Glossary

Works Cited

Index

GLOSSARY

'aal: bravo!

'aba: short for *'abaya*

'abaya: women's black, all-covering veil

abra sec: a dry tree

'agal: cord wound around a kaffiyah to hold it in place

'agha: Kurdish leader

al-hamdu lillah: Thanks be to God

anderun: harem

'arabana: two-horse carriage

'arak: colorless intoxicating liquor made from grapes or dates

bakhsheesh: bribe, gift

balam: boat

balek: take care; watch out

beg: respectable title for a man (Turkish)

burghul: boiled, dried, and ground wheat

chaichi: one who prepares and serves tea

chaikhana: teahouse

Dar al-Hikmah: House of Wisdom

darbuna: alley

debki: folk dance

dehasha: flat, blue, buttonlike charm used to counteract the "eye of envy"

dhow: an Arabian vessel with two or three masts

dinar: paper currency, equivalent to a 1940s English pound

diwan: a guest room; a council chamber

diwankhana: a gathering place for visitors or elders

fallahin: peasants. Singular, *fallah*

fardaws: paradise

farhud: mob violence

farrash: janitor

fatiha: opening sura (chapter) of the Qur'an

fez: red cylindrical felt hat with black silk tassels

fi 'aman Illah: May you be in Allah's protection

fils: basic Iraqi copper currency; 1,000 fils = 1 dinar

finjan: narrow-waisted glass teacup

franji: a Frank, a Westerner

guffa: boat built like the arc of Moses, made of wicker, daubed outside with
   bitumen

hajji: a Muslim who has made a pilgrimage to Mecca

hakamen: rabbis

hammal: porter

hilhal: joy-cry

'Id: feast

'Idak mubarak: may your 'Id be blessed (singular form)

'Idkum mubarak: may your 'Id be blessed (plural and formal form)

'Id al-Fitr: great feast which follows month-long fast of Ramadan during which
   an observing Muslim does not eat, drink, or smoke from dawn until after
   sunset

'ijma': consensus of Muslims on the rightness of a belief or practice

'imam: commonly, one who leads a group of Muslims in prayer; the leader of a
   mosque and the community. In Shi'ism, an imam is one of a succession of
   seven, or twelve, religious leaders after the Prophet Muhammed; they are
   considered to be divinely inspired.

Inglezi: English; Englishman

'izar: garment worn by married Christian or Jewish women which hung from
   the head; made of solid colors with borders of deep and contrasting colors
   interwoven with threads of gold

kaffiyah: traditional Arab men's head scarf held in place by ropelike *agal*

katib: clerk

killidar: keeper of the treasures

kitab: book

laban: yogurt

lala: tall, slender lamp, burning a candle

lemonata: lemonade

mahailah: type of vessel used on the Tigris

majlis: council, national assembly

manna min sama: manna from heaven

mudir: mayor; manager; director

muluk: kings

mustow: Kurdish *laban* (yogurt) thinned with water

nadi: a club

nargila: tobacco pipe in which smoke is drawn through a jar of water, cooling it

nawab: a Muslim Indian prince

pasha: title of high officials (Turkish)

qalabaaligh: Arabic word borrowed from Turkish, general confusion

qasr: literally, a castle or palace, commonly applied to a large and commodious house

Qasr al-Zuhur: Palace of Flowers, Iraqi royal residence

ruh: a brusque way of saying "Go"

salaam; salaaming: greeting, peace

serai: municipal building

serdab: room in large Baghdadi homes, below the level of the court, where the temperature is lower

shaitan: Satan

shamm al-hawa: "smelling" the air

shura: consultation

sidara: type of hat introduced in Iraq in the 1920s. It became the emblem of the Iraqi governing and professional classes. It went out of fashion after the overthrow of the monarchy in 1958.

sisu: Finnish word to describe endless energy and vitality

Sitt: Miss

tarbush: see fez

vali: governor

wazir: government minister

zanbur: a heavy and hardy variety of wasp

zibil: garbage

zikr: state of ecstasy induced by a group of dervishes, usually by chanting rhythmically a phrase that contains a name of God

WORKS CITED

Allen, W. E. D., and Paul Muratoff. 1953. *Caucasian Battlefields*. Cambridge, UK: Cambridge Univ. Press.

Appiah, Kwame Anthony. 2008. "How Muslims Made Europe." *New York Review of Books* 55, no. 17: 59–62.

Bird, A. E. C. (American Consulate, Baghdad). 1909. To Secretary Chase Knox Philander, Sept. 9. Department of State, Consular Bureau, 20 178/1-6, Enclosure 1. National Archives, Washington, DC.

Chiha, Habib. 1908. *La Provence de Baghdad*. Cairo: Imp. El-Maaref.

Coakley, J. F. 1992. *The Church of the East and the Church of England: A History of the Archbishop of Canterbury's Assyrian Missions*. Oxford, UK: Oxford Univ. Press.

Cohen, Stuart A. 1976. *British Policy in Mesopotamia, 1903–1914*. Oxford, UK: Ithaca Press.

Great Britain. 1905. Foreign Office. F. O. 195/2188, no. 152/16, Mar. 6, and no. 241/29, Apr. 6.

Great Britain. 1912. India Office. London. Document no. LP and S/10/212, vol. 211 (1912–14).

Hourani, Albert. 1991. *A History of the Arab Peoples*. Cambridge, MA: Harvard Univ. Press.

Joseph, John. 2000. *The Modern Assyrians of the Middle East: Encounters with Western Christian Missions, Archaeologists, and Colonial Powers*. Leiden: Brill.

Kazemzadeh, Firuz. 1951. *The Struggle for Transcaucasia*. New York: Philosophical Library.

Kedourie, Elie. 1974. "The Sack of Basra and the Farhud in Baghdad." In *Arab Political Memoirs and Other Studies*. London: Routledge.

Khadduri, Majid. 1951. *Independent Iraq*. Oxford, UK: Oxford Univ. Press.

O'Leary, De Lacy. 1923. *Comparative Grammar of the Semitic Languages*. London: Paul, Trench, Trubner.

247

Ruthven, Malise. 2009. "Divided Iran on the Eve." *New York Review of Books* 56, no. 11: 53.

Stewart, Rory. 2007. "The Queen of the Quagmire." *New York Review of Books* 45, no. 16: 10–14.

Tibawi, A. L. 1967. "Syria in War Time Agreements and Disagreements." *Middle East Forum* 43, no. 2: 84–85.

Tripp, Charles. 2002. *A History of Iraq*. Cambridge, UK: Cambridge Univ. Press.

Tschanz, David. 2004. "Journeys of Faith, Roads of Civilization." *Saudi Aramco World* 55, no. 1: 2–11.

Wallach, Janet. 2005. *Desert Queen, the Extraordinary Life of Gertrude Bell*. New York: Anchor Books.

Willkie, Wendell. 1943. *One World*. New York: Pocket Books.

Wright, William. 1966. *Lectures on the Comparative Grammar of the Semitic Languages*. 1890. Reprint. Amsterdam: Philo Press.

INDEX